Frommer's®

23 GREAT drives in NEW ENGLAND

WILEY

Wiley Publishing, Inc.

Written by Kathy Arnold and Paul Wade

Additional research: Lans Christensen, Gael May McKibben, Tom Arnold and Harlan Levy

First published 1997
Revised second edition 1999
Revised third edition 2001
Revised fourth edition 2003
Revised fifth edition 2005
Revised sixth edition 2007
Revised seventh edition 2009

Edited, designed and produced by AA Publishing.

Published by AA Publishing

Published in the United States by
John Wiley & Sons, Inc.
111 River Street, Hoboken, NJ 07030

Find us online at Frommers.com

Frommer's is a registered trademark of Arthur Frommer.
Used under license.

ISBN 978-0-470-42338-7

Cataloging-in-Publication Data is available from the Library of Congress.

Color separation: Daylight Colour Art, Singapore

Printed and bound by G. Canale & C. s.p.a., Torino, Italy

A03666
Atlas mapping in this title produced from map data supplied by Global Mapping, Brackley, UK. © Global Mapping

CONTENTS

ABOUT THIS BOOK

This book is not only a practical touring guide for the independent traveler, but is also invaluable for those who would like to know more about New England. It is divided into the 6 states, each with its own city and driving tours. The driving tours start and finish in those cities considered to be the most interesting centers for exploration. There are special features on Boston and the American Revolution, the beauty of the fall, and the rich heritage of the arts and the surrounding seas. Each tour has details of the most interesting places to visit en route. Boxes catering to special interests follow some of the main entries – for those whose interest is in history, or walking, or those who have children. There are also boxes which highlight scenic stretches of road and which give details of special events, crafts and customs. The simple route directions are accompanied by an easy-to-use map at the beginning of each tour, along with a chart showing how far it is from one town to the next in miles and kilo-meters. This can help you to decide where to take a break and stop overnight. (All distances quoted are approximate.) Before setting off, it is advisable to check with the information center listed at the start of the tour for recommendations on where to break your journey, and for additional information on what to see and do, and when best to visit.

★ This symbol on the maps represents other attractions seen along the routes, often mentioned in the panels.

Torrington, Connecticut

ATMs (cash machines) are plentiful.

Currency
The American unit of currency is the dollar, consisting of 100 cents. Bills are mainly green, are the same size and have similar appearance, so be careful, though the $10, $20 and $50 have been redesigned. They range from one to 2, 5, 10, 20, 50 and 100 dollars. Coins are in denominations of 1 cent, (penny), 5 cents (nickel), 10 cents (dime), 25 cents (quarter), 50 cents and a dollar.

Customs Regulations
Non-U.S. residents may take in, duty-free, one carton of cigarettes, a liter of alcohol and $100 worth of gifts. Customs officials are very strict about banning any fresh meat, fruit, plants and, of course, drugs (unless on prescription). Check for updates on www.cbp.gov.

Electricity
Standard voltage is 110–120V, 60 cycles AC, using flat two-pin plugs. Bring the right adaptor.

Emergency Telephone Numbers
If you have an emergency, telephone 911 to be put in touch with

Tour Information
See pages 167–76 for addresses, telephone numbers, websites and opening times of attractions plus telephone numbers and websites of tourist offices.

Accommodations and restaurants
See pages 160–6 for a list of recommended hotels and restaurants for each tour.

Motoring
For information on aspects of motoring in New England see pages 158–9.

INFORMATION FOR NON-U.S. RESIDENTS
Banks
Banks set their own hours, opening at 9 and closing between 3 and 5 on weekdays. Some open on Saturday mornings.

Although foreign currency can be changed at big hotels or airports, U.S. dollar travelers' checks are recommended as they are accepted as cash everywhere from restaurants to gas stations.

Credit Cards
Major credit cards are accepted in New England. However, many small bed-and-breakfasts will accept only cash or travelers' checks.

the right service. Otherwise, dial "0" and consult the operator.

Entry Regulations
Citizens of most European countries, plus Japan, Australia and New Zealand, do not need visas if they are visiting the U.S. on holiday, the stay will not exceed 90 days and they have a return or onward ticket.

However, requirements for travel to the US can change, so check the current situation with your tour operator or travel agent, as well as such official websites as www.travel.state.gov and www.dhs.gov. Some of the newer requirements relate to machine readable passports and being able to provide information such as the full address of your destination, where you will spend your first night in the US.

Health Matters
It is essential to have adequate health insurance before traveling to the U.S. While hospitals are usually excellent, treatment can be expensive. It may be delayed or refused without proof of proper insurance. Your hotel will be able to recommend a doctor or hospital. Alternatively, call the local hospital. No special inoculations are required.

See also Health Services on page 158.

Holidays
See page 158.

Post Offices
Stamps for postcards and letters are on sale in many stores and hotels; for larger packages, go to a post office. It is cheaper to send postcards and aerograms than letters. See also page 159.

Telephones
Since payphones are being phased out in the USA, consider buying a cheap prepaid cellphone (mobile phone) if you are visiting for more than a few days. These are sold at drugstores, as well as phone shops.

To call abroad, dial 011, then the country code:
Australia 61
Canada 1
New Zealand 64
Republic of Ireland 353
U.K. 44

Time differences
New England is on Eastern Standard Time (EST), 5 hours behind the U.K., 6 hours behind mainland Europe, and 15 hours behind Sydney, Australia.

Daylight Saving Time alters the time by one hour in mid-March and early November.

Travelers Aid Society
The Travelers Aid Society, 17 East Street, Boston, Massachusetts 02111 (tel: 617/542-7286; www.taboston.com), is dedicated to helping travelers. Staff provide crisis intervention, counseling, referrals to community sources, and emergency financial assistance to travelers in crisis.

Useful Addresses
As well as the listings on pages 160–6, these agencies and associations have a selection of places to stay:
Select Registry, Distinguished Inns of North America (tel: 800/344-5244; www.SelectRegistry.com);
Bed and Breakfast Agency of Boston. Tel: (in U.K.) 0800 895128 (in U.S.A. and Canada) 800/248-9262; www.boston-bnbagency.com.

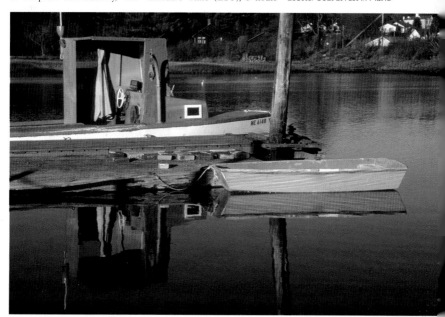

Lobster boat at rest in Maine

MASSACHUSETTS

After 385 years of permanent European settlement, Massachusetts has acquired a "little history." Here, the Pilgrims landed and built their communities. A century and a half later, patriotic passion exploded in a series of events culminating in the American Revolution. Not surprisingly, that heritage has been preserved. Conservation has encompassed old houses and bridges, churches and farms, even entire villages.

Massachusetts is known as the Bay State because of the gaping Atlantic gulf enclosed by the flexed arm of Cape Cod. The shape of the state ensures a variety of landscapes. It stretches from the storm-tossed Atlantic to the rolling, wooded hills of the Berkshires, with the rich meadows of the Connecticut River Valley in between.

The seasons are distinct: crisp, clear winter days melting into an explosion of spring greenery and flowers, followed by muggy, soporific summers and, finally, the fall with its dazzling multicolored leaves (see pages 102–3).

Massachusetts, especially around Boston, was also America's cultural cradle (see pages 56–7). Artists and writers, poets and musicians have long been drawn together by the web of academia. Harvard University, founded in 1636, is the oldest American institute of higher learning, but there are numerous other colleges to be found throughout the state, as well as boarding schools (called "prep schools" because they prepare students for college).

Concord is a beautiful town with a rich and varied history

Outdoor festivals of music and drama are a bonus for visitors during the summer months.

But the region's focus always returns to history. Many of America's most treasured icons are here, from Plymouth Rock to Boston's Old North Church and Concord's historic bridge. Thanksgiving is celebrated with justifiable pride; after all, the tradition of eating turkey and pumpkin pie was "invented" here. They even have the cranberry bogs nearby to provide the accompanying sauce.

Tour 1

*"Listen, my children, and you
shall hear,
Of the midnight ride of
Paul Revere ..."*

Paul Revere is one of the best-known messengers in history, thanks to Henry Wadsworth Longfellow's poem. His ride from Boston to warn the Americans that the British were on the march has become legendary. The patriots assembled and took on the trained soldiers, first in Lexington and then in Concord. All the British wanted to do was capture the rebels' arms cache; they had no idea that the skirmishes of April 19, 1775 would spark the American Revolution. In both towns, historic sites have been preserved, while the visitor information centers provide details of "who did what and when." The route for this tour also has a literary focus. In the 19th century, Concord was the home of some of the best-known writers of the day: Henry David Thoreau, Louisa May Alcott, Nathaniel Hawthorne and Ralph Waldo Emerson.

Tour 2

Although Cape Cod has long been recognized as a playground for Bostonians, the North Shore, with its rugged, rocky outcrops is also a popular place to relax by the sea. Add to that atmospheric fishing villages and the gruesome history of witches in Salem, and this drive is fun as well as scenic. The sparkling light has long attracted artists, especially in Rockport. Castles and underwater rocks, whales, frozen peas and even clam chowder are threads in the rich tapestry of America's history which unravels along this shoreline drive.

Tour 3

Cape Cod enjoys a mystique matched by few holiday destinations. The names of its 300-year-old villages are reminders of English fishing ports, its history peopled with Native Americans and fishermen, whalers and sea captains. On Cape Cod Bay, the sands are sheltered and the water is warmer than on the Atlantic Ocean shore, where strong waves buffet the dunes of the Cape Cod National Seashore.

This 40-mile (60km) coastline stretches from the elbow of the peninsula up to Provincetown, known for its bohemian lifestyle. The popularity of the Cape has taken its toll: roadside development sprawls around Hyannis on the south shore and traffic can be bumper to bumper on summer weekends. Off season, it is easier to get away from it all, and find what aficionados call "the old Cape Cod."

Tour 4

Western Massachusetts has an intriguing mixture of the rural and sophisticated, the historic and eccentric. The rolling Berkshire Hills inspired authors

Chatham Light, Cape Cod. Lighthouses are an important part of New England's heritage

such as Herman Melville and Edith Wharton, and attracted millionaires, who built vacation homes away from the seaside. Now the hills resound to summer festivals of music and theater. Attractive towns and villages range from Deerfield, with its perfectly preserved 18th-century houses, to Williamstown with its excellent college and astonishing art collection. Stockbridge thrives on its "traditional America" image, ably reinforced by *Saturday Evening Post* cover artist Norman Rockwell, whose paintings are on display here. Drive down lazy back roads to old covered bridges arching over rocky streams; there are surprises around every corner.

BIRTHPLACE OF A NATION

The American perspective of the War of Independence is simple: the Colonists were oppressed by King George III and Parliament and justifiably rebelled. The issues were a little more complex. In the early days, there were no "states" as such. The Colonies differed in population and style of government: some depended on fishing and trade, others on farming and tobacco. Although links with the Mother Country were strong for economic and cultural reasons, the Colonists had become increasingly independent-minded during the century-and-a-half since the first settlers arrived.

A turning point in American history was the defeat of the French and the Native Americans in the war from 1756 to 1763. This gave the New Englanders, and the colonies along the coast to the south, a vision of vast lands stretching westward and a sense of "new" country to be developed. Relations with Britain, however, became strained when Parliament decided that the colonies should help pay for the seven years of war; after all, the English reasoned, they were defending Colonial lands. Moreover, a 10,000-strong army was still needed to protect the Colonies. A monopoly on trade was proclaimed, restricting Colonists to dealing only with Britain and other British possessions (notably the West Indies). Further, a ban was issued on new settlements west of the Appalachians.

Although these restrictions rankled, what inflamed Colonial passions was direct taxation. Traditionally, Britain had raised money by customs duties on shipping; the Stamp Act in 1765 set a new precedent. This placed a charge on all contracts, deeds, newspapers and legal documents. Protests forced its repeal within a year, but other revenue-raisers followed, only to be repealed. Parliament decided to stand firm on one, however. That was the tax on tea.

After the French and Indian War, economic times were hard for the Colonists, and the new rules hurt financially. But the

Colonists also protested on principle. "No taxation without representation" was the cry at public meetings and in pamphlets. Articles questioned the legality of such taxes, claiming that they infringed the charters of some of the Colonies.

Boston was an important focus of militant feelings, which periodically exploded into riots. One relatively minor event, on March 5, 1770, became a legend. A lone British sentry on duty at the Custom House was harassed by a crowd. Reinforcements arrived, but the mob continued to bait the soldiers, heckling them and throwing stones. Shots were fired; five Colonists died. This incident became known as the "Boston Massacre" and was used by leaders such as Samuel Adams to whip up emotions.

Three years later, in December, came one of the most colorful incidents of the era, the Boston Tea Party. As a protest against the tax of 3 pence per pound on tea, about 100 men, disguised as

Native Americans, boarded the newly arrived HMS *Dartmouth*. Its cargo of 300 chests of tea was thrown overboard. In response, General Gage and four British regiments were sent to Boston, and the port was closed down in 1774.

Below: the Boston Massacre, in which five Colonists died

Bottom: the "Sons of Liberty," disguised as Mohawks, throw East India Company tea into the water

The scene was set for the smoldering coals of resentment to be ignited. In April, 1775, it was reported to General Gage that farmers in Concord, a small village west of Boston, were stockpiling firearms. He ordered 700 British troops to march out, confiscate and destroy the Patriots' illegal cache. On route, they skirmished with the Minute Men (locals who could be ready "in a minute" to fight) in Lexington before being outnumbered in Concord. Instead of withdrawing in an orderly manner, the British confronted the militiamen, lost three soldiers and had to beat a hasty, undignified retreat to Boston.

cost was hundreds of lives. The psychological victory belonged to the Americans. King George III replied savagely by declaring the Colonies to be in rebellion. Mercenaries were hired in Europe and transported across the Atlantic to augment the troops.

Not all the Colonists were ready for war. About one-third remained loyal to the crown and another third were neutral. The rest, however, were vociferous and demanded to sever links with the Mother Country. Further British attacks on Falmouth (now Portland, Maine) in October, 1775 and on Norfolk, Virginia in January, 1776, only

Boston, never to return. Fighting, however, continued elsewhere. In May, representatives of all 13 Colonies met in Philadelphia, Pennsylvania. Freedom was the agenda of this Continental Congress. A short document drafted by Thomas Jefferson of Virginia set out the grievances and proclaimed that "these united colonies are, and of right ought to be, free and independent states." This was the Declaration of Independence, accepted unanimously by the delegates and signed on July 4, 1776.

Liberty did not come immediately, however. War raged for five years and even after the

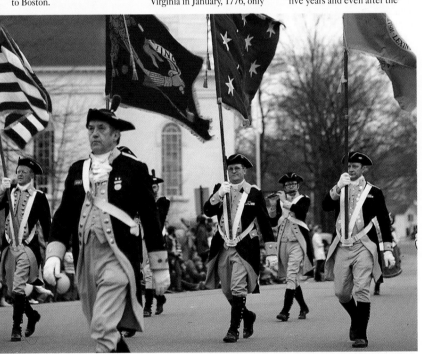

Some 20,000 Minute Men rushed to Boston, penning the British forces in. In May, 1775, artillery powder and ammunition captured at Fort Ticonderoga in New York State was hauled overland by the Colonists and used to capture Bunker Hill. Although the Redcoats soon stormed and recaptured it, the

served to fan the fury. *Common Sense*, a pamphlet written by Thomas Paine, became a best seller, with 120,000 copies sold in January, 1776 alone. Although he was an Englishman who had lived in the Colonies for only a year, he argued strenuously for independence. In March, 1776, the British withdrew from

The citizens of Lexington reenact the events of April 19, 1775

formal British surrender in 1781, London refused to recognize the Colonies' independence. Finally, in September, 1783, a peace treaty was signed in Paris, acknowledging that a new nation had been born.

Lexington
& Concord

Concord and Lexington are two of the most famous towns in the United States, due to the skirmishes between locals and British soldiers in 1775 that triggered the American Revolution. Concord has an additional claim to fame: it was home to some of the great writers of 19th-century America. Today, Lexington feels like a residential suburb of Boston, while Concord has retained more of its historical flavor. The main themes of this route are liberty and literature, but at the end, the focus is strictly contemporary.

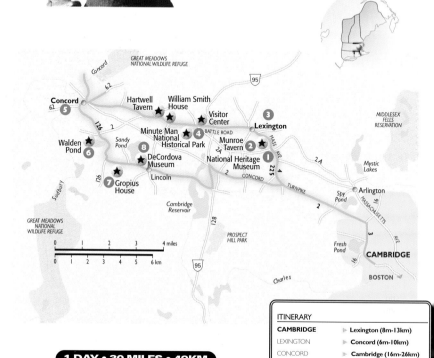

1 DAY • 30 MILES • 49KM

ITINERARY	
CAMBRIDGE	▸ **Lexington (8m-13km)**
LEXINGTON	▸ **Concord (6m-10km)**
CONCORD	▸ **Cambridge (16m-26km)**

Headquarters of the Lexington Minute Men, 1775

i Cambridge Visitor's Information Center, Harvard Square

▶ From Cambridge, take the Fresh Pond Parkway (**Routes 16** and **3**) to **Route 2** west. Take this for 3.7 miles (6km) and then at Exit 56, turn right onto **Routes 4** and **225**. At the first stop sign, turn left onto Massachusetts Avenue (always known as "Mass Ave"). This was the route taken by Paul Revere on his way to Lexington. At the junction with the **2A**, turn left onto **2A West** to reach the National Heritage Museum.

❶ National Heritage Museum

This bright and airy museum provides a useful background to the rest of the tour. As well as regular new exhibitions, a long-term display explores the background to the events that "sowed the seeds of liberty," including the notorious Stamp Act of 1765 – a major trigger of unrest in the Colonies. The museum's Heritage Shop has a wide range of American history books, plus cultural souvenirs.

▶ Return to the Massachusetts Avenue junction and turn left to reach Munroe Tavern.

❷ Munroe Tavern

On the afternoon of April 19, 1775, this fine old pub (1695) was the site of the temporary hospital and headquarters for British soldiers retreating from the battle at Concord. Fourteen years later, George Washington dined here in an upstairs room, while on tour in New England. Today it is the headquarters of the Lexington Historical Society.

▶ Follow Massachusetts Avenue for about a mile (1.5km), straight into Lexington to the triangular green.

❸ Lexington

This cradle of the American Revolution is dotted with significant sites, not least of which is Battle Green. Here, a bronze statue of Captain John Parker stands on a stone cairn, facing the line of the British approach. Behind him the Lexington militia would have stood. "Ye villains, ye rebels, disperse!" ordered the arrogant Major John Pitcairn. Faced by the superior numbers and strength of the British, Parker wisely told his men: "Don't fire unless fired upon, but if they mean to have a war, let it begin here!"

A shot rang out, no-one knows from where. Suddenly fire was exchanged; two British soldiers and eight Minute Men were killed or wounded. Seven of them are buried under the Revolutionary Monument farther along on the Green. The British, having beaten off this minor attack, marched on toward Concord.

In the nearby Visitor Center there is a diorama giving an overview of the events of that day. Next door to it is Buckman Tavern, a handsome three-story tavern (1710) where, in the early hours of April 19, 1775, several Lexington Minute Men had gathered to drink ale. Around 4am came the news that 700 British troops were just minutes from the Green. Bells rang out, drums rolled and the Minute Men, under the command of

Captain John Parker, filed out of the tavern. As the sun rose, they assembled on the Green, more as a protest than looking for a fight. The Tavern looks exactly as it did in 1775, with bar orders chalked on the tap room wall. The front door has a hole in it, allegedly from a bullet shot during the encounter.

From here go to the right of the Green and turn right on Hancock Street. Number 36 is the Hancock-Clarke House, where, at around 1am on April 19, 1775, John Hancock and Samuel Adams were awakened by a knock on the door. Paul Revere had arrived to warn these two important leaders that the British were on the march. This 1698 house is furnished as it would have been on that night. You can see Major Pitcairn's

The Old North Bridge, Concord

pistols (see previous page) and a drum belonging to Minute Man William Drummond.

i *1875 Massachusetts Avenue or Battle Green*

▶ *Return to the Minute Man statue and bear left. At the second stoplight, turn right on 2A West, which takes you into the Minute Man National Historical Park.*

❹ Minute Man National Historical Park

Although the actual road followed by the British troops has been largely covered over by Route 2A, a small section has been preserved in the Minute Man National Historical Park. Start at the Visitor Center, with its excellent "Road to Freedom" multimedia theater program. About a half mile (800m)

SPECIAL TO...

The events of April 19, 1775 are re-enacted each year on Patriots' Day. At sunrise, latter-day Minute Men from communities around Concord march through the woods much as their ancestors did. Historically accurate 1775 uniforms are *de rigueur*, both for the "farmers" and the "Redcoats." In a brief but moving ceremony near the Old North Bridge, officials from Britain and America pay their respects to those who died, as the *Last Post* rings out. Patriots' Day is also a state holiday on the Monday closest to April 19, with parades and ceremonies throughout the long weekend in Boston, Lexington and Concord. Details on www.battleroad.org

beyond is the site where Paul Revere was captured by a British patrol. His fellow messenger, Dr. Samuel Prescott, eluded them and rode on to Concord.

In another half mile (800m), a narrow winding section of the original Battle Road bears off to the right. This is a typical "two rod road," named because of the 32-foot (10m) distance between the stone walls on either side of the road (a rod measures 16 feet/5m). Here, the William Smith House and the Ephraim Hartwell Tavern are fine examples of Colonial architecture.

ⓘ *Minute Man Visitor Center, Route 2A, Lexington*

▶ *Continue on Route 2A, and at the Battle Road and Route 2A split, bear right for Concord.*

⑤ Concord
Concord was founded in 1635, and is redolent with history, from its historic houses (many with date plaques) to its reminders of the Revolution, to its fine literary heritage.

The approach to the center of Concord is along Lexington Road, where two on the right were the homes of famous writers. The Wayside, with its distinctive red brick chimneys, was originally the home of the muster master, whose job was to summon the Minute Men if the British attacked. In the 19th century, it became first the residence of the Alcott family, then in 1852, Nathaniel Hawthorne bought it and changed the name from Hillside to The Wayside. He completed *Tanglewood Tales* in his study in the tower at the top of the house.

A little way farther up the street is Orchard House, to which the Alcott family moved after leaving The Wayside. It was here that Louisa May wrote much of *Little Women*. Researchers for the 1992 movie of the book took photographs here and made sketches here, then built a house in Canada especially for the filming. It was not

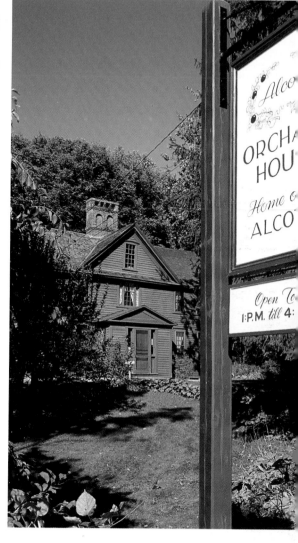

an exact replica, however, and those taking the guided tour may notice a number of differences, particularly in the bedrooms. Carefully preserved furnishings and costumes reflect the family's 20 years here.

Closer to the town center, make a left onto the Cambridge Turnpike for the Concord Museum. This is a fine example of a small museum, and it encompasses all aspects of Concord's history in a particularly engaging way. Relics of the

Orchard House, the home of novelist Louisa May Alcott

Revolution include Paul Revere's signal lantern and the sword that belonged to Colonel Barrett, commander of the Concord militia. Literary mementos include Louisa May Alcott's tea kettle and doll, Henry David Thoreau's bed, writing desk and rocking chair from his cabin at Walden Pond (see below), and Ralph Waldo Emerson's study, brought from his former home across the street and reconstructed here.

When Emerson's original house was destroyed by fire in 1872, the philosopher-poet's reaction was unusual, to say the least: "But isn't it a lovely blaze!" was all he said. Sent away to recover from the shock, he returned after a year to find that his home had been rebuilt by his friends and neighbors. Emerson's life here was characterized by "plain living and high thinking" but he is less remembered for his essays than for quotes such as, "If a man can write a better book, preach a better sermon, or make a better mousetrap than his neighbor, though he builds his house in the woods, the world will beat a path to his door." The reconstructed house is exactly as he left it – except for the study, of course.

Off Concord's Green, along Route 62 East, is Sleepy Hollow Cemetery, every bit as peaceful as it sounds. Here, on top of "Author's Ridge," are the last resting places of Louisa May Alcott, Ralph Waldo Emerson and Nathaniel Hawthorne. The grave of Henry David Thoreau is marked by a simple headstone, inscribed with only one word: "Henry."

The most famous site in Concord is undoubtedly the Old North Bridge on Monument Street, the "rude bridge" where, on April 19, 1775, "... the embattled farmers stood, And fired the shot heard round the world." These words are from the *Concord Hymn*, written by Emerson in 1837 to celebrate the completion of the Battle Monument. One of the most powerful American icons, it was sculpted by Daniel Chester French, who also created the figure of Abraham Lincoln for the Lincoln Memorial in Washington D.C.

On the day of the battle, some 400 Minute Men were waiting here to confront the 700 tired and worried British Regulars. As they advanced across the bridge, the famous

shot rang out. The sloping fields would have looked much as they do now, though the bridge is a modern replica. Nearby, at the edge of an open field, stands the Old Manse. It was from a window of this three-story wooden house that the parson, William Emerson, watched the bloody events. He was the grandfather of Ralph Waldo Emerson, who lived here as a little boy. In later years the house was rented to Nathaniel Hawthorne, and some of his possessions are still there, including his writing desk.

[i] Concord Visitor Center, 58 Main Street; North Bridge Visitor Center, 174 Liberty Street

▶ *Return to the Green. Leave Concord following the sign for Route 2A . After a short distance, turn right on Heywood Street, then left on Walden Street (Route 126 South). Continue for 1 mile (1.5km), crossing Route 2, to the Walden Pond parking lot.*

6 Walden Pond

Henry Thoreau came here and "lived alone, in the woods, a mile from any neighbor, in a house I had built myself, on the shore of Walden Pond." This two-year "back to nature" experience was the basis of his most famous work, *Walden*, published in 1854.

Seeking the solitude that he found may be difficult in summer, when families swim and picnic at "this pond ... so remarkable for its depth and purity ... a clear and deep well, half a mile long and a mile and three quarters in circumference ..." A replica of his cabin is conveniently close to the parking lot; to avoid the crowds, walk around to the far side of the water, where a cairn marks the site of the real cabin. The pond is surrounded by the 462-acre (187-hectare) Walden Pond State Reservation.

▶ *Follow Route 126 south for a short distance to Baker Bridge Road and turn left. At No. 68 is the Gropius House.*

7 Gropius House

This is the home of the German architect Walter Gropius, founder of the Bauhaus Movement, who moved to the U.S. in 1937 and lectured at Harvard for 14 years. The house was far ahead of its time, combining traditional architecture with the innovative use of modern materials, such as welded steel, glass blocks, and chrome. The house looks lived in: Coats hang in the hall, towels in the bathroom.

▶ *Continue to the end of the road and turn right onto Sandy Pond Road. On the left is the DeCordova Museum.*

8 DeCordova Museum

Dedicated to the work of contemporary American artists, this museum is located in 35

The Old North Bridge, actually a modern replica

Around 1845, Concord was the literary epicenter of America, with four of the country's most revered writers living near one another. Ralph Waldo Emerson (1803–82) was a philosopher, poet and magnetic speaker. Today, he is best remembered for the *Concord Hymn*, encapsulating the events of the Old North Bridge (see page 14). In 1837, he struck up a friendship with Henry Thoreau (1817–62). Thoreau came to live in Concord and spent two years in a small cabin that he constructed himself at the edge of Walden Pond. It was here that he wrote his most memorable book, *Walden*. The Salem-born novelist Nathaniel Hawthorne (1805–64), a Concord resident for a few years, was also part of the group. At that time, though Louisa May Alcott (1832–88) was just a child, she was already writing poems and romantic stories.

acres (14 hectares) of open fields and woods overlooking Sandy Pond. Around 75 works stand in New England's largest sculpture park. The museum store sells original works of art.

▶ *Return to Sandy Pond Road, turn left and drive to the first*

RECOMMENDED TRIPS

Canoes can be rented at the South Bridge Boathouse (on Main Street, Concord) for trips through Concord and the Great Meadows National Wildlife Refuge. Although there are 18 miles (29km) of navigable water, the paddle to the North Bridge and the 1.5 miles (2.5km) back is an easy two hours and is an excellent way to see parts of the town that haven't changed significantly since the Revolution.
If paddling is not your style, you can take the marked nature trail (3 miles/5km) in the wildlife refuge.

*intersection. Cross Lincoln Road, and continue on Trapelo Road for 2¹/₂ miles (4km) to **Route 128**. Go north on **Route 128** to **Route 2** east, the first exit, and return to Cambridge.*

FOR HISTORY BUFFS

"March with the Corps of Grenadiers and Light Infantry ... to Concord, where you will seize and destroy all Artillery, Ammunition, Provisions, Tents, Small Arms, and all Military Stores ... but you will take care that the Soldiers do not plunder the Inhabitants, or hurt private property."
Unfortunately the orders of General Gage were leaked to patriots in Boston and, as the British prepared to cross the Charles River on the night of April 18, two lanterns appeared in the belfry of the Old North Church. A waiting Paul Revere saw the signal and set off on horseback to tell the men of Lexington and Concord to be ready.

The North
Shore

One famous seaport after another follows the curve of the coast north of Boston, from the towns of Gloucester and Marblehead, to Salem and Newburyport. There are hundreds of handsome old houses, and dozens of high-quality museums and art galleries.

1 DAY • 134 MILES • 215KM

ITINERARY

BOSTON	▶ **Marblehead** (17m-27km)
MARBLEHEAD	▶ **Salem** (5m-8km)
SALEM	▶ **Manchester-by-the-Sea** (7m-11km)
MANCHESTER-BY-THE-SEA	▶ **Gloucester** (8m-13km)
GLOUCESTER	▶ **Rockport** (5m-8km)
ROCKPORT	▶ **Pigeon Cove** (2m-3km)
PIGEON COVE	▶ **Essex** (10m-16km)
ESSEX	▶ **Ipswich** (5m-8km)
IPSWICH	▶ **Plum Island** (21m-34km)
PLUM ISLAND	▶ **Newburyport** (11m-18km)
NEWBURYPORT	▶ **Boston** (43m-69km)

Salem Custom House where
Nathaniel Hawthorne worked

ℹ️ *Boston Common Visitor
Information Center, 147 Tremont
Street*

▶️ *Leave Boston via the Callahan
Tunnel, and follow **Route 1A** to
Lynn. After 8 miles (13km),
pass a rotary (roundabout),
and bear right onto Carroll
Parkway. Follow **Route 129**
along the sea wall to
Swampscott, and bear right
onto Puritan Road for 1 mile
(1.5km) until it rejoins **Route
129**. Go right on **Route 129** to
Ocean Avenue and turn right
to Marblehead Neck.*

❶ Marblehead Neck

On the road across the causeway,
look right for a view of the
Boston skyline. To the left, a
fleet of sailboats sits anchored in
Marblehead harbor. Bear right
and follow signs for the Bike
Route for about 2 miles (3km) to
Chandler Hovey Park and the
lighthouse.

From the park there are spectacular views all the way to
Manchester and Gloucester
harbors. Marblehead Neck itself
is all quiet residential streets.

▶️ *Return to **Route 129** and turn
right to Marblehead.*

❷ Marblehead

The up-hill-and-down-dale style
of Marblehead's old town
reflects the West of England
origins of the fishermen who
settled here in 1629. On Front
Street, the oldest houses cluster
round the harbor of what was
soon known as the "greatest
Towne for fishing in New
England."

As overseas trade developed,
merchants built bigger and
better houses, such as the 1768
Jeremiah Lee Mansion. A few
steps away is the Marblehead

Museum and Historical Society.
Marblehead sailors played a vital
role in the Revolution, and a
local boat, the *Hannah*, takes
pride in being America's first
warship. Today luxury yachts fill
the moorings.

ℹ️ *Information Booth, Pleasant and
Spring streets*

▶️ *Leave Marblehead on **Route
114**, then join **Route 1A North**
and drive 5 miles (8km) to
Salem.*

❸ Salem

One short period of hysteria in
the 17th century singled Salem
out from the rest of the North
Shore coastal ports. Now, more
than 300 years later, witchcraft
trials and executions have
become big business.

Those wanting to relive the
gruesome spectacles can visit
the Witch Museum, Witch
Village and Witch House, but
there is much more to see in this
historic town. The fine mansions
were so impressive that future-
president John Adams wrote in
1766: "the houses are the most
elegant and grand that I have
seen in any of the maritime
towns." Examples can be found
on Chestnut, Essex and Federal
streets.

Statue of Puritan Roger Conant, who founded Salem in 1626, outside the Salem Witch Museum

The Peabody Essex Museum, arguably America's oldest museum, is also one of New England's largest. It was started in 1799 by a group of sea captains wishing to display their souvenirs from far-flung voyages. The richest and most impressive section is the Asian Export Art Collection, which contains beautiful oriental objects that were made specifically for sale to the West. Don't miss the Native American collection, with its contemporary and historic works, and the Oceanic collection, whose 20,000 pieces date back to the museum's founding.

The town's nautical traditions are portrayed in the admirable Salem Maritime National Historic Site, which snakes along the harborfront.

$\boxed{i}$ *New Liberty and Essex streets*

FOR HISTORY BUFFS

Salem comes from the Hebrew word *Shalom*, meaning peace. But the calm of Salem was shattered in 1692 when several young girls began to have fits and accused three women of casting spells on them. Panic followed, other accusations were made, and before common sense prevailed, 19 people had been hanged, and one man, Giles Corey, was crushed by rocks. The hysteria was stamped out the following year, when the governor ordered all the "witches" to be released from prison, probably because his wife had been one of the accused!

▶ *Take **Route 1A North** across the bridge over Beverly Harbor, and follow **Route 127** through Beverly for 4 miles (6km) to the Prides Crossing railroad station.*

SPECIAL TO...

Salem's gloomy past inspired two authors in particular – Nathaniel Hawthorne and Arthur Miller. Born here, Hawthorne reflected the hypocrisy of Puritan Salem in *The Scarlet Letter* (the subject of a movie in 1995) and set *The House of the Seven Gables* in his cousin's home, which still stands. Three hundred years later, Arthur Miller wrote *The Crucible*, where he used the hysteria of the Salem witch trials as a symbol for the McCarthy anti-Communist trials that took place in the early 1950s.

---

4 Prides Crossing

When the railroad from Beverly was extended to Manchester in 1840, it crossed land once owned by the Pride family, who supposedly received the grant in the early 1700s from the King of England. The route was used by wealthy Bostonians who left the city and came out to spend the summers by the water in their large mansions. The railroad depot still has separate benches marked for use by Democrats and Republicans. Residents of this small village still commute to Boston's North Station. It's a 45-minute ride.

▶ *Continue on **Route 127** for 3 miles (5km) into the center of Manchester-by-the-Sea.*

5 Manchester-by-the-Sea

Originally settled by Englishmen from Manchester, the town's name was amended in 1990 to emphasize its position at the head of a pretty harbor, graced with its flotilla of sailboats. On one side of the town square is First Parish Church, dating from 1809, with a clock face on each side of its distinctive steeple. Visitors come in summer, not just to walk along the waterfront, but also to spend the day on Singing Beach, where the wind "sings" as it whistles along the sand.

▷ *Continue on* **Route 127** *for 3 miles (5km), then bear right for Magnolia. Continue through the town center and up the hill on Norman Avenue to Hammond Castle.*

❻ Hammond Castle Museum

Whenever you use a remote control button to switch television channels or open the garage from your car, the man to thank is Dr. John Hammond (1888–1965). This genius thought up over 800 inventions and was granted 400 patents, mainly to do with electronics. His quirky mind is reflected in the clifftop mansion he built in the mid-1920s, which incorporates bits of European buildings: there is an archway built with lava rock from Mount Vesuvius, and a Roman bath. There are even secret passages and a laboratory. Hammond is buried on the grounds with two of his cats and, as requested, poison ivy grows over his grave.

▷ *Return to* **Route 127** *and continue to Gloucester.*

❼ Gloucester

The first landmark in town to meet your eye is *The Man at the Wheel*, the statue of a ship's pilot staring out toward the mouth of the harbor. The statue was set in place in 1923 to commemorate Gloucester's 300th birthday, and as a reminder that the town continues to be a working port, America's oldest. Learn more at the Gloucester Maritime Heritage Center.

The loss of the *Andrea Gail* in the early 1990s was the inspiration for the book *The Perfect Storm*. Visitors still come to see where the movie (2000) was shot, as well as for whale-watching excursions and the annual Schooner Festival at the end of August or early September. The Cape Ann Museum is a tribute to artist Fitz Henry (Hugh) Lane, who lived out his life here and specialized in seascapes.

ⓘ *Stage Fort Park Information Center, Hough Avenue (seasonal) and 33 Commercial Street (year-round)*

FOR CHILDREN

At the Gloucester Maritime Heritage Center, kids can handle sea stars, sea urchins, crabs and sand dollars in the touch tanks of the aquarium. They can also explore the Stellwagen Bank National Marine Sanctuary, between Gloucester and Provincetown. Using the latest technology, they can learn about shipwrecks and the marine life, particularly the whales that come to feed in the waters in summer.

SPECIAL TO...

There really was a Cap'n Birdseye. As early as 1912, Clarence Birdseye of Gloucester was intrigued to see how the Inuit people of Labrador preserved their food by freezing it. By 1924, he had perfected the bulk deep-freezing technique that is taken for granted today. The company concentrated on fruit and vegetables in the early days, but as demand for his products grew, Birdseye needed to speed up the process, so he invented the multiple plate freezer, which is still used. In the 1950s, the company developed fish sticks, or fish fingers, a great favorite with children.

The pier at Gloucester
Inset: *The Man at the Wheel*

WHALE WATCHING...

Up and down the coast of New England, boats still set off to hunt for whales. Unlike the 19th century, however, the purpose is not to shoot the majestic mammals with harpoons, but with cameras. Tours depart regularly from Boston, but they also leave from Newburyport and Gloucester on the North Shore, from Portsmouth, New Hampshire and from Cape Cod towns such as Provincetown. The favorite places for spotting whales are the Stellwagen Bank and Jeffreys Ledge, both popular feeding grounds. Harbor porpoises and Atlantic white-sided dolphins, relatives of the whales, are also abundant, and have teeth rather than the baleen plates of the whales.

RIGHT WHALES

Named by Yankee whalers, because they were the "right" whales to catch, this is the most endangered species in the world. The whales are easily recognized by the callosities, crusty growths, on their backs. Reaching up to 50 feet and 60 tons (16m and 61,000kg), they can be spotted offshore from April through January.

HUMPBACK WHALES

The name comes from their habit of arching their backs before diving. They are also known to "breach," leaping clear out of the water, a particularly impressive sight, since humpbacks grow up to 50 feet (16m) long and 30 tons (30,500kg) in weight. They are resident off New England from spring through fall.

FIN WHALES

The largest whales in New England waters are also the most common. Reaching up to 70 feet (21m) in length and 50 tons (51,000kg), fin whales can be identified by their dorsal fin, as well as the white chevron on their backs. Like the humpbacks, they are resident from spring through fall.

SPECIAL TO...

The third weekend in May is Motif No. 1 Day in Rockport. It celebrates an old fishing shack, dating from the mid-1800s, that stands at the end of Bradley Wharf in Rockport Harbor. Local lore has it that, back in the 1920s, art teacher Lester Hornby was confronted by yet another student's sketch of this dark red hut, festooned with lobster traps and colorful lobster floats. "What? Motif number one again!" he exclaimed despairingly to the pupil. Would-be photographers and painters should walk to the end of the wharf to compose their own version of this picturesque icon.

▶ Follow **Route 127** for 1 mile (1.5km), then bear right onto East Main Street for Rocky Neck.

8 Rocky Neck and Beauport

The little peninsula of Rocky Neck traces its artistic tradition back to Fitz Henry (Hugh) Lane's 1844 painting, *Gloucester Harbor from Rocky Neck*. Among the galleries and artists' studios, the Bryan Gallery shows works by members of the Rocky Neck Art Colony.

Farther toward Eastern Point lighthouse is Beauport. From the turn of the century, big spenders such as R. T. Vanderbilt and J. D. Rockefeller, as well as such stars as Joan Crawford, came out here to consult Henry Davis Sleeper (1878–1934), *the* interior decorator of his day. In Beauport, his own summer home, he gave

The town of Gloucester

each of the 40 rooms a design theme, from the Lord Byron and Paul Revere Rooms to the China Trade and India Rooms. The house is now a museum, full of his collection of antiques and art.

▶ Return to Gloucester and follow signs for **Alternate Route 127A** to Rockport.

9 Rockport

As its name implies, Rockport's early fame was founded on rock, in particular the granite quarried for many of America's 19th-century monuments, bridges, and civic buildings. For the past century, however, Rockport has been better known for its artists' colony and the town is full of galleries and craft shops exhibiting their work, principally the Rockport Art Association's galleries on Main Street.

The heart of the action in this popular resort is Bearskin Neck, where old fishing lofts have been turned into studios and galleries, restaurants and stores.

Until 2005, Rockport was famously "dry," so liquor was not allowed to be sold. Years before Prohibition, Hannah Jumper led 200 women of Rockport in the Hatchet Gang raid of 1856. These militant teetotallers imposed their own ban on booze by smashing every cask, bottle, and flask they could find. And the men of Rockport didn't ask for one day after that. Now visitors can order drinks in many restaurants – as long as they are "in conjunction with the consumption of a meal."

ⓘ 3 Whistlestop Mall

▶ Leave town, rejoining **Route 127**, and follow signs for Pigeon Cove (2 miles/3km).

10 Pigeon Cove

Just off Route 127, this small community boasts an unusual building. At No. 52 Pigeon Hill Street stands the Paper House, built between 1922 and 1942 by Elis Stenman and his family. It took two decades and both the house and the furniture have been constructed out of 100,000 old newspapers. The walls are

215 sheets thick, the desk is made from the *Christian Science Monitor*, and a bookshelf uses only foreign papers!

▶ *Continue on* **Route 127** *and after 1 mile (1.5km) is the turning for Halibut Point State Park.* **Route 127** *continues past rocky points of land and art galleries to the rotary (roundabout) at* **Route 128**. *Go west on* **Route 128**, *then turn right onto* **Route 133** *west for Essex.*

⑪ Essex
The 30 or so antiques shops that line Main Street in this small, sleepy-looking town draw dealers and collectors from all over America for the quality and excellent value of their wares. The small Shipbuilding Museum, also on Main Street, recalls the town's heyday in the days of sail.

SPECIAL TO...

Woodman's of Essex is credited with inventing fried clams back in 1916, and is still one of the best-known clam shacks in New England. "Woodie's" is known for serving fresh, delicious fried clams, clam cakes, and New England clam chowder made with milk, butter, lots of potatoes, and clams.

▶ *Continue to Ipswich.* **Route 133** *north joins* **Route 1A**.

⑫ Ipswich
Ipswich has several fine houses, particularly the 1677 John Whipple House, one of the oldest Puritan homes still standing, and the Heard House. This Federal-style mansion retains its period furnishings and has collections of art, toys, carriages and sleighs.

Out of town, some 6 miles (10km) along Argilla Road, is the home of Chicago industrialist Richard T. Crane, on the crest of Castle Hill. This 59-room Great House recalls the stately homes of England, with its 63-foot

(18.9m) long gallery and 16-foot (4.8m) high ceilings. It is open for tours, and there are also concerts and a popular Fourth of July event on the grounds in summer.

Down below, the 5-mile (8km) long beach is one of the most beautiful north of Cape Cod. Beware of the three weeks from mid-July to early August when the voracious, biting "greenhead" flies take over the strand.

▶ *Continue north on* **Route 133** *and* **Route 1A** *for 11 miles (18km) to Rolfe's Lane. Turn right for Plum Island and the Parker Refuge.*

BACK TO NATURE

Located about 1 mile (1.5km) north of the turn-off to Crane's Beach on Route 133, Wolf Hollow is home to five North American wolves. On weekends, visitors have an hour-long presentation and then watch the wolves as they respond to commands from their trainers. Fear not, for although they are at close range, a strong fence separates observers from the observed.

---

⑬ Plum Island and the Parker River National Wildlife Refuge
Plum Island, first visited by Samuel de Champlain in 1601, is a 6-mile (10km) long beach that acts as a breakwater to the coastal towns. With its vast expanse of salt marsh, this is a major stopping point for birds migrating north and south each year. Early spring and late fall are the ideal times to see some of the 300 species.

On the way to the island, stop for information on recent sightings at the Joppa Flats Education Center and the visitor center of the Parker River National Wildlife Refuge.

Once in the refuge, follow the boardwalks across the dunes, but remember that swimming can be dangerous here because of

the cold water and the strong undertows.

▶ *Return to* **Route 1A** *and continue into Newburyport (11 miles/18km).*

⑭ Newburyport
This town at the mouth of the Merrimack River is an attractive, busy place. The Custom House on Water Street has a museum of all things maritime, including an extensive collection of model ships. The boat-building tradition continues over the river in Amesbury, where Lowell's Boat Shop has been making fishing dories since 1793. Recent years have seen a growth in the arts scene, with a dozen or so galleries and the Firehouse Center for the Performing and Visual Arts.

Two centuries ago, the town commissioned Charles Bulfinch, the architect of the State House in Boston, to design the Courthouse on High Street. This street is often called "sea captain row," with mansions such as the three-story Cushing House, built in 1808 by John Cushing. His son, Caleb, was the first emissary sent by the United States to China, and his collection of fine porcelain, paintings, and cabinetware from China fills the 21 rooms.

▶ *Leave on High Street (***Route 113***) and follow signs to I–95 south and* **Route 128**. *(Do not take* **Route 1**.) *Take I–95 south, then west. After about 30 miles (48km), turn south onto I–93 for Boston.*

RECOMMENDED WALKS

Halibut Point State Park is a delightful place to stop and stretch your legs, with well-maintained nature and walking trails. The point is not named for fish; it was originally called "Haul About Point" because sailing ships had to "come about" here and tack to sail around Cape Ann.

Cape Cod

2 DAYS • 241 MILES • 387KM

This 62-mile (100km) long peninsula is one of the `country's eminent vacation playgrounds. Route 6A, the Old King's Highway, passes through 300-year-old communities where every other house seems to be a craft shop, antiques store or bed-and-breakfast.

Fine example of Sandwich's famous glass, highly valued by collectors
Page 23: Scargo Tower

[i] *Cape Cod Chamber of Commerce, Hyannis*

▶ *Leave Boston on **I-93**; take **Route 3** south to the Sagamore Bridge, crossing the Cape Cod Canal.*

❶ Cape Cod Canal

Sailing from Boston around the outside of Cape Cod has always been dangerous. Indeed, even just a century ago, some 25 ships a year foundered on the 135-mile (216km) journey. Traders welcomed the opening of the canal in 1914, 300 years after Myles Standish of the Plymouth Colony first proposed the idea. Running 17 miles (28km) from Cape Cod Bay to Buzzard's Bay, the Canal is 160 yards (150m) wide. Nowadays, recreational yachtsmen take the short cut, watched by fishermen and cyclists on the Cape Cod Canal Bikepath.

[i] *70 Main Street, Buzzards Bay*

▶ *Now on **Route 6A**, continue to Sandwich (4miles/6km).*

❷ Sandwich

Sandwich reeks of old-world charm, due to its fine collection of 18th- and 19th-century houses, the Wren-like spire on the First Church of Christ, and tree-lined streets. Overlooking Shawme Pond is the 1654 Dexter Grist Mill, still in working order, and one of the oldest houses on the Cape, the 1675 Hoxie House. In classic "salt box" style, with diamond window panes, it contains 17th-century furniture, tools, and tableware inside. The Eldred House, next door, is now a museum dedicated to the children's author Thornton W. Burgess, best remembered for his *Peter Cottontail* stories.

Despite its 300 years of history, however, Sandwich is no living museum: You can still

charter a boat to go fishing offshore for cod.

▶ *Continue on **Route 6A** to Barnstable (12½ miles/20km).*

❸ Barnstable

Off the road to the left, 4 miles (6km) before Barnstable, Sandy Neck is a rich nature reserve where the dunes were trampled by U.S. soldiers training for the North African Desert campaign during World War II. When a north wind blows, watch for windsurfers skimming across Barnstable Harbor.

In town, drop into the Sturgis Library to see the original home of the Reverend John Lothrop, one of the first residents of the 1639 settlement. The library's genealogical records are useful for those searching out family roots, especially if they are descended from the Lothrops, who occupy much of the cemetery. The main industries in the 19th century were growing cranberries, and making bricks, some of which are now collector's items.

▶ *Continue on **Route 6A** to Yarmouth Port.*

4 Yarmouth Port

The Captain Bangs Hallet House reflects the affluence and sophistication of a successful sea captain's life in the 19th century. Located near the Yarmouth Port Post Office, its handsome Greek Revival façade hides the original 1740 structure. It is now the headquarters of the local historical society, and the starting point for pleasant walks through a nature preserve along the Botanic Trails of Yarmouth.

The 1680 Thacher House and the 1780 Winslow-Crocker House next door, now run by Historic New England (formerly SPNEA), are filled with high-quality furniture and household objects made in Colonial and Federal times by New England craftsmen.

i Yarmouth Area Chamber of Commerce, 424 Route 28, West Yarmouth

▶ Continue on **Route 6A** to Dennis and East Dennis.

5 Dennis and East Dennis

Few men can match Josiah Dennis' claim of having five villages named for him. This 17th-century Congregational minister is immortalized in East, West and South Dennis, as well as Dennisport and Dennis. In his home, the Josiah Dennis Manse, visitors can see his portable pulpit and browse round the small maritime museum.

Nearby is the Cape Cod Center for the Arts, whose campus includes three cultural venues. Best known is the Cape Playhouse, the oldest summer theater in the U.S. Here, Bette Davis worked as an usherette and Gregory Peck and Henry Fonda trod the boards. The Cape Cod Museum of Art focuses on artists associated with the Cape and nearby islands. The church-like building nearby is an art deco cinema, with leather seats and a mural by 20th-century American artist Rockwell Kent.

Take time to see the lie of the land from the Scargo Tower

where, on a good day, you can see Provincetown, 20 miles (32km) to the north.

i Dennis Chamber of Commerce, Junction Routes 134 and 28, West Dennis

▶ Continue on **Route 6A** to Brewster (7 miles/11km).

6 Brewster

On and behind Route 6A, which doubles as Main Street in Brewster, stand the elegant clapboard houses of 19th-century sea captains. At the height of New England's trading with China, as many as 100 lived here, and many are buried in the graveyard next to the "Captains' Church," the First Parish Church. Memories and records of that era are in the Brewster Historical Society Museum, East Brewster.

The society also looks after the Higgins Farm Windmill and the Harris-Blake House. Both these 18th-century structures are in West Brewster, in Drummer

You can watch the process of corn being ground at Brewster

FOR CHILDREN

The Cape Cod Museum of Natural History at Brewster is popular for its aquarium and lively exhibitions, lectures and tours explaining the Cape's bird and animal life. As well as two short trails in the wildlife sanctuary, the longer John Wing Trail is a fine walk to the unspoiled beach. Remember, though, to check times of tides before setting out. The museum also organizes KidSummer, a range of nature-oriented programs for 3–12 year olds.

Boy Park. Children can let off steam in the park's Playground by the Sea, and there are also band concerts on Sunday evenings in summer.

i Brewster Chamber of Commerce, 2198 Main Street

BACK TO NATURE

The alewife, a type of herring, spawns in fresh water every three or four years. In spring, these silvery fish swim up the narrow Stony Brook creek, using the fish ladder to bypass the water-powered Grist Mill on Stony Brook Road, just north of Brewster, off Route 6A, and return to the ponds where they were conceived.

▶ Continue on **Route 6A** to the Orleans roundabout.

�７ Orleans

The name rhymes with "beans," even though it commemorates the French Duke of Orléans, who fled here from the French Revolution in 1797. This busy town has been the "hub of the Outer Cape" for two centuries. Back then fish, and salt for preserving the catch, were shipped direct to Boston from tiny Rock Harbor on Cape Cod Bay.

▶ Continue north for 4 miles (6km) on what is now **Route 6** to Eastham. Just before the town, the road to Fort Hill, on the right, provides panoramic views above the cupola-crowned Victorian house of whaling captain Edward Penniman.

🄇 Eastham

The windmill opposite the Town Hall in Eastham, pronounced East-Ham, was built in Plymouth in 1688, rebuilt in Truro, then moved to its present site in 1808. The oldest windmill on the Cape, it is celebrated on Windmill Weekend in September. Samoset Road leads to Cape Cod Bay. Here, First Encounter Beach is the legendary site of the first meeting between the Pilgrims and the Native Americans. A metal plaque explains how arrows and musket fire were exchanged when the newcomers encountered the tribe, who remembered a slave trader kidnapping some of

their people six years before. Don't expect to find any arrowheads, though; the Pilgrims gathered up the arrows and sent them back to England as curiosities.

From here to Provincetown, the Cape is a landscape of steep dunes tufted with grass. On the Atlantic side, breakers pound the flat beaches while lighthouses emphasize the sense of solitude.

At the Salt Pond Visitor Center, beyond Eastham, displays and films explain the ecology and wildlife of the 43,600-acre (17,650-hectare) Cape Cod National Seashore, a stretch of unspoiled coastline some 40 miles long (64km). A road leads to Coast Guard Beach where, in 1929, Henry Beston spent a year writing his classic nature journal, *The Outermost House*. The book is evocative, and perhaps more readable than Henry Thoreau's *Walden*. The beach is superb.

Eye-catching façade on Cape Cod

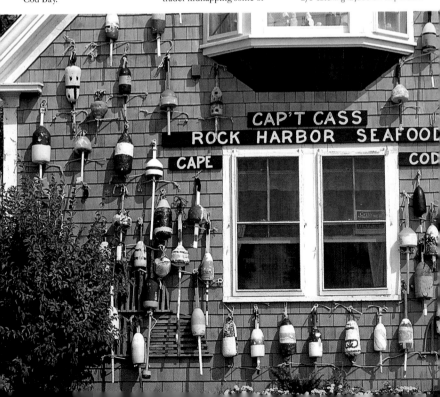

The Nauset Light is a reminder of the region's seafaring heritage

ℹ️ *Eastham Tourist Information Booth, Route 6 at Governor Prence Road (seasonal)*

▷ *Detour east to Coast Guard Beach, on Doane Road, then turn left on Ocean View Drive to Nauset Light Beach.*

SPECIAL TO...

The local Native Americans taught the Pilgrims how to cook shellfish and New Englanders still use the same method for a clambake on the beach. Dig a shallow pit into the sand, line it with stones and build a wood fire. When the wood has burned down, cover the hot stones with layers of damp seaweed, clean clams, more seaweed, corn on the cob and bluefish. Seal with a tarpaulin. Leave for an hour to steam, then uncover and eat.

9 Nauset Light Beach

As you drive through the typical scrub oak and pine that is the natural vegetation of Cape Cod, you will catch glimpses of the ocean to the right. You can venture down to a stretch of seemingly unending sandy beach, where the Atlantic waves thunder in, and you can get away from other people simply by taking a walk.

SCENIC ROUTES

The Cape Cod Central Railroad runs by cranberry bogs and marshes between Hyannis and the Cape Cod Canal. This should not be confused with the Cape Cod Rail Trail, where there is no longer a train. The Rail Trail follows the former Boston to Provincetown railroad route between South Dennis and Wellfleet. Here, the rail bed has been replaced by a smooth, 22-mile (35km) path. Its flatness makes it ideal for joggers, hikers, and cyclists.

▷ *Loop back to **Route 6** via Cable Road and Nauset Road to Wellfleet (7 miles/11km).*

10 Wellfleet

Famous for its oysters since Samuel de Champlain's Gallic taste-buds were tickled in 1606, this charming town, complete with picturesque harbor and photogenic old houses, now attracts artists. You can view their work in a dozen or more galleries. Fishing still goes on, and the clock on the First

Fishermen on the pier in Truro as the sun sets

Congregational Church reflects Wellfleet's nautical tradition by following ships' time, confusing landlubbers considerably by chiming, for example, two bells at one, five and nine o'clock. It is reportedly the only clock in the world to do so.

i Wellfleet Chamber of Commerce, off Route 6, South Wellfleet

RECOMMENDED WALKS

The Great Island Trail is an 8-mile (13km) round-trip walk along a narrow spit of sand. The trail is covered at high tide, and has views up to Provincetown and down to Brewster. To get there, follow Holbrook Avenue from Wellfleet Center. Turn right on Commercial Street, keep the water on the left, continue to Chequesset Neck Road and drive to the parking lot.

▶ Continue north on **Route 6** for 5 miles (8km) to Truro.

11 Truro
Originally named Dangerfield, this is a small, quiet neighborhood. For a taste of Pilgrim lore (and great views up to Provincetown), follow Castle Road, then Corn Hill Road, to Corn Hill Beach. Soon after the Pilgrim Fathers' arrival, Captain Myles Standish came across a cache of corn buried by a Native American in the sand. Desperate for food, he took it, but on meeting with the owner about a year later, Standish repaid him what was owed.

On the Ocean side of Route 6, the Cape Cod Highland Light stands on the site of the Cape's first lighthouse (1791). Climb to the top for panoramic views, then visit the small museum next door. Nearby, Highland Links is the oldest golf course on the Cape.

Farther north, park the car and hike the short Pilgrim Spring Trail to the spot where legend has it that the Pilgrim Fathers first found "springs of fresh water" after their grueling transatlantic crossing.

▶ Continue north on **Route 6** to Provincetown (10 miles/16km).

12 Provincetown
Although the Vikings are reckoned to have landed here long before, in AD 1004, this is where it all started for the Americans on November 11 or 21, 1620, depending on which calendar you use. The *Mayflower* dropped anchor in what is now Provincetown Harbor, after a 65-day voyage. Of the 102 passengers, one had died, but a baby had been born. Myles Standish, a soldier of fortune hired by the Pilgrims for protection, rowed ashore. These days, a rather unimpressive plaque on Commercial Street marks the event. After five weeks, the Pilgrims continued on their way, hoping to find a more hospitable site for settlement. They are remembered with the town's famous landmark, the Pilgrim Monument. Built in 1910, the granite tower soars 252 feet (76m) high. The stairs are a real test of stamina, but climbers can read the plaques noting the founding dates of Massachusetts towns. The reward is the observation platform at the top. The museum at the base tells the story of Provincetown.

The town's main industry of deep-water fishing for cod, mackerel and whales was established in the early 18th century. Although the fishing heyday passed over a century ago, boats still go out each morning to supply New York and Boston with fresh fish, and whale watching is popular in summer.

Today, in Provincetown, known almost universally as P-town, the fun really begins after the day-trippers have gone home. Artists have been coming here since Charles Hawthorne arrived in 1899. He taught for 30 years and his painting, *Fish Cleaners*, can be seen in the Town Hall.

Edward Hopper and Jackson Pollock are among the famous who joined the amateurs, working in the dazzling light on the shore. Playwright Eugene O'Neill wrote and produced his earliest plays in what was, and still is, a surprisingly bohemian town where everyone comes to have a good time.

[i] *307 Commercial Street*

▶ *Return on* **Route 6**, *but before the Orleans rotary (roundabout), turn off on* **Route 28** *for Chatham (32 miles/52km).*

B Chatham
Sitting right on Cape Cod's "elbow," Chatham relies on more than just tourism, thanks to its busy fishing fleet. The bounty of the sea is represented by the striking 1992 sculpture *Provider* on Fish Pier. Here, each afternoon, crates of flounder and

haddock, cod and squid are transferred straight from the boats to waiting trucks. Take a walk along Main Street, with its clapboard houses, restaurants, stores, and 180-year-old Mayo House, restored and open to the public. Chatham Lighthouse is an active Coast Guard station, continuing a 200-year-old tradition of warning mariners. Tours are offered once a week, in season.

[i] *533 and 2377 Main Street*

▶ *Take* **Route 28** *out of Chatham. Turn north on* **Route 137** *and rejoin* **Route 6** *at Exit 11. Follow* **Route 6** *back to the Sagamore Bridge, then* **Route 3** *to I-93 and back to Boston.*

Provincetown, overlooked by the Center Methodist Church
Inset: cranberries at Plymouth

2 DAYS • 181½ MILES • 292KM

The Berkshire
Hills

The Berkshires were once the exclusive playground of the rich. Now
these forested slopes are a vacation destination for everyone, particularly
music lovers who are drawn to the numerous summer festivals.

ITINERARY		
SPRINGFIELD	▶	**Monterey (32m-51km)**
MONTEREY	▶	**Gt Barrington (9m-15km)**
GREAT BARRINGTON	▶	**Sheffield (7½m-12km)**
SHEFFIELD	▶	**Stockbridge (20m-32km)**
STOCKBRIDGE	▶	**Lenox (7m-11km)**
LENOX	▶	**Pittsfield (6m-10km)**
PITTSFIELD	▶	**Williamstown (22m-35km)**
WILLIAMSTOWN	▶	**North Adams (3m-5km)**
NORTH ADAMS	▶	**Shelburne Falls (29m-46km)**
SHELBURNE FALLS	▶	**Deerfield (11m-18km)**
DEERFIELD	▶	**Northampton**
		(16m-26km)
NORTHAMPTON	▶	**Springfield (19m-31km)**

i 1441 Main Street, Springfield;
Riverfront Park Information
Center, West Columbus Avenue

SPECIAL TO...

Basketball was invented in
Springfield, and the town
boasts the Basketball Hall of
Fame. Desperate to exercise
bored young men during the
winter of 1891, Dr. James
Naismith nailed up a couple
of peach baskets in the gymnasium of the Springfield YMCA
and tossed them a soccer ball.
Basketball was born. At first,
the players had to put up a ladder to retrieve the ball every
time there was a score. Then
someone had a brilliant idea:
remove the bottom of the baskets. First accepted at the 1936
Olympics, basketball has
become the world's most
popular indoor sport.

FOR CHILDREN

South of Springfield on Route
159 is the Six Flags New
England theme and water park.
Its thrill rides include
Superman: Ride of Steel, a
combination of height, speed
and weightlessness, and
Batman: The Ride, with its
sensation of flying. Gentler
rides for younger children
include Harold the Helicopter
and *Looney Tunes* Animation
Department.

▶ From Springfield, take **Route
20** west across the
Connecticut River, through
West Springfield, passing the
Exposition grounds, site of the
huge "Big E," New England's
largest fair, held every
September. Bear left on **Route
23** west at Woronoco. Drive
through Blandford and Otis to
Monterey.

❶ Monterey

The Mexican name of this town
honors General Zachary Taylor, a
hero in the Mexican-American

War (1846–8). So popular was
"Old Rough and Ready" Taylor
after his victories at Monterey
and Buena Vista, that one
Kentuckian predicted (correctly)
that the general would win the
1848 presidential election "by
spontaneous combustion." Born
in Virginia, Taylor had no known
connections with the village.

▶ Continue on **Route 23**, past
the Butternut Ski Area.

❷ Great Barrington

Local inventor William Stanley
assured that this small town
would have its place in the
history books. He first demon-
strated the potential of using
alternating current here in 1886
by lighting up 24 stores on the
main street. Stanley's system,
more efficient than Edison's
cumbersome direct current

lighting, led to more widespread
use of electricity. A lamp and
plaque in the small park at the
corner of Main and Cottage
streets tell the story.

On six weekends in summer,
Simon's Rock College hosts the
Aston Magna Festival. It is the
oldest festival in America
devoted to baroque, classical and
early romantic music, all played
on period instruments.

▶ Leave town on **Route 7** and
head south for 7½ miles
(12km) to Sheffield.

❸ Sheffield

Back in the 18th century, two
minor events helped shape
American democracy. In 1773,

A cover image from the *Saturday
Evening Post*, painted by Norman
Rockwell

BACK TO NATURE

A few miles south of Sheffield is one of several small, flat-topped hills known locally as "cobbles." Barthlomew's Cobble is a 500-million-year-old lump of limestone and marble, doubling as a nature reserve.
Ledges Interpretive Trail (20 minutes) winds through rugged, glacially formed rocks. Here, some 45 species of fern, many of them rare, grow in the summer. A small museum records some of the 900 types of plants and wildlife in the area.

the Sheffield Declaration demanded freedom for the individual, while in 1787, Shays' Rebellion ended here. Poor farmers, many of them Revolutionary War veterans, thought they were being over-taxed and rebelled under Captain Daniel Shays. The seven-month protest brought the end of imprisonment for debt, and also strengthened the case for federal and state laws. A century or so ago, local people carved a large slab of marble into a monument honoring the rebellion. It stands in a field north of the town. Today, antiques shops line the main street.

▶ *Leave Sheffield west on Berkshire School Road to* **Route**

41 and turn north. Join **Route 23** *and take it through South Egremont to Great Barrington. Rejoin* **Route 7** *and head north to Monument Mountain.*

4 Monument Mountain

This jumble of huge boulders has long been a favorite for picnickers and hikers. Back in 1850, two of New England's best-known authors, Herman Melville and Nathaniel Hawthorne, first met here. Caught in a thunderstorm, they took shelter, drank champagne with their companions, and listened to a recitation of *Monument Mountain*. The poem relates the local legend of a love-lorn girl who leapt to her death from this mountain.

▶ *Continue north on* **Route 7** *to Stockbridge.*

5 Stockbridge

Stockbridge was created in 1722 as a well-meaning experiment by the London Society for the Propagation of the Gospel in Foreign Lands. The local Native Americans were invited to settle alongside the English Colonists in the hope that they would become "civilized," and follow Christian and English customs. Despite the support given by the Native Americans during the Revolutionary War, the Colonial ambitions of the settlers put an end to the experiment. Even today, Stockbridge remains picture-postcard pretty, with tall maples and elms. There is hardly a telephone or electricity pole in sight, the cables have been buried underground. The Red Lion Inn is the heart of the town, as it has always been since pre-Revolutionary days. Although this old coaching inn burned down in the 19th century, the Victorian replacement retains the wide porches, with rocking chairs for watching life pass by.

At the beginning of the 20th century, the Berkshires became a resort for millionaires. Up Prospect Hill is Naumkeag, the Choate family's magnificent estate. The 44-room mansion vies for attention with the land-

FOR HISTORY BUFFS

The charming wooden Ashley House near Sheffield is named after Colonel John Ashley who campaigned for The Sheffield Declaration of equal rights in the late 18th century. His slave, Mum Bet, is better remembered, since she used her master's arguments to gain her own freedom in 1783. The woodwork and paneling in Ashley's upstairs study show the skill of the craftsmen who built the house in 1735.

RECOMMENDED WALKS

Two trails lead to Squaw Peak, the 1,735-foot (520m) summit of Monument Mountain. One is steeper and shorter; the other is easier and longer. Check the map of the mountain in the parking lot. Enjoy the oaks, white pines, laurels and chestnuts, the mysterious caves under overhanging rocks and the rushing streams. A fine view can be had from the top.

The Norman Rockwell Museum in Stockbridge

scaping, especially the famous "Blue Steps."

As you leave Stockbridge to continue the itinerary, look for the Berkshire Botanical Garden, 2 miles (3km) out of town at the junction of Routes 183 and 102. One of the oldest botanical gardens in the U.S., it is a beautiful and relaxing place to visit, with 15 acres (6 hectares) of colorful landscaped gardens that include water features, annual and perennial beds, vegetable plots, a children's garden and a woodland trail.

From the Berkshire Botanical Garden, Take Route 183 south to the Norman Rockwell Museum. Installed on the old Linwood estate, the museum has 600 of the illustrator's works, and contains his studio, which was moved here lock, stock, palette, and paintbrush. Rockwell's *Saturday Evening Post* magazine covers made him a household name, and many favorites are here. Freckle-faced boys, cuddly grannies and Thanksgiving turkeys all appear bathed in the glow of nostalgia.

Near by is Chesterwood, the summer home and studio of sculptor Daniel Chester French. The best known of his 1,000 works are national symbols: the solemn, seated figure of

Abraham Lincoln in the Lincoln Memorial in Washington D.C. and *The Minute Man* statue in Concord, Massachusetts.

[i] *Main Street*

▶ *After see all the Stockbridge area attractions, head north on* **Route 183** *for 6 miles (10km) to Tanglewood.*

❻ Tanglewood

The former country estate of the Tappan family is now synonymous with music. Although the New York Symphony first performed here in 1934, it is the Boston Symphony Orchestra that has made Tanglewood its summer home since 1936. Over the years, millions have come to

---

SPECIAL TO...

The 1969 film *Alice's Restaurant* was based on an incident that has become a legend. After folk singer Arlo Guthrie and friends had enjoyed their Thanksgiving dinner in an old church in Housatonic, they deposited the leftovers outside the Stockbridge town dump.

Guthrie was arrested by Officer Obie, and ended up in jail. The conviction meant that Guthrie, a Vietnam protester, could not be drafted for the war. As for Alice and her restaurant, she had several in the area; one is now the Main Street Café in Stockbridge.

---

picnic on the grounds before listening to concerts in the 5,000-seat Koussevitzky Music Shed. Great conductors such as Leonard Bernstein and Seiji Ozawa have directed here. In 1994, the 1,200-seat Seiji Ozawa Hall was added: the rear wall opens on to a grassy hillside. Jazz is also on the program, along with performances by musicians, singers and conductors attending the prestigious Tanglewood Music Center. Also on the grounds is a reproduction of author Nathaniel Hawthorne's Little Red House, the summer cottage where he wrote *The Tanglewood Tales* and *The House of the Seven Gables*.

▶ *Follow* **Route 183** *to Lenox.*

❼ Lenox

Because of the movie *The Age of Innocence*, there has been renewed interest in the Pulitzer Prize-winning writer Edith Wharton (1862–1937). Visitors come to this attractive town because it was the haunt of some of America's richest families more than a century ago. The Vanderbilts, Carnegies, and other stars of New York's upper crust summered in what they referred to as "Berkshire cottages." Some of these grand estates still exist, others are charming small hotels such as Wheatleigh and Blantyre. The Mount, Wharton's 35-room mansion, was built to

Enjoying one of the summer concerts at Tanglewood

Williamstown's Gothic cathedral
Inset: Hancock Shaker Village

her own rigid specifications. She spent her happiest years here (1902–11), writing such novels as *Ethan Frome* in bed each morning. Shakespeare & Company, the popular theater group, has performances all year long. Its three venues include an outdoor space for free plays and concerts. As well as works by the Bard, it produces contemporary plays.

☒ *Chamber of Commerce, 5 Walker Street*

▶ *Continue north on* **Route 7A/7** *toward Pittsfield. On the right, just before the town, are signs for Arrowhead.*

8 Arrowhead

Author Herman Melville (1819–91) was inspired by the Berkshires. Between 1850 and 1863, he lived on this farm where the views reminded him of his seafaring days: "I look out of my window in the morning when I rise as I would out of the porthole of a ship in the Atlantic." He could see the humpbacked, whale-like shape of Mount Greylock, a constant influence as he wrote *Moby-Dick*. The novel did not sell, so Melville was forced to leave

Arrowhead and take a job as a customs officer in New York. He died a poor man.

☒ *Pittsfield Visitor Information Center, 109 South Street*

▶ *Continue north for 2 miles (3km) to Pittsfield, turn left on* **Route 20** *and drive 6 miles (10km) to Hancock Shaker Village.*

9 Hancock Shaker Village

The Shakers, a socialist Christian sect, are remembered for their use of dance in religious services, and their exquisitely simple but practical furniture and architecture. The last of the Shakers left Hancock in 1960, after 170 years, but their homes, workshops, herb gardens, and farm have been restored and revived.

Typical is the three-story round barn, built in 1826, where one man standing in the center can feed 54 cows with ease. Special events include Shaker suppers and timber-frame building demonstrations. The tranquility of the 1,200 acres (480 hectares) of meadows and woodlands clearly reinforces Hancock's original Shaker name: the City of Peace.

▶ *Return to Pittsfield and* **Route 7**. *Continue north to Williamstown on* **Route 7**.

10 Williamstown

Revolutionary soldier Colonel Ephraim Williams' gift of money ensured that both the town and college would bear his name. With that, he outdid earlier educational benefactors such as John Harvard and Nicholas Brown, who only have schools named for them. Today, Williams College is one of the country's most distinguished small colleges, and the town is one of the most attractive in New England.

There is plenty here for culture addicts. First on anyone's list should be the Sterling and Francine Clark Art Institute. The art collection was

created by the Singer sewing machine heir and his French wife and features works by European and American painters. Included are *At the Concert*, one of 30 paintings by Pierre Auguste Renoir; a study of Rouen Cathedral by Claude Monet; and *Rockets and Blue Lights* by J. M. W. Turner.

Next is the college's own Museum of Art, which concentrates on modern and contemporary art. Contemporary works, such as Andy Warhol's yellow and black self-portrait are on display. For 50 years, the Williamstown Theatre Festival has attracted such star names as Kathleen Turner and Roger Rees to participate in the summer season.

☒ *Routes 2 and 7; also 70 Denison Park Drive*

▶ *Drive east on* **Route 2** *for 4 miles (6.5km) to North Adams.*

11 North Adams

The term Museum of Contemporary Art will never be the same after you have been to the innovative Massachusetts Museum of Contemporary Art (MASS MoCA). Contemporary in every sense of the word, the museum embraces a dynamic approach to putting visual, performing and media arts on show. The whole process of creativity is explored here, and the center not only stages exhibitions and performances by renowned artists, but also shows work in progress in its art fabrication shops, production

---

BACK TO NATURE

Halfway between Lenox and Pittsfield is the Pleasant Valley Wildlife Sanctuary. With its hummingbirds and beavers, this is a delightful place for a stroll. Some 7 miles (11km) of marked trails meander through the 1,400 acres (560 hectares) of meadow and forest.

studios, performance rehearsals and the use of multimedia technologies. The museum is housed in a converted mill complex consisting of some 26 buildings, linked by covered bridges and elevated walkways.

▶ Continue east on **Route 2**.

⑫ Shelburne Falls
Hamlets dot this rugged road as it passes through forests and along the edges of gorges where the gushing water once drove the mills. Shelburne Falls is enjoying a renaissance, and members of the local horticultural society have had

SCENIC ROUTE

Three hundred years ago, Native Americans crossed the Berkshire Hills by walking a trail cut through the forest. Later, pioneer settlers broadened the route on their way through to what is now New York State. Opened in 1914 as one of America's first "scenic highways," the Mohawk Trail is a popular drive these days, especially in the fall (see pages 102–3). The Mohawk tribe is remembered with *Hail to the Sunrise*, the statue of a serene Native American brave, his arms raised to the east.

the ingenuity to disguise a 400-foot (120m) long trolley bridge with a hanging flower garden, the Bridge of Flowers.

ℹ️ *75 Bridge Street*

▶ *Continue to Greenfield and turn south on **Route 5** to Historic Deerfield.*

⑬ Deerfield
Called simply "The Street," Deerfield's main thoroughfare is lined with the most impressive

The *Hail to the Sunrise* memorial at the entrance to the Mohawk Trail State Forest collection of original Colonial houses in New England. The surrounding fields and absence of advertising completes the film-set effect. A dozen of the 65 18th- and 19th-century houses are open to the public for guided and self-guided tours.

Don't miss the Flynt Center of Early New England Life, which provides insights into the life of this community back in the 18th and 19th centuries. Rotating exhibits of fine American-made furniture and silver reflect the affluence of local families, while the costume collection shows that, even in western Massachusetts, staying fashionable was important.

In 1675, Native Americans massacred farmers as they paused to eat grapes, giving a nearby stream its present name of Bloody Brook. In 1704, the French and Native Americans ravaged the town in the depths of winter, carrying off 112 prisoners to Canada.

The Indian House Door, with its gaping hole hacked by a tomahawk, is preserved in the Memorial Hall. The hall was once used by students at the 200-year-old Deerfield Academy, a well-known boarding school.

▶ *You can either continue south for 16 miles (26km) on* **Route**

FOR CHILDREN

Butterflies never fail to delight children, and they are sure to be captivated by Magic Wings, a butterfly conservatory and garden. Lush gardens house 4,000 colorful, free-flying tropical butterflies and moths, and outdoor gardens have been planted specially to attract indigenous species.

5 to Northampton or use the faster route, I–91.

14 Northampton

With its mixture of industrial and educational heritage, Northampton is a pleasant, balanced sort of town. Little evidence remains that it was first settled in 1654.

In the 1980s, a vigorous program of downtown renewal sprouted restaurants and boutiques. It is the home of one of America's first women's colleges, founded in 1875 by Sophia Smith, and Smith College is still one of the nation's most prestigious schools.

ℹ️ *99 Pleasant Street*

▶ *Return to* **I–91** *south and drive to Springfield.*

Dwight House is a delightful example of early 18th-century architecture in Deerfield

FOR HISTORY BUFFS

"This is my letter to the world, that never wrote to me ..." penned the poet and recluse Emily Dickinson (1830–86) who lived in Amherst, northeast of Northampton, on Route 9. Of her 1,700 poems, only 11 had been published by the time she died. Hundreds were later found in her bedroom. Dickinson rarely left the house, but was a favorite with local children, lowering baskets of her home-baked gingerbread to them from her window. Most of her papers and belongings are kept at Harvard University and Amherst College, but her white dress hangs in her house. The garden at Amherst is a delight.

SPECIAL TO...

Sylvester Graham of Northampton was a 19th-century food fanatic who gave his name to Graham flour, a type of wholewheat flour later used for Graham Crackers.

BOSTON

With its unique blend of history and modern development, its "walkable" downtown and efficient public transport system, Boston is a delight for the visitor. Words like "sophisticated" and "civilized" are often used to describe this city that feels European but is the birthplace of American liberty. Balancing all this is a lively student population of more then 250,000, from around 60 colleges and universities.

The city owes its foundation to the sea. When the Puritans settled here in 1630, they found poor soil, but a fine harbor. By 1700, only the ports of London and Bristol outranked Boston. Until 1755, Boston was the largest city in North America. Its place on the American stage was guaranteed less by wealth and more by its independent thinkers, who had been in the forefront of the Independence movement (see pages 8–9).

Boston's great strength is that it has moved with the times. After the Revolution, Beacon Hill was developed for elegant housing, followed by Back Bay, a landfill project that is now an area of chic stores, galleries and cafés. In the 1960s, a bold plan of urban renewal revitalized Quincy Market. Most recently, a project nicknamed the Big Dig has transformed downtown. North-south traffic has been diverted to a tunnel; the ugly elevated highway that once divided the harbor area from the rest of the city has been torn down; the result is a mile of airy, clean parkland, with lawns, trees and benches.

As well as theater, music and art galleries, sport plays a major part in the life of the city. The professional teams boast proud histories in the nation's four favorite sports: baseball (the Red Sox), hockey (the Bruins), basketball (the Celtics) and football (the New England Patriots).

As for getting around, that is easy. "The T," as locals call the MBTA (Massachusetts Bay Transport Authority), was the country's first such subway system, opened in 1897.

The USS *Constitution*

Tour 5

The Boston Freedom Trail is a "must" for anyone interested in American history. A red line on the pavement leads visitors along the world's first self-guided walking tour of its kind. Along the route are buildings that played an important role in the uprising against British Colonial rule over 200 years ago. This is no dry re-run of history, however.

There is also tantalizing trivia, from America's oldest restaurant to the nation's oldest commissioned vessel. Plaques and cemeteries, sculpture and bullet marks are also pointed out to give a fascinating insight into the history of the city, known as the "Cradle of the American Revolution."

Tour 6

There is more to Boston than Revolutionary history. This walk shows off the contrasts in Boston, starting down by the water and the modern aquarium and ending at Copley Square, where the Boston Marathon ends. In between are the cobbled streets and Georgian front doors on Beacon Hill, the chic stores of Newbury Street, and the open-air elegance of the Public Garden. Always a city that has welcomed strangers, there are also moving tributes to African Americans and victims of the Holocaust.

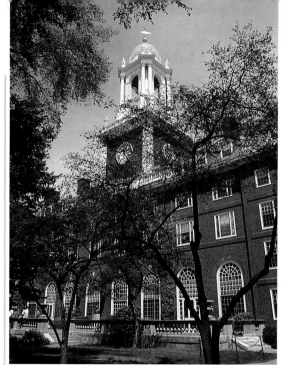

Tour 7

Harvard University is one of the world's great educational institutions. Its libraries and museums boast some of the finest collections in the world, housed in magnificent examples of architecture from the 18th century to the present day. At the same time, the student body, which numbers 6,700 undergraduate men and women, adds zest to Cambridge, where coffee shops and boutiques, bookstores and

Harvard University is one of the pre-eminent Ivy League establishments in the country

art galleries are a pleasure for students and visitors alike. With huge mature trees along the Charles River, and New England clapboard houses, Cambridge retains its own character, totally distinct from Boston, just a bridge or two away.

Boston's impressive skyline at night

The Boston
Freedom Trail

A local journalist, William Schofield, came up with the simple idea of linking Boston's historically important sites with a walking trail in 1951. Since then, millions have taken the route, marked sometimes by a painted red line, at other times by red bricks.

HALF A DAY

NORTH SHORE

Bunker Hill Monument ★ 19

PLEASANT ST
MONUMENT AVE
WARREN ST
COLEY ST
MAIN ST

CHARLESTOWN
NEW HAMPSHIRE

CHELSEA STREET

Charlestown Navy Yard ★
USS *Constitution* Museum ★
18 USS *Constitution* ★

Hoosac Pier

Boston Inner Harbor

Charles River

93

CHARLESTOWN BRIDGE

TIP O'NEILL TUNNEL

COMMERCIAL S
17 Copp's Hill Burying Ground ★
16 Old North Church ★
PAUL REVERE MALL

CAUSEWAY STREET

HULL STREET
PRINCE ST

NORTH END

HANOVER STREET
NORTH STREET
RICHMOND ST

15 Paul Revere House ★

Haymarket 14 ★

BEACON HILL

Union Oyster House
Haymarket
CONGRESS ST
MARSHALL ST
NORTH ST

13 Boston Stone ★

Burying Ground

King's Chapel 7 ★
Park Street Church
6
State House Church
Shaw Memorial
2 ★
3
BEACON STREET
PARK ST
SCHOOL STREET
WASHINGTON STREET
TREMONT ST

12 ★
State Old State
COURT ST House ★
10 ★
STATE ST
8 ★ Old Corner Bookstore

11 Faneuil Hall ★

NEW ATLANTIC AVENUE

FINANCIAL DISTRICT

Granary Burying Ground ★
1
Visitor Center
Park Street
9 ★ Old South Meeting House

CONGRESS STREET

93

Boston Common
1 ★

0   250   500 yards
0   250   500 m

CAPE COD

Allow half a day, longer if you want to explore the Charlestown Navy Yard, located near the end of the trail, home of the USS *Constitution*. Remember that in summer long lines build up to see this historic ship.

▶ *Start at the Visitor Center on Boston Common, just a few steps down the hill from the Park Street MBTA stop.*

❶ Boston Common

Often called America's first public park, this common land in the very heart of Boston was set aside in 1634 for "the feeding of Cattell" and as a "trayning field" for militia. Once the cattle left around 1830, the Common was used for recreation and oration. In 1851, Amelia Bloomer, wearing her manly "bloomers," campaigned for women's rights.

In the 20th century, charismatic speakers such as Martin Luther King, Jr. and Pope John Paul II addressed large crowds here. Today it is an area of lawns, trees, and even baseball diamonds.

▶ *Follow the red line to the State House.*

❷ State House

Built in 1795, this "new" seat of state government replaced the Old State House of 1713. The original red-brick structure was designed by Charles Bulfinch, the most able and sought-after architect of his day. His original dome of wood was replaced first with a copper one, then gilded with 23-carat gold leaf in 1861.

▶ *Just across Beacon Street is a large monument.*

❸ Shaw/54th Regiment Memorial

The lively bronze bas-relief by Augustus Saint-Gaudens pays tribute to the local black soldiers who volunteered to fight for the North in the American Civil War. Prejudice confined blacks to the ranks, but wealthy white Bostonian Robert Gould Shaw led what became the 54th Massachusetts Regiment. He was killed, along with 32 of his soldiers, in the assault on Fort Wagner, South Carolina. Their heroism inspired the 1989 movie *Glory*, which won three Academy Awards.

The Robert Gould Shaw/54th Regiment Memorial

▶ *Walk back down the Common to Park Street Church.*

❹ Park Street Church

Founded in 1809, this is where anti-slavery campaigner William Lloyd Garrison made his first speech in 1829. Two years later, the hymn *America* was first sung on the steps, and it remains part of the church's Fourth of July tradition. It is ironic that the melody is the same as the British national anthem.

▶ *Adjacent to Park Street Church, facing Tremont Street, is the Granary Burying Ground.*

❺ Granary Burying Ground

Buried here are some of the best-known leaders of the patriot cause: John Hancock, Samuel Adams, John Otis, and Paul Revere (see page 12). One of the most popular graves, however, is that of Mary Goose, also called Elizabeth Vergoose, and supposedly the original Mother Goose. The mother and step-mother of a total of 20 children, she was buried here in 1757. Her son-in-law is

SPECIAL TO...

The Omni Parker House, a hotel since 1855, overlooks King's Chapel and the Burying Ground. Parker House rolls became widely known and served, perhaps because they were considered the "patrician accompaniment to formal dining." Ironically, these popular rolls were served to customers by two of the 20th century's most radical figures who both worked here as waiters: Ho Chi Minh, later leader of North Vietnam, and Malcolm X, the 1960s militant black leader.

supposed to have published *Mother Goose's Melodies* (*Songs for the Nursery*).

▶ *Continue on Tremont Street. Cross to King's Chapel, on the corner of School Street.*

❻ King's Chapel

Dating from 1749, King's Chapel was seen as a symbol of British rule in North America. The colony's governors worshipped in a special canopied pew. George Washington also used it in 1789; perhaps one reason that it has survived. Today's congregation follows a mixture of Church of England and Unitarian liturgy.

▶ *Walk down School Street. Beside the chapel is the graveyard.*

7 Burying Ground

This cemetery contains the graves of several historic figures, including Mary Chilton, the first of the *Mayflower* pilgrims to reach Plymouth Rock, and John Winthrop, first governor of the colony. Others buried here include William Dawes, who joined Paul Revere in his "midnight ride," as well as Elizabeth Pain, who provided the inspiration for Hester Prynne in Nathaniel Hawthorne's *The Scarlet Letter*. The oldest gravestone in Boston remembers William Paddy, who died in 1658.

▶ *Walk down School Street, passing Old City Hall.*

8 Old Corner Bookstore

Once a famous bookstore (now a jeweler), this is one of Boston's oldest buildings. Starting out as an apothecary shop in 1712, it became famous in the mid-19th century as the publishers Ticknor and Fields. Their best-selling authors included Nathaniel Hawthorne, Henry Wadsworth Longfellow, Henry David Thoreau, and Julia Ward Howe, who penned *The Battle Hymn of the Republic*, the anthem of the North during the Civil War.

▶ *Turn right on Washington Street.*

9 Old South Meeting House

Standing in the quiet simplicity of this 1729 Congregational church, it is hard to imagine the fiery debates that inflamed political passions and led to the Revolution. Back then, "Old South" was the largest space

available for public assemblies. After the Boston Massacre in 1770, protesters marched from here to confront the lieutenant-governor.

More than three years later came the meeting that triggered the Boston Tea Party (see page 8). Today, the second-oldest church in Boston is a museum recording those tumultuous days.

ⓘ *Boston National Historical Park Visitor Center, 15 State Street*

▶ *Turn back and follow Washington Street past the Corner Bookstore. Just before State Street, a walkway to the right leads to the Old State House.*

10 Old State House

The lion and unicorn symbolize the connection with the Mother Country, a link which James Otis demanded be cut as early as 1761. Five years later, the hated Stamp Act was debated here and, on July 18, 1776, Colonel Thomas Crafts stepped on to the balcony to read the Declaration of Independence. Two hundred years later, Queen Elizabeth II stood on the same spot and spoke in celebration of the American bicentennial. Note the ring of cobblestones outside

the seat of the Massachusetts Assembly, recording the Boston Massacre of 1770, when five Bostonians were shot by British soldiers (see page 8). The museum inside tells the story.

▶ *Cross Congress Street diagonally.*

11 Faneuil Hall

In Boston, Faneuil rhymes with Daniel, and the name recalls the French merchant who funded the construction of Boston's marketplace in 1742. In the meeting hall above, freedom of speech was a prerogative. Locals congregated in 1764 to object to the Sugar Act. In the following years, their topics of protest were taxation and English troop movements. Samuel Adams' rebellious speech in 1772, stirring up anti-British feelings, was particularly provocative. But debate did not stop with Independence.

Over the centuries, Bostonians have spoken their minds here on issues such as slavery, alcohol, the Vietnam War and women's rights. Like the Old State House, there is a reminder of England: the grasshopper that tops the building is thought to be a copy of the weathervane on the Royal Exchange in London.

Union Oyster House where Daniel Webster used to dine

Boston's oldest public building, the 1713 Old State House

▶ *Turn right into Hanover Street, Walk back to Blackstone Street.*

🄸 Haymarket

Vendors still set out their produce here on Fridays and Saturdays as they have for 300 years. In contrast to modern air-conditioned supermarkets, this is a noisy, bustling market, with a huge variety of fruit and vegetables, locally grown and from around the world.

▶ *Follow the Freedom Trail red line to Hanover Street, crossing the Rose Kennedy Greenway. Turn right on Richmond Street, then left on North Street to North Square.*

🄸 Paul Revere House

Revere's talent as a silversmith, bell-maker, engraver, and even false teeth-maker fade away in the light of his fame as messenger. He rode to Lexington on the night of April 18, 1775 to warn that "the British are coming!" (see page 12). His tiny wooden home, at No. 19, is the oldest in Boston (1680) and is as plain and simple inside as Revere left it.

▶ *Leave North Square on Prince Street, turn right on Hanover Street, then left on Paul Revere Mall to the Old North Church.*

SPECIAL TO...

For almost 50 years, an elevated expressway cut off downtown Boston from the harbor. The multi-billion dollar project nicknamed 'the Big Dig' banished cars and trucks to tunnels. Where the steel structure that carried traffic once stood is now a mile-long series of parks, the Rose Kennedy Greenway. Each of the four sectors has its own theme and design. Once more, the financial district is just a few steps away from the waterfront.

▶ *Follow the red line across North Street to Union Street. (For the Holocaust Memorial, see page 46.)*

🄸 Union Oyster House

Dating back to 1826, this place enjoys the title of the "oldest continuously operated restaurant in America." It started life as a store, but became a place to eat in 1826. Lawyer Daniel Webster used to sit at the bar, consuming up to six glasses of brandy and three dozen oysters at a sitting.

▶ *Turn onto Marshall Street for the Boston Stone.*

🄸 Boston Stone

Myth insists that this millstone marked the true center of Boston, and that all distances were measured from here. This is a tribute to the public relations skills of a tavern owner who set the stone up as a publicity stunt back in 1737. The stone itself was used originally for grinding pigment by Thomas Child, a painter from London.

Paul Revere's House, restored to its original appearance, now operates as a small museum

16 Old North Church

Sexton Robert Newman had to flash lanterns ("One if by land, and two if by sea") to fellow patriots across the Charles River to warn them of British troop movements. He hung up two from the 191-foot (58m) steeple that is still visible in many parts of the city.

Supposedly, one John Childs *flew* from the steeple in 1757, though contemporary reports do not explain how. Officially named Christ Church, it is the oldest in Boston (1723), and remains a place of worship. On the "Behind the Scenes" tour, you can go up into the bell-ringing chamber and down into the crypt. Here is the tomb of British Major John Pitcairn (see page 11).

▶ *Go uphill on Hull Street.*

17 Copp's Hill Burying Ground

This is not a resting place of famous historic figures, though Sexton Newman is buried here, as is early African American

community leader Prince Hall. The old headstones are worth a look, particularly that of Daniel Malcolm. Used for target practice by the British soldiers who camped here, the scars are still clear to see.

▶ *Continue downhill on Hull Street; turn left on Commercial Street, then right across Charlestown Bridge. At the north end of the bridge, follow the red line, turning right on Chelsea Street.*

18 USS *Constitution*

Like HMS *Victory* in England, this is still a commissioned ship and an icon for the navy. A magnificent example of a wooden warship, her greatest glory came in the war of 1812

against the British, who were then masters of the sea. She destroyed four enemy frigates and sloops and earned the nickname, "Old Ironsides," when, as cannonballs bounced off her hull, a seaman shouted "Huzzah! Her sides are made of iron!" In fact, the ship is made of live oak, a particularly tough wood from southeastern U.S.A.

▶ *Follow the trail to the Bunker Hill Monument.*

19 Bunker Hill Monument

A 221-foot (67m) obelisk commemorates the first major battle of the Revolutionary War, which was fought on this hill on June 17, 1775. Facing a mighty British force, the ill-equipped Colonists stood their ground, mindful of the now legendary order, "Don't fire until you see the whites of their eyes!" Though the Colonists were eventually routed, they reduced the British army's numbers considerably and the battle was significant in their ultimate victory. There is an exhibition across the street.

▶ *Return to the bridge or take the MBTA water shuttle to Long Wharf.*

FULL DAY

Boston
Old & New

Boston's development started by the water, then moved inland to Beacon Hill where the wealthy lived. Later, it included Back Bay, which was reclaimed land. Allow a full day for this tour, which traces highlights of that growth, from narrow streets to grand boulevards, with Georgian houses and modern skyscrapers.

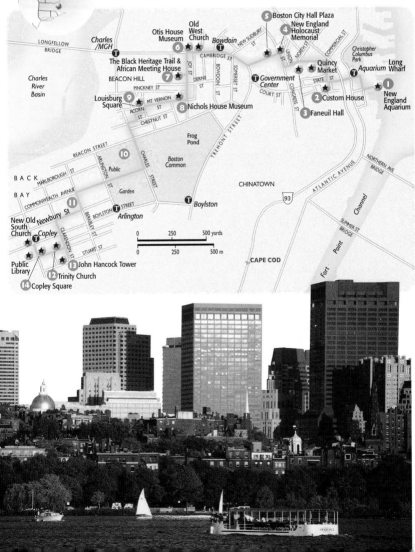

i 147 Tremont Street; 15 State Street

▶ Start at the Aquarium MBTA stop. Walk to the New England Aquarium on Central Wharf.

❶ New England Aquarium

The "greeters" at this "world of water" are two families of harbor seals, whose habitat is by the front door of this aquarium, which has long been a landmark of the city's waterfront. Indoors, the centerpiece is a huge four-story-high glass salt-water tank (200,000 gallons/757,000 liters), one of the largest in the world, where sharks and eels prowl up and down past Myrtle, a 500-pound (227kg) green sea turtle who likes to have her back scratched by the aquarium's divers.

Spending a day here is like taking a tour of the world's oceans. Get to know the inhabitants, from giant Pacific octopuses to tiny seahorses. Pick up a sea urchin or horseshoe crab; watch penguins dive; learn all about jellyfish. In addition, there are animal presentations, IMAX movies and whale-watching cruises that leave daily from Long Wharf (April to late October). Special programs include being a trainer for an afternoon.

▶ Return to the Aquarium MBTA Stop. Cross to State Street. At McKinley Square is the Custom House.

❷ Custom House

This massive 1847 granite building was described as "one of the noblest pieces of commercial architecture in the world" by 19th-century poet Walt Whitman. Certainly it is one of the biggest Greek Revival structures in the country and took ten years to build, with 3,000 pilings each weighing more than 40 tons (36,363kg) being driven into the soggy soil. In 1915, the 495-foot (148.5m) high tower was added. This shattered the city's height limit and won it the title of the "tallest building in New England." The 26th-floor open-air observation desk is open at 2pm Mon–Sat.

▶ Turn right on Commercial Street and continue into Quincy Market. Turn left.

❸ Faneuil Hall/Quincy Market

The well-traveled visitor may see nothing remarkable about this array of stores and restaurants in restored 19th-century buildings. Yet this 1976 urban redevelopment was the first of its kind, and its success has been copied all over the world ever since.

In Colonial days, when sailing ships tied up at Long Wharf, the Marketplace was used by vendors of fruits, vegetables, and other commodities. By 1825, Faneuil (rhymes with "Daniel") Hall was too small, so Mayor Josiah Quincy authorized the construction of the Quincy Market and its two offspring, the North and South markets.

Today, restaurants, pubs, and fast-food counters satisfy the hunger of over 14 million visitors a year. (See also page 42.)

▶ Behind Faneuil Hall is a plaza with a statue of Samuel Adams. Cross North Street; walk through the park to the Holocaust Memorial.

Quincy Market, a lively collection of eating places and stores

❹ New England Holocaust Memorial

This memorial, both dramatic and intimate, is located on a busy traffic island between City Hall Plaza and the 18th-century Blackstone Block. The six glass towers are lit from within at night. Each is six stories high and etched with six million random numbers, symbolizing the victims of the concentration camps. On the base of each tower are quotes from survivors, which tell of love, hope, and despair. One, from Gerda Weissman Klein, recalls a 13-year-old's gift to her best friend in the camp: "Imagine a world in which your entire possession is one raspberry, and you gave it to your friend."

▶ Cross Congress Street and continue up the steps to the City Hall Plaza.

❺ Boston City Hall Plaza

This enormous open space dates from an urban renewal project back in the 1960s. On one side is City Hall, a pyramid standing on its head; on the other are the John F. Kennedy federal office buildings. At the west end of the plaza, a stone plinth commemorates the birth of the telephone in nearby Court Street. That was where Alexander Graham Bell had his laboratory and, along with Thomas A Watson, "first transmitted sound over wires. In

winter the plaza looks barren, but in summer it becomes a lively meeting-place, with push-cart vendors, office workers, and free evening concerts on the stage behind City Hall.

▶ *Continue through the Plaza to Cambridge Street; turn right.*

6 Otis House Museum

Beacon Hill, with some of the most elegant homes in Boston, dates back to just after the Revolution, when Harrison Gray Otis started to build houses here. This lawyer, mayor of Boston, and U.S. senator was also a prop-erty developer, so he could afford to have Charles Bulfinch, the noted architect of the day, design a home for him here at 141 Cambridge Street. Often called the First Otis House, its perfectly proportioned, if rather dull, brick exterior hides a sophisticated and surprisingly colorful interior. At the top of a handsome staircase, the grand drawing-room looks much as it did 200 years ago. Today this is the headquarters of Historic New England (formerly SPNEA), an organization that looks after some 36 historic properties throughout New England.

▶ *Cross Cambridge Street and go up Joy Street.*

7 The Black Heritage Trail

At this point the itinerary and Boston's Black Heritage Trail meet. Celebrating the history of the city's African-American community, the Trail tells the stories of the men and women who worked to change the system, whether it was slavery in the south or discrimination in the north. The route encompass-es 14 significant sites. Two are on this route and are part of the Museum of African American History, which traces the civil rights movement. The Abiel Smith School has changing exhibits, which reflect the African American experience in Boston and eastern Massachusetts. The school itself was established with an endow-ment from white businessman Abiel Smith. From its opening in 1835, it educated African American children until segrega-tion in the city's schools was finally abolished 20 years later.

Next door is the African Meeting House (closed for reno-vation), which is the ending point of the Trail. It was built by black Americans in 1806 as a place where they could worship without being relegated to the gallery, as was the case in "white" churches. The meeting house was the birthplace of the New England Anti-Slavery Society – such a force in the Abolitionist Movement that the building became known as the Black Faneuil Hall.

▶ *Continue up Joy Street; turn right on Mount Vernon Street. At No. 55 is Nichols House.*

8 Nichols House Museum

Red-brick houses line Mount Vernon Street, one of the loveli-est streets in Boston. The museum is a time-warp, where nothing has been changed since the owner, Rose Standish Nichols, died in 1960. Her will ensured that "people from around the world without a letter of introduction could see

the inside of a fine house." From a wealthy Boston family, she is remembered as a land-scape gardener and a fervent worker for international peace. Her needlework and paintings lend a personal touch to the 1804 mansion, which also has bronzes by her uncle, the sculp-tor Augustus Saint-Gaudens.

▶ *Continue west along Mount Vernon Street to Louisburg Square.*

9 Louisburg Square

The name of this square recalls the struggle between France and Britain for supremacy in North America. Even though local troops had fought success-fully for the Crown against the French at the Fortress of Louisburg, Nova Scotia, back in 1745, this elegant square, named after their victory, was built a century later. Much like a London square, the grassy quad-rangle is a private park for owners of the surrounding smart homes. Residents included celebrities such as writer Louisa May Alcott (No. 10). Opera singer Jenny Lind, the "Swedish Nightingale," was married at No. 20.

▶ Across from Louisburg Square
is Willow Street. Take the first
right, Acorn Street, then go left
on West Cedar Street, then
right on Chestnut Street and,
finally, left on Charles Street.
Across Beacon Street is the
Public Garden.

10 Public Garden

Boston can thank a group of
public-spirited green thumbs for
America's first botanical garden.
From 1837 until their success
over 20 years later, they battled
to protect the city's green heart
from developers. Today, their
triumph provides a retreat for
locals and visitors alike. In spring
and summer, flowers bloom by
the paths, while the swish of
fountains masks the noise of the
traffic.

Children plead for rides on
the slow, stately, foot-pedaled
swan boats, introduced in 1877,
and peer at the fountain sculpture of Bagheera, the panther
immortalized in Kipling's *Jungle
Books*. A home-grown favorite is
the sculpture of Mrs. Mallard
and her eight ducklings, at the
corner of Charles and Beacon
streets. Robert McCloskey's
Make Way for Ducklings is a
much-loved children's tale of a
mother duck stopping Boston
traffic as she shepherds her
brood from the Charles River to
the pond in the Boston Public
Garden. A children's parade
each spring retraces the ducklings' route.

▶ Cross the Garden using the
suspension bridge and exit
through the Arlington Street
gate onto Commonwealth
Avenue Mall. Walk one block,
turn left on Berkeley Street,
then right on Newbury Street.

11 Newbury Street

Water covered this area of
Boston until the second half of
the 19th century when Back Bay
was filled in and transformed
into a residential district. The
backbone is Commonwealth
Avenue, a Parisian-style boulevard, lined with fine trees and
grand statues of long-forgotten
worthies. Running parallel to
"Comm Ave" is Newbury Street,
known for its upscale and trendy
art galleries, boutiques and cafés.
Yet, the apartments on and
around the street create a neighborhood atmosphere. Old buildings have new uses: What was
built as a Temple for the
Working Union of Progressive
Spiritualists is now a major bookstore. Boston's former Museum
of Natural History is full of
expensive clothing for men and
women; and the severe face of

The pedal-powered swan boats
on the pond in Boston's Public
Garden are popular in summer

49

Trinity Church reflected in the John Hancock Tower

glass fell off decades ago, but this minimalist skyscraper is now a feature of the Boston skyline. Its unusual rhomboid shape stretches up for 62 storys

▶ *Copley Square is a huge plaza, bounded by the Boston Public Library, Trinity Church, New Old South Church, the Fairmont Copley Plaza Hotel and the John Hancock Tower.*

14 Copley Square

Copley Square was described by one observer as a "desert of dirt, dust, mud, and wind." Now it is a pleasant place of fountains, benches...and skateboarders. The bronze sculpture, *Tortoise and Hare*, commemorates all those who have run in the Boston Marathon, the world's oldest, which finishes here on the square. The Boston Public Library, the first in America to lend books for free, is Charles McKim's adaptation of an Italian Renaissance palazzo. Constructed with a quarryful of yellow Siena marble, the 1895 building was decorated with works by then-contemporary artists and sculptors such as John Singer Sargent and Daniel Chester French.

▶ *There is an MBTA stop at Copley Square to return to the Aquarium, or travel elsewhere in the city.*

the New England Insurance Company fronts trendy fashion stores. You will also find fashion in the former American Academy of Arts and Sciences.

▶ *After one block, turn left on Clarendon Street and continue to Boylston Street. Turn right, left and onto Copley Square.*

12 Trinity Church

Henry Hobson Richardson designed Trinity Church in the late 19th century. His design was inspired by medieval Europe, while the interior coloring was a tribute to William Morris's pre-Raphaelite movement. On the Boylston Street side of the church, the statue of the Rev. Phillips Brooks commemorates the passionate preacher who used to ride his horse at break-neck speed. He also wrote *O Little Town of Bethlehem* in 1867.

▶ *Across Stuart Street is the John Hancock Tower.*

13 John Hancock Tower

Once the tallest building in New England, the former headquarters of the John Hancock Life Insurance Company was designed by architects I. M. Pei and Henry N. Cobb. Locals still recall that some of the panels of

SATURDAY, NOV 13
5:00 - 7:00 PM
BAKED BEAN SUPPER
ADULTS $5 CHILDREN $2
CHRIST CHURCH, UNITED METHODIST

HALF A DAY

Cambridge &
Harvard University

Established as Newtowne back in 1630, this was the first capital of the colony. Two years after Harvard College was founded in 1636, the town changed its name to Cambridge, to give it the same kudos, no doubt, as the English university city. Today, the mixture of grand museums, historic houses, wealthy residents, and student *joie de vivre* makes it one of the most vibrant and attractive places in New England.

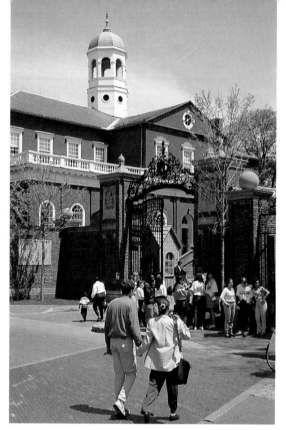

Johnston Gate, the main entrance to Old Harvard Yard

i Cambridge Visitor's Information Center, Harvard Square; Harvard Information Center, Holyoke Center (for tours)

▷ *Start at the Harvard Square MBTA stop.*

1 Harvard Square

All around the traffic island is the bustle and noise of "the square." Here you can buy international newspapers at the kiosk, eat international cuisine at the numerous restaurants, then buy all-American sportswear at the Harvard Cooperative, the large department store, known locally as "the Coop" (rhymes with hoop).

▷ *Walk up Massachusetts Avenue and turn right through Johnston Gate, the entrance to Old Harvard Yard.*

2 Old Harvard Yard

Harvard is not only the oldest university in America, but also one of the most influential. From its earliest days, it has symbolized the independent attitude of the Colonists and, significantly, America's first printing press was set up here in 1640.

Harvard Yard, the center of the campus for more than 350 years, is really two vast, open quadrangles, totalling 22 acres (8.8 hectares). The first yard is the home of the Freshmen (first-year students) who live in the red-brick dormitories. On the right is Massachusetts Hall, the university's oldest surviving building. Established as a laboratory and dormitory in 1720, it housed American troops at the start of the Revolution.

3 John Harvard Statue

Directly across the yard, in front of the granite University Hall (1815), this seated statue is labeled "John Harvard, founder 1638." The sculpture is wittily referred to as the "Statue of the Three Lies." Harvard was a benefactor rather than a founder, the foundation year was 1636, and the statue is actually of Sherman Hoar, a Harvard student who modeled for 19th-century sculptor Daniel Chester French.

▷ *Continue past University Hall and enter New Yard.*

4 New Yard

The second, larger portion of the Yard is also called Tercentenary Theater because it was here that the 300th graduation ceremonies were held in 1936. Criss-crossed by walking paths, a figurative bridge links the spiritual and intellectual centers of the university. To the left is Memorial Church, "Mem Church." It was completed in 1932 as a tribute by Harvard alumni to classmates killed in World War I, and has been updated for victims of World War II and, later, the Korean and Vietnam conflicts.

▷ *To the right is the Widener Library, the world's largest university library.*

5 Widener Library

In this temple to the written word, information spans the centuries, from a first folio of Shakespeare and a Gutenberg

FOR HISTORY BUFFS

America's oldest university is also one of its most prestigious. One of the seven so-called Ivy League schools (so old that ivy grows on their hallowed walls), Harvard emphasizes academic excellence, shunning the sports scholarships and razzmatazz of the country's younger universities. The 7,000 undergraduates now include the women of Radcliffe (see page 55), but there is also an impressive graduate program ranging from the prestigious Harvard Law and Medical Schools, to newer disciplines, such as Business Administration and Government.

Bible, to microfilm files and computer screens. Built between 1913 and 1915, the library was given in memory of Harry Elkins Widener, a wealthy graduate who drowned on the *Titanic*. Unfortunately the library is not open to the public.

▶ *Straight ahead is Quincy Street with its cultural icons.*

6 Carpenter Center for the Visual Arts

This glass and concrete block at No. 24 Quincy Street is the only example in America of a building by the 20th-century Swiss architect Le Corbusier. As well as art exhibitions, it houses the extensive Harvard Film Archive.

7 Fogg and Busch-Reisinger Art Museums

In 2008, Harvard University's four research centers and three museums were renamed as the Harvard Art Museum. The Fogg Museum, Busch-Reisinger Museum and Arthur M. Sackler Museum are all included in a major reorganization, due to

finish in 2013. With the sixth largest collection in the USA, the Fogg is vast, with only 0.5 per cent of its treasures ever on display. These include a Van Gogh self-portrait, and Claude Monet's *Red Boats*.

The Busch-Reisinger is renowned for its Expressionist works by Franz Marc, Paul Klee, Wassily Kandinsky, and Emile Nolde.

Eventually, across the Charles River in Allston, a new gallery will be devoted to the university's modern and contemporary art. While the Fogg and Busch-Reisinger are closed, the Sackler is displaying highlights from all three collections.

▶ *Go north on Quincy Street, cross Broadway, and the Arthur M. Sackler Museum is on the right.*

8 Arthur M. Sackler Museum

This is the university's third art museum, in British architect James Sterling's strikingly contemporary building, opened

in 1985. Famous for its exquisite collection of Chinese ceramics, bronzes and jades, it specializes in Ancient Greek, Islamic and Asian art, from Indian miniatures to Japanese prints. On the fourth floor, among the Greek art, are several large ceramic vases dating from about 340 BC. There are also jade dragons, bronze ritual bells and a large bronze wine container, more than 3,000 years old, from China.

▶ *Continue along Quincy Street, crossing Cambridge Street. Memorial Hall is on the left.*

9 Memorial Hall

Memorial Hall reopened after a major restoration in 1996. Built in 1878 to honor the Harvard men who died in the Civil War, it epitomizes the Gothic Revival style, with a Great Hall soaring up to a jig-saw puzzle roof of carved beams and timbers. Here, Winston Churchill was given an

During closure, the Fogg Museum's finest works will be shown at the Sackler Museum honorary degree in 1943. The stained-glass windows portray stories and heroes from the Bible, American history and Greek mythology. In a controversial move, "Mem Hall" has been made into a dining room. Where nervous undergraduates once took exams, first-year students gossip at mealtimes under the chandeliers. To one side is Sanders Theater, an intimate auditorium finished in dark wood. It was the setting for Harvard graduations up until 1911, but is now used for the performing arts.

▶ *At the end of Quincy Street bear left across Kirkland Street, then turn right onto Oxford Street.*

⑩ Museums of Natural History

Don't be put off by the fusty-sounding names of the four museums: there is plenty to fascinate adults and children alike in this brick building. Highlights include the 22-pound (10kg) meteor which fell from the sky in 1992, and landed on a car in Peekskill, New York, and the life-size skeleton of a 42-foot long (12.5m) *Kronosaurus*. This gigantic crocodile lived 135 million years ago.

Best known of all is the unique Ware Collection of Glass Flowers, 3,000 scientifically accurate, life-size models of flowers and plants made out of blown glass.

▶ *From Oxford Street, go into Harvard Law School. Pass under the arch to the right of Pierce Hall, and bear left on the path along Langdell Hall.*

⑪ Harvard Law School

The Law School was started in 1817, with six students. Today, each new class of 540 students has been selected from over 7,000 applicants. Langdell Hall, on the right, has the largest law library in the world, and a public reading room on the fourth floor that stretches the length of two football fields.

Next is Austin Hall, a small brownstone building completed in 1881 by Henry Hobson Richardson. Each spring in the Ames Courtroom, on the second floor, finalists in the third-year competition argue their cases before a Justice of the U.S. Supreme Court. In the sessions, seating is by ticket only; students have priority.

▶ *Bear right upon leaving Austin Hall and follow the path between Hemenway Gymnasium and Gannett House. Cross Massachusetts Avenue at the traffic light and walk across Cambridge Common.*

Longfellow House: this clapboard building was abandoned by its Loyalist owner in 1774

⑫ Cambridge Common

This small green park is all that remains of the fields and pastures where the American army assembled after the 1775 battles of Lexington and Concord (April) and Bunker Hill (June). On July 3, George Washington took command of the American army here. A granite stone and flagpole, next to three cannons, mark the site of the fated Washington Elm.

▶ *On the far side of the Common, turn right on Garden Street, then left on Mason Street. Turn right on Brattle Street and continue to No. 101.*

⑬ Brattle Street

All along Brattle Street are fine houses, built before the American Revolution. Since most were then occupied by supporters of the Crown, it was called "Tory Row." The owners left hastily, and all that remains are their names, recorded on blue plaques. Hastings House, No. 101, is a fine example, as are Nos. 113 and 115, which belonged to the daughters of Henry Wadsworth Longfellow, who lived at No. 105.

Built in 1685, the Hooper-Lee Nichols House at No. 159 is now the headquarters of the

Cambridge Historical Society, who also organize guided walks.

14 Longfellow House
The Tory, or British sympathizer, John Vassall lived in this yellow clapboard mansion. He built it in 1759, in anticipation of his marriage to Elizabeth, the sister of the last Royal Lieutenant Governor. In 1775, he was thrown out by the patriots, who moved in with the wounded from the Battle of Bunker Hill. Next, the hospital became George Washington's headquarters for nine months. Washington enlarged it to make room for guests.

In the following century, the celebrated American poet Henry Wadsworth Longfellow rented a room here. Later, he received the house as a wedding present and lived here from 1837 to 1882. During that period he wrote *Hiawatha* (1855) and *The Village Blacksmith* (1839) here, and completed his translation of Dante, among other works. Here, also, he entertained fellow writers Dickens, Emerson, Hawthorne, Twain, and Wilde. Longfellow was particularly fond of the view across to the Charles River, and it remains unspoiled, thanks to his children, who gave the land to the City of Cambridge in 1913.

Tours of the Longfellow House are offered in summer, but the grounds and historic garden are open year-round for visits during daytime hours.

▶ *Retrace your steps on Brattle Street and turn left into Radcliffe College through the Gilman Gate.*

15 Radcliffe Yard
Radcliffe College started out in 1879 with just 27 women students in a small two-story house. It was named in honor of Londoner Lady Anne Radcliffe, who gave £100 to Harvard back in the 17th century. Admissions to Radcliffe have always been highly competitive, and many "Cliffies" have become well known, including Helen Keller,

whose life was portrayed in the movie *The Miracle Worker*. Nearly a century after its founding, Radcliffe merged with Harvard. The name, however, lives on thanks to the Radcliffe Institute for Advanced Study, founded in 1999. In Radcliffe Yard, the Federal-style Fay House was built in 1807 and was the first building acquired by the college. Today it is used as an administration building.

▶ *After crossing the Yard, exit onto Garden Street, and bear right to Christ Church.*

16 Christ Church and the Old Burying Ground
In the lobby, just inside the outer door of Christ Church, a plaque behind the door marks a bullet hole made, so the story goes, when the British were

Christ Church, designed by Peter Hamson, the architect of King's Chapel in Boston

marching to Lexington in April, 1775. Later that year, George and Martha Washington attended services here, using the pew directly below the pulpit, on the left. Between the Christ Church and the First Church is Cambridge's oldest cemetery, God's Acre. The earliest grave is that of Anne Erinton, a settler who passed away on December 24, 1635. Eight presidents of Harvard are also buried here.

▶ *Continue down Garden Street to Massachusetts Avenue and bear right to Harvard Square and the MBTA stop.*

SPECIAL TO...

Close by the sidewalk is a stone milestone, carved in 1734. On the back are the words: "Boston 8 miles." Today that distance is covered in 8 minutes on the MBTA.

CULTURAL CRADLE

America's culture, as well as its sense of history, started in New England. The 19th century, in particular, saw the development not just of American themes but of a distinctive American "voice" and viewpoint. What binds the most talented artists and writers together is their sense of New England, in print and on canvas, set to music or presented on stage. Names such as Robert Frost (poet), Nathaniel Hawthorne (novelist), Winslow Homer (painter), Norman Rockwell (illustrator), and Eugene O'Neill (playwright) conjure up bleak landscapes and clapboard houses, glistening seas and "salt-of-the-earth" families, while Charles Ives' music interprets the moods of the countryside.

Literature

The first New England writer to make an international name for himself was Henry Wadsworth Longfellow (1807–82), a poet who was also a professor at Harvard. Hugely popular, his narrative poems told home-grown tales, from *The Song of Hiawatha*, a story of Native Americans, to *The Midnight Ride of Paul Revere*, which encapsulates the start of the American Revolution. Nathaniel Hawthorne (1804–64) also took inspiration from New England history, though he explored the psychological effects of Puritanism in novels such as *The Scarlet Letter* and *The House of the Seven Gables*. His friend Herman Melville (1819–91) received little critical acclaim in his lifetime. A New Yorker who wrote at Arrowhead in Western Massachusetts, Melville's most famous novel was *Moby Dick*, an allegory of good and evil which drew on his experiences aboard a New England whaler as a young man.

While Hawthorne and Melville relied on the realism of history, two authors, Emerson and Thoreau, took a more spiritual path. Transcendentalism was a movement led by Ralph Waldo Emerson (1803–82), a charismatic speaker and writer whose philosophy is best summed up by his often quoted saying: "who so would be a man must be a non-conformist." He appealed to Americans to throw off the yoke of European tradition and to look at their individual experiences. His friend, Henry David Thoreau (1817–62), did just that, going "back to nature." The result of his simple life by Walden Pond, on the edge of Concord, was the idealistic book *Walden: Or Life in the Woods* (1854).

Both men spent time in Concord, where Louisa May Alcott (1832–88) also lived and wrote *Little Women*, a huge best-seller, based on family life. Another woman writer, Harriet Beecher Stowe (1811–96), brought the issue of slavery to thousands of homes with *Uncle Tom's Cabin*. The book, which was originally published as a weekly serial, sold 300,000 copies. While Stowe wrote to further a cause, Emily Dickinson (1830–86) wrote for herself. A recluse whose poems were only discovered after her death, she lived her entire life not just in Amherst in Western Massachusetts, but also in the same brick Federal house where she had been born.

New England also attracted writers from elsewhere in the States. Samuel Longhorne Clemens, better known as Mark Twain (1835–1910), was born in

Left: Henry Wadsworth Longfellow
Below: Topsy, from Harriet Beecher Stowe's *Uncle Tom's Cabin*

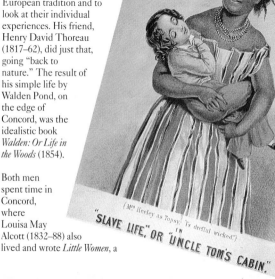

("Mrs Keeley as Topsy. "I's drefful wicked.")

"SLAVE LIFE," OR "UNCLE TOM'S CABIN."

Missouri, but many of his best-loved stories, such as the antics of Huckleberry Finn and Tom Sawyer, were written in his Hartford home. His tales of the American West, written with humor and an easy style, brought him a wide audience. By contrast, high society was the subject of novelist Edith Wharton (1862–1937). The author of *The Age of Innocence* did much of her writing at The Mount, her retreat in Lenox, Massachusetts.

The quintessential New England poet was Robert Frost (1874–1963), who spent most of his life in New Hampshire and Vermont. So great was his stature that he was the first poet to participate in a presidential inauguration. In 1961, he read his poem *The Gift Outright* at President John F. Kennedy's swearing-in. His descriptions of a Vermont snowstorm and swinging on birch trees are easily remembered; his forthright expression of universal truths have a darker side.

Theater

New York was always the cradle of American theater, but America's first major playwright, Eugene O'Neill (1888–1953), learned his craft in New England. The New Yorker studied at the 47 Workshop of George Pierce Baker in Harvard before making an impact with the Provincetown Players on Cape Cod. Ten of his plays were produced from 1916 to 1920. A Nobel and Pulitzer prize winner, O'Neill is remembered at the theater bearing his name near New London, Connecticut. The cottage where he spent his boyhood summers was the setting for *Long Day's Journey into Night*.

Music

While Puritan influences restricted early New Englanders to music in churches, the region was a powerhouse of classical music in the 20th century. The best known composer is Charles Ives (1874–1954), born in Danbury, Connecticut, the son of a bandmaster. Fiercely proud and independent, Ives bucked

The Boston Symphony Orchestra performs at Symphony Hall from the beginning of October to the end of April

European tradition to draw on traditional American folk songs, hymns, and marches. The result was works such as his *New England Symphony*, *Three Places in New England*, and *Sonata No. 2* for piano and flute. The last was nicknamed *Concord, Mass 1840–1860*, perhaps because of its dedication to the town's literary circle of Emerson, Thoreau, Hawthorne, and the Alcotts.

New Englander Colonel Henry Higginson enjoyed the Austrian attitude to music so much that he set up the legendary Boston Pops in 1885, based on the romance and fun of Viennese orchestras. In 1929, the Pops went outdoors to perform, as they still do to this day. The Boston Symphony, long one of the world's great orchestras, has extended its popularity and fame thanks to the summer season in Tanglewood, in western Massachusetts.

CONNECTICUT

Connecticut has much to offer as a vacation destination. Although popular with Manhattanites for weekends, many Americans and overseas visitors overlook it when planning a trip to New England. Yet it has a history dating back to 1635, a rich tapestry of villages and towns, countryside that looks softer than elsewhere in the northeast, and miles of unspoiled shoreline. Contrasts are to be found everywhere. Although well over half the state is heavily forested, Connecticut is also heavily populated. Most residents live in the suburbs, on the southwest coast and along the Connecticut River that cuts through the middle of this rectangular state.

From the early days, the state has been the home of a host of inventors whose ideas still provide employment. Eli Whitney's cotton gin brought mass production techniques to the world. Sam Colt, inventor of the Colt 45 revolver, set up an arms and ammunition industry that survives today. Clocks and door locks, tires and the pay telephone were all developed here. Now, chemicals, jet engines, and insurance are major employers. One of the wealthiest states in the country, in 2007 it also boasted the highest per capita income.

Fall foliage in the Litchfield Hills

The affluent southwestern corner of Connecticut is virtually a suburb of New York City. Farther north, the Litchfield Hills, idyllic for artists and craftsmen, are also a retreat for show business celebrities. Two hundred years ago, the same wooded hills were stripped to fuel the furnaces and forges that processed iron for the guns used during the Revolution.

The coast, especially the eastern strip, is most popular with visitors. Mystic Seaport is an admirable re-creation of an early 19th-century seafaring village, complete with sailing ships.

There is a rich cultural heritage, because of the influence of Yale University and writers such as Mark Twain, Harriet Beecher Stowe, and dictionary-writer Noah Webster. Painters and actors have also made their homes here, and antiques shops and art galleries abound.

Tour 8

Hartford is known as the "Insurance Capital of America." The business began in 1794. It is also a city of "firsts" and "oldests." It claims the first municipal rose garden and development of the first American dictionary; the oldest newspaper, the *Hartford Courant*, and oldest state house. Two of America's most revered writers also lived here: Mark Twain and Harriet Beecher Stowe, who was Twain's neighbor. Twain's Victorian house is one of the most intriguing you'll see, deliberately designed to be unusual.

Tour 9

When it comes to universities, Yale and Harvard go together like Oxford and Cambridge, in England. Just as Harvard and Cambridge are in attractive towns, so Yale and Oxford are in industrial cities. Yale, with its ivy-covered buildings, is one of the finest academic institutions in the country, with impressive museums and art galleries. Countering all this culture, the Frisbee was supposedly invented here, along with two of America's most popular fast foods: the hamburger and the pizza.

Tour 10

Western Connecticut has bumpy, wooded hills dotted with villages that don't seem to have kept up with the 20th century, let alone the 21st. Although New York City is within commuting distance, urban frenzy is banned here. This is the countryside the way urban folk prefer it, with waterfalls and covered bridges, pleasant stores and small art galleries. Litchfield boasts the first American law school, which was set up in a tiny house over 200 years ago. The innocent-looking town of Lakeville turned out tons of arms to fuel the battle against Britain, winning itself the nickname of the "Arsenal of the Revolution."

Tour 11

Connecticut's coast was settled in the early 17th century by British emigrants who named the small towns after their homes: New London, Guilford, Essex and Old Lyme. The oldest stone house in New England, complete with fortifications, was built back in 1640. Later, locals turned their hand to building ships and submarines. The finest maritime museum in the States is at Mystic, where boats, docks and a variety of craftsmen at work recreate the life of a shipbuilding village in the 19th century.

Later, the seaside attracted artists and writers, while the Eugene O'Neill Theater Center outside New London gave actors such as Al Pacino and Meryl Streep their early opportunities. Despite the popularity of the bigger towns, there are still sleepy corners where visitors can sit and munch a sandwich in peace, overlooking tranquil Long Island Sound.

Mystic Seaport is a re-creation of a 19th-century seaport

Hartford

One of the oldest cities in the country, Hartford was founded in 1636 by a native of Hertford, England. There is an English flavor to the narrow streets and parks of Hartford, downtown is easily navigable, and skyscrapers rise high above the Connecticut River with its renovated riverfront. In this state capital are well-preserved historic places, the nation's oldest public art museum, a world-famous rose garden, and the homes of two of America's best-known and best-loved writers, Harriet Beecher Stowe and Mark Twain.

HALF A DAY

The Senate Chamber of the Old State House – the first state house in a newly independent United States

ℹ️ *45 Pratt Street*

▶ *Park your car in the XL Center garage, entrance on Asylum Street.*

❶ XL Center

Downtown Hartford is undergoing a vigorous program of regeneration. Off Trumbull Street, at the side of the XL Center is brick-paved Pratt Street, with its variety of restaurants and shops. Inside the XL Center, the outstanding University of Connecticut basketball squad consistently fills the arena, while the Hartford Wolf Pack, an affiliate of the New York Rangers hockey team, now faces off here.

▶ *Leave the XL Center and walk east on Asylum Street to Main Street. Cross and enter the Old State House.*

❷ Old State House

Abandoned in 1878, the US's oldest state house has been carefully restored. Designed in 1792 and completed in 1796 by New England's star architect Charles Bulfinch, it stands on Meeting House Square, where the Colony was founded in 1636. This is where the first written constitution guaranteeing the right to representative government was enacted by the English colonists. That is why Connecticut is nicknamed "The Constitution State". Lafayette was made a citizen here, and the trials of Cinque and the *Amistad* opened here in 1839. One of the highlights of a visit is to see the original version of Gilbert Stuart's famous portrait of the first president of the US, George Washington. Also in the Old State House is Mr. Steward's Museum of Natural and Other Curiosities, established in 1797, featuring a two-headed calf and an 8.5-foot (2.5m) alligator. In summer, a farmers' market follows the Colonial tradition of setting up stands by the meeting house (Mon, Wed, Fri mornings).

▶ *Walk south one block to Travelers Tower, on the corner of Gold Street.*

SPECIAL TO...

The Connecticut Freedom Trail was established in 1995 to honor the history of the state's African American community, and covers a series of buildings and sites that represent the concept of freedom. Hartford's Old State House features in the trail for the part it played in the famous *Amistad* trials, a two-year legal battle that ultimately set free and repatriated to Sierra Leone a group of Africans who, in 1839, had taken control of the Spanish vessel carrying them to a life of slavery in Cuba. The story was told in Steven Spielberg's movie *Amistad* (1997).

🔳 Travelers Tower

Soaring 527 feet (160m) above
street level, the "free
Renaissance"-style, pink-granite
Travelers Tower is capped by a
prominent beacon light. From
the observation deck atop the
tower, visitors are rewarded
with a breathtaking view of
downtown Hartford, the
Connecticut River and the
entire Connecticut Valley from
Mount Tom to Meriden
Mountain in the south.

▶ *Across the street, on the corner
of Main and Gold streets, is
the Wadsworth Atheneum.*

🔳 Wadsworth Atheneum

One of New England's leading
"must-see" museums, "the
Wad" was founded in 1842, so it
takes the title "the nation's
oldest public art museum."
Housed in an impressive neo-
Gothic building, it boasts
masterpieces from the 16th
through the 20th centuries,
including classics by Picasso

(*Harlequin*) and Van Gogh (*Self
Portrait*). The most intriguing
painting is *House Fronting New
Milford Green* by Ralph Earl,
painted in 1796. The house still
stands. Other home-grown
talent includes members of
the Hudson River School, the

The Hartford Fire Insurance
Company building in Hartford,
America's insurance industry capital

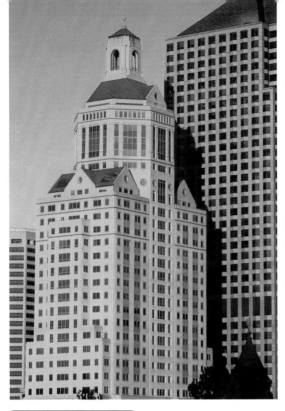

Downtown Hartford is dominated by high-rise office buildings

show dates of birth from the 1590s to the early 1600s, in Hartford, England.

▶ *Continue walking down Gold Street to Bushnell Park. Turn right along the border, Jewell Street. Opposite Ann Street, across from the YMCA, the Bushnell Park Carousel is in the park.*

7 Bushnell Park Carousel

The carousel is a Stein and Goldstein, hand-carved merry-go-round built in 1914, with 48 prancing horses and chariots rollicking to the tunes of a 1925 Wurlitzer band organ. At only $1 a ride, it is one of New England's bargains. Hot dogs and other snacks are available when the park is open.

▶ *Walk a few steps west to Trinity Street. Look right to the Sailors and Soldiers Memorial Arch, built in 1886 to honor the 4,000 Hartford citizens who served in the Civil War. Turn left and proceed up the hill half a block to the State Capitol. A statue of the French General Lafayette, ally of George Washington, sits on horseback in the middle of the street at the driveway entrance.*

8 State Capitol

Another refurbished landmark (built 1878), the Capitol is the home of the House of Representatives and Senate, Connecticut's legislature. Against a backdrop of white Connecticut marble are Gothic spires, a gleaming gold dome, statues, medallions, and bas-reliefs commemorating important people and events in state history. Gaudy to the point of being brash, architect Frank Lloyd Wright called it "The most ridiculous building I know of." Open to the public, the assemblies are in session from February through May in even years and January through June in odd years. More statues and historical relics decorate the interior.

SPECIAL TO...

Hartford is America's insurance capital, thanks to its history of paying up quickly and in full. Originally, companies covered merchant vessels, but later specialized in insuring homes against fire. In 1835 and 1845, major blazes in New York bankrupted many firms. But the Hartford Fire Insurance Company and fellow companies settled "all just claims" and so made their reputations. Now, some of the world's biggest insurance companies are based here.

19th-century group of landscape painters who achieved a definite American style. There is also a fine collection of African-American art, decorative arts, costumes and textiles.

▶ *Cross the street diagonally to the north side of Gold Street and proceed down Gold Street, stopping at the Stone Field Sculpture and the adjacent Ancient Burying Ground.*

5 Stone Field Sculpture

"$250,000 for a pile of rocks? That's ridiculous!" That was the reaction of many locals when the Hartford City Council voted to fund the sculpture created by Carl Andre in 1977. His work of art consists of 36 large stones laid out in rows to form an isosceles triangle. A similar furor erupted in England when London's Tate Gallery bought "a pile of bricks," a total of 120 bricks in two layers which the American sculptor entitled *Equivalent VIII*.

6 Ancient Burying Ground

Center Church, built in 1632, is Hartford's oldest church. Behind it, the Ancient Burying Ground is one of the city's few surviving historic sites from the 17th century. In the small, green, fenced-in graveyard, more than 400 brownstone markers stand at attention, marking the final resting places of Hartford's founding families. Epitaphs record lives that were only occasionally lengthy, more often short. Many

▶ *Cross Capitol Avenue to No. 231.*

❾ Museum of Connecticut History

The State Library and Supreme Court sandwich this museum, which contains the Fundamental Orders of Connecticut, the Royal Charter of 1662, issued by King Charles II and the Colt Firearms Collection. The latter showcases Samuel Colt's genius for the invention, making and marketing of his patented revolvers and rifles. The museum also has a variety of political, industrial and military artifacts.

▶ *Return to the Capitol. Walk through it (round it, if closed) to the rear exit and continue north down the hill and through the park to Asylum Street. Turn right and walk one block back to the Civic Center to retrieve your car. Leave downtown, driving west on Asylum Street under the railroad bridge. Bear left at the fork onto Farmington Avenue. After 1 mile (1.6km), on the left is the home of Mark Twain (park at the rear).*

❿ Mark Twain House and Museum

The internationally known writer and wit Samuel Clemens, alias Mark Twain, lived in this

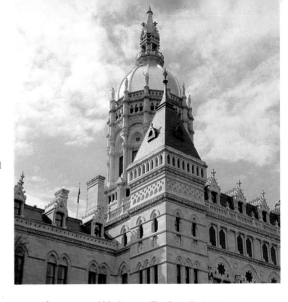

The State Capitol; its exuberant design reflects Victorian pride

spectacular orange and black brick Victorian mansion for 17 years. He commissioned this Gothic eccentricity in 1871, when he settled in Hartford with his family. In 1881, he had the 19-room home completely refurbished by Louis Comfort Tiffany. The library is the epitome of Victorian opulence, with carved wood, patterned carpets, and lavishly decorated walls and ceilings. Guides describe the life of the writer, his soirées with guests such as English writer Rudyard Kipling, and the way he retired to the billiard room to write books such as *The Adventures of Tom Sawyer* and *Huckleberry Finn*, because his

children had commandeered his study. One of the first private citizens in Hartford to have a telephone, Twain had so many problems with the new-fangled instrument that he kept a chart to record its inefficiencies.

In the spacious, modern museum alongside, you can watch Ken Burns' revealing documentary on Twain.

▶ *Next door to the Twain house, at Forest Street, is the home of Harriet Beecher Stowe.*

⓫ Harriet Beecher Stowe Center

The "little lady who started the big war" (Civil War, 1865–70), was how President Abraham Lincoln referred to the author of *Uncle Tom's Cabin*. Published in 1852, the book was a blockbuster, selling over 300,000 copies in the first year alone. The sentimental story of slaves in the south was unabashed, though successful, propaganda for the Anti-Slavery Movement. Nowadays, no-one remembers any of her other 30 books. Moreover, the term "Uncle Tom" has come to mean an African American who doesn't stand up for the rights of his race.

This house, in what was quiet farmland a century ago, was Stowe's home from 1873 until she died in 1896. Her home is

---

SPECIAL TO...

Samuel Colt (1814–62) was a self-taught and persistent inventor who revolutionized hand guns. Aged 21, he patented his Colt Paterson revolver and used the assembly-line techniques of fellow Connecticut inventor Eli Whitney to mass produce weapons. His 1848 Colt Dragoon was the first U.S. Army regulation revolver and, years later, the American West was won with what was, ironically, called the Colt Peacemaker.

FOR HISTORY BUFFS

On the Mississippi River, when a boatman called out "*Mark Twain*," the pilot knew that the depth was two fathoms. This was the pseudonym taken by Samuel Clemens, in 1862, when he became a newspaper reporter. Born in Missouri in 1835, Twain popularized life in the West with books such as *The Adventures of Tom Sawyer* (1876) and *The Adventures of Huckleberry Finn* (1884). Despite his folksy stories, he was no hayseed, but a well-traveled man, awarded an honorary degree by Oxford University in England in 1907.

now restored and paintings by her and her writing table, plus memorabilia of her career and her family lend a personal touch.

▶ *Exit car park, turn right, then immediately left on Woodland Street. Take the first left onto Asylum Avenue. Just before the first traffic light, the Connecticut Historical Society is on the left.*

12 Connecticut Historical Society Museum

Inside, the museum has exhibits on state history, plus permanent displays of furniture and the decorative arts from Connecticut craftsmen of the 17th, 18th and 19th centuries. The exhibition "*Amistad* – A True Story of Freedom" tells the story (popularized by Stephen Spielberg's 1997 movie) of the African slaves who gained their freedom.

Mark Twain's House, in the Nook Farm district of Hartford

▶ *Back on Asylum Avenue, continue through the traffic light and take the right fork. After a mile (1.6km), having passed through two more traffic lights, the Elizabeth Park Rose Garden is on the left (see **Back to Nature** panel).*

▶ *Return to Asylum Avenue and drive for 1½ miles (2.2km), through two traffic lights. At the third light, turn left on North Main Street and go 2 miles (3km) through the West Hartford Center shopping district. North Main becomes South Main. Continue to No. 227, on the right.*

13 Noah Webster House

Born in 1758, Noah Webster graduated from Yale and became a teacher. He soon saw the need to standardize spelling, so published his *Bluebacked Spellers*, which sold some 70 million copies and became the basis for elementary education

throughout the country. The "Schoolmaster of the Republic" did not stop there. He recognized that the language of America was evolving from the original English words, spelling and pronunciation, and spent 20 years compiling *An American Dictionary of the English Language*. Published in 1828, the two volumes contained some 70,000 words.

Inside the house are a first edition of his dictionary, his spellers and some 200 editions of his works. Guides in 200-year-old Colonial dress lead the way through the authentically furnished rooms. On special days there are demonstrations of carding wool, weaving on the massive loom, cooking, bread baking and butter churning.

▶ *Continue south on South Main Street and turn left onto I–84 eastbound at exit 41 to return to downtown Hartford.*

HALF A DAY

New Haven &
Yale University

Founded in 1638 by a group of settlers, the town first depended on seafaring. In the 19th century, thanks to inventors such as Eli Whitney, assembly lines turned out clocks, carriages, and guns by the thousand. More recently, New Haven has undergone a downtown regeneration, with Crown and Chapel streets particularly busy with bars, restaurants and shops. At the heart of the city is Yale, one of America's leading universities, adding an enviable cultural dimension to the city.

ⓘ *1000 Chapel Street*

▶ *Start on The Green, corner of Temple and Elm streets.*

❶ The Green

New Haven has been called "the first planned city in the U.S.A." because of its original (1638) grid-like street design, visible from the 16-acre (6.4-ha) Green. Here, residents came to gossip, to debate, and to pray at the trio of handsome churches, each with its different architectural style, but all built in the early 1800s.

The United Church, with its distinctive cupola, has long held public meetings and debates on topics ranging from slavery in the 1800s to Civil Rights in the 1970s. It is also sometimes referred to as the North Church.

In the middle of The Green is Center Church, and ever since the mid-1600s, a meeting house or church has stood on this site. Cool and elegant within, handsome Tiffany stained glass fills the arched window above the altar. Trinity Church, the third, was the first Gothic Revival church in the country, and was constructed with materials allowed to pass through the British blockade of New Haven harbor during the War of 1812. On Church Street, in front of

New Haven City Hall, is the three-sided Amistad Memorial, marking the site of the jail where the African slaves were imprisoned in 1839.

▶ *Walk diagonally north across The Green toward the imposing battlements and towers of*

Neo-Gothic Harkness Tower, a New Haven landmark

Yale University and enter the Old Campus through the Phelps Gate.

SPECIAL TO...

Ever wondered who invented the hamburger? One of the strongest claims comes from Louis Lassen of New Haven who served them here at Louis Lunch. That was back in 1900, and the simple brick house with a communal table and two booths probably looks much now as it did then. It stands in the middle of a parking lot at 263 Crown Street. The hamburgers, however, come as a surprise. Forget the griddle and the buns, these beef patties are cooked in front of diners on a vertical gas grill and served on toast.

2 Old Campus

Phelps Gate, the front door to Yale, leads to the Old Campus, a typical university quadrangle. The oldest building here is also the oldest in town. Connecticut Hall, with its handsome windows and brick, was built between 1750 and 1753. Nathan Hale, Class of 1773, whose green patina statue sits outside, lived here during his student years. Three years later he was hanged in New York by the British, who caught him spying. His last words: "I only regret that I have but one life to lose for my country" became a rallying cry. He was only 21. The left foot of Theodore Woolsey's statue is particularly shiny thanks to superstitious students giving it a rub before exams.

Off to the right, before leaving the quadrangle, is a rough-hewn granite bench. Here, A. Bartlett Giamatti, a former president of the college would sit, philosophizing about life and comparing it to a baseball game. His best loved essay, *Green Fields of the Mind*, is baseball-oriented.

So keen was he on baseball, America's favorite summer game, that he gave up academia to become the Commissioner for Baseball and run the professional sport. Sadly, he died soon after taking up the appointment.

▶ *Cross the quadrangle and exit onto High Street.*

SPECIAL TO...

Among the contributions Yale students have made to the world, nothing is quite as much fun as the Frisbee. Since 1947, students supposedly have whizzed flat aluminium pie dishes at one another across the Old Campus. When Wham-O, inventors of the hula-hoop, bought the patent for a plastic flier, they called it a Frisbee because those dishes came from Bridgeport's Frisbie Baking Company. Such major inventions are often in dispute: Middlebury College in Vermont (see page 117) also claims to be the home of the Frisbee.

The Old Campus at Yale is an architectural showpiece

FOR HISTORY BUFFS

Like its perennial rival Harvard, near Boston, Yale is one of America's Ivy League schools. Originally started by the Puritans in 1701 to train clergymen and administrators, the first Collegiate School moved to New Haven 15 years later, and changed its name to Yale in recognition of wealthy benefactor Elihu Yale. Students were nicknamed the "Elis" in honor of the merchant, whose donation of books was sold to finance the institution. The roll call of famous Yale students ranges from dictionary compiler Noah Webster and architect Eero Saarinen to movie star Jodie Foster, Class of 1984. From the renowned graduate schools, especially the Law School, recent celebrities include former President Bill Clinton and his wife, Hillary, who first met here.

❸ Branford/Saybrook Colleges and the Harkness Tower

Above the stone gate ahead of you is an inscription: "For God, For Country and For Yale." The seal of the college has the Latin words *Lux et Veritas* (Light and Truth), but these jollier words are also the last lines of Yale's student song, *Bright College Years*, composed in 1888.

Across the street are the twin buildings of Branford and Saybrook Colleges, reminders of the school's locations before it moved to New Haven. Yale consists of a dozen separate and self-governing colleges. Their buildings were funded by the Harkness family, commemorated by the tall, dark, Gothic Harkness Tower that soars 216 feet (66m), and houses a 54-bell carillon, one of the largest in the world. Its partner, the Wrexham Tower, is modeled on the church steeple in Wrexham, Wales, where Elihu Yale is buried.

▶ *Turn left and continue on High Street.*

❹ Skull and Bones Society

Just before walking under the arch, the windowless and ominous-looking stone building on the right is the Skull and Bones Society. Founded in 1832, it is Yale's oldest secret society. Although the membership is never publicized, it supposedly included former president George Bush, Snr. Among many "Bones" legends is one that the remains of the great Apache chief, Geronimo, are interred within its walls.

▶ *Pass under the arch and then turn right for the Yale University Art Gallery and Yale Center for British Art.*

❺ Yale University Art Gallery

The nation's oldest college art gallery dates back to 1832 and is one of several fine museums here, some of which offer free admission. A replica of the original gallery is named for John Trumbull (1756–1843), the founder, and exhibits his work. This artist depicted major moments of the Revolution, such as the Battle of Bunker Hill in Boston, and the signing of the Declaration of Independence.

Today, the museum boasts an enormous international collection. From the past are Greek, Roman, Egyptian, and pre-Columbian antiquities. From 19th- and 20th-century Europe are paintings by Manet, Millet, Matisse and Magritte. Of the museum's two buildings, the 1953 addition is the work of architect Louis Kahn. He also designed the Yale Center for British Art, across Chapel Street.

▶ *Cross Chapel Street.*

❻ Yale Center for British Art

The center's enormous collection, the gift of Paul Mellon in 1966, traces the development of British art over the centuries and includes a roll call of the great: Van Dyck, Gainsborough, Reynolds and Turner. For more specialist tastes are the works of visionary William Blake and animal painter George Stubbs (*A Lion Attacking a Horse*).

▶ *Continue on Chapel Street, passing the Atticus Bookstore.*

Here browsers and buyers are joined by sippers of exotic teas and coffees served in the small café. Walk to the corner of Chapel and York streets.

❼ Yale Repertory Theatre

Since 1966, a small professional company, boosted by students from the graduate school, has presented avant-garde, cutting-edge work in this 500-seat, converted Victorian gothic church.

▶ *Diagonally across from the theater on York Street is the Yale School of Architecture. What looks like nine stories on the outside actually hides 36 floors, and caused much discussion when it was put up in the 1960s. Turn right on York Street and walk to the University Theatre, home of Yale's illustrious graduate schools.*

8 Yale School of Drama

Students who have attended a three-year course here include Paul Newman and Meryl Streep. Contrary to popular myth, Jodie Foster did not attend the Drama School: she was a liberal arts undergraduate.

▶ *Continue on York Street to Elm Street. Turn left, then veer right onto Broadway. Look up to the right.*

9 Payne Whitney Gymnasium

Dominating the skyline is the tower of what looks like a Gothic cathedral. Inside, however, are neither pillars nor pews but "Yalies" in sweat pants and sneakers. The Trophy Room contains memorabilia dating back to 1842. Although the university does not award athletics scholarships, sports facilities are as good as anywhere in the country, and "The Game," the annual football game against Harvard, is both a passionate match and a social occasion.

▶ *For fun shopping, walk up Broadway, or return to York*

FOR HISTORY BUFFS

Eli Whitney, the Yale graduate who became "father of mass production," made his name by inventing the cotton gin, which separated cotton fibers from the seeds. Although he patented the design in 1794, it was much-copied, so he did not make his deserved fortune. Next, his analytical brain turned to the making of guns. By standardizing components, he produced guns faster and cheaper in his factory than craftsmen could by traditional methods.

The impressive Gothic-style Payne Whitney Gymnasium

Street and turn left. Halfway down the block, at No. 300, is Toad's Place, well known to rock music fans. Next door is Mory's, one of the most popular spots in town.

10 Mory's

Today, Mory's is a private club for eating and drinking, but it started out as a bar and inspired a famous ballad, the Whiffenpoof song:

"To the tables down at Mory's
To the place where Louis dwells ... "

Louis Linder was the club's proprietor in 1909 when four students, members of the Yale Glee Club singers, formed the barbershop-style Varsity Quartet. They took the name of the Whiffenpoof, a mythical half-bird, half-dragon that was a character in a contemporary Broadway show. The 14-strong Whiffenpoofs are the oldest a cappella choir in the country, giving 150 concerts a year. They still meet at Mory's every week.

▶ *Turn right on Wall Street and walk to the corner of Wall and High streets to the Beinecke Library.*

11 Beinecke Rare Book and Manuscript Library

This three-star building alone is worth the journey to New Haven: the exterior, the most memorable of the university's modern buildings, looks like an unbroken cube of white Vermont marble supported at four corners by the lightest of steel pads. Even more memorable is the interior, glowing with bronze-hued light filtering through the translucent marble. The central stack is a six-story glass tower of rare books. On the mezzanine level are two large cases: one holds a rare 1455 Gutenberg Bible, one of only 22 known, the other a complete edition of *Birds of America* by naturalist John James Audubon (1785–1851).

▶ *Continue on Wall Street, to the corner of College Street.*

12 Scroll & Key

Enigmatic and bearing no name or sign, this stone building, with minarets and mystical carved figures, is home to another of the private secret societies.

▶ *Turn right on College Street, left on Elm Street, and return to the Green.*

The Litchfield
Hills

1 DAY • 151½ MILES • 245KM

The rolling Litchfield Hills and the Housatonic River give a special character to the scattered villages that dot the peaceful northwest corner of Connecticut, among the thick woods.

ITINERARY	
HARTFORD	▸ Litchfield (34m-55km)
LITCHFIELD	▸ New Preston (11m-18km)
NEW PRESTON	▸ New Milford (8m-13km)
NEW MILFORD	▸ Kent (16m-26km)
KENT	▸ Cornwall Bridge (9m-15km)
CORNWALL BRIDGE	▸ West Cornwall (4m-6km)
WEST CORNWALL	▸ Salisbury (12½m-20km)
SALISBURY	▸ Norfolk (14m-23km)
NORFOLK	▸ Hartford (43m-69km)

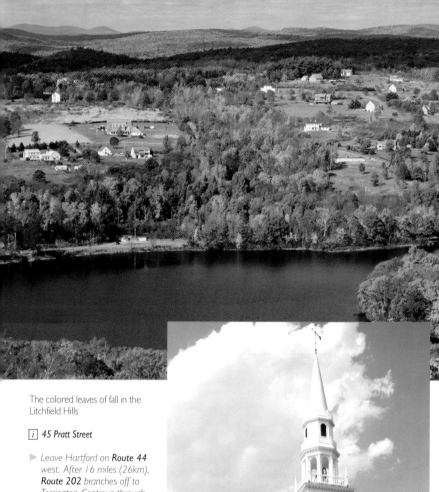

The colored leaves of fall in the Litchfield Hills

i 45 Pratt Street

▶ *Leave Hartford on **Route 44** west. After 16 miles (26km), **Route 202** branches off to Torrington. Continue through Torrington and drive 6 miles (10km) to Litchfield.*

❶ Litchfield

Rather as a judge surveys his court, so Litchfield dominates the local landscape. Appropriately, the Tapping Reeve House on South Street was owned by Judge Tapping Reeve, who had America's first law school built in the grounds. Opened in 1773, it produced judges by the score, as well as three justices of the U.S. Supreme Court, 28 senators, and two vice-presidents. Exhibits here relate the importance of the school and its students to the new nation. During that era, Litchfield was also famous for its leather goods, mills, and factories. Townspeople have proudly maintained their homes and the common to re-create the classic

The First Congregational Church

New England village seen today. The First Congregational Church, with its white columns, has a stately position at the head of the Green with North, South, East and West streets reaching out in their appropriate compass headings. North Street, often labeled one of the country's most beautiful, boasts textbook examples of late 1700s Georgian and Federal architecture, such as the Sheldon Tavern. The red-brick building at the corner of North

Grill is known for its celebrity customers, from politicians to movie stars.

i *Litchfield Hills Information booth, The Green*

▶ *Drive west for 11 miles (18km) on* **Route 202**.

❷ New Preston
The road climbs abruptly to New Preston, alongside the waterfalls of the Aspetuck River, which give a clue to the town's industrial background. In the early 1800s, no less than 21 water-driven mills operated between New Preston and Marble Dale, barely a mile (1.5km) away. The mills did not survive the transition to steam power, but New Preston thrives on a new economy centered on its chic antiques shops.

▶ *Continue through New Preston to Lake Waramaug.*

❸ Lake Waramaug
To the Indians, Lake Waramaug was the "place of good fishing." Today, most visitors just come to catch the view, and to visit the Hopkins Vineyard, where the red-painted Yankee barn houses the winery and store.

SPECIAL TO...

Between Preston and New Milford, the Henderson Cultural Center at Hunt Hill Farm is an unusual combination of cooking school, art gallery, and gourmet kitchenware and food store. Set in former stables and a barn, The Silo is always associated with the late Skitch Henderson, the British-born broadway veteran and founder-director of The New York Pops. His Henderson American Music Archive is an important source for 20th-century American culture.

▶ *Return to New Preston and take* **Route 202** *south for 8 miles (19km) to New Milford.*

❹ New Milford
The Town Hall on The Green stands on the site of Roger Sherman's birthplace. He is the only native of Connecticut whose signature appears on all the significant documents concerning America's independence. Near the bandstand is a tank whose small scale and Victorian styling make it an unusually decorative armed forces memorial.

▶ *Drive through New Milford on* **Routes 202** *and* **67** *southwest, cross the Housatonic River bridge, turn right at the traffic lights onto* **Route 7** *north and continue through peaceful countryside to Bull's Bridge.*

❺ Bull's Bridge
Bull's Bridge, one of just two covered bridges in the state that still see daily use, is barely longer than a large car. Beneath, the Housatonic River rushes through a particularly rugged gorge. Raging waters and winter ice jams destroyed four successive bridges until the present one, which has lasted since 1842. Back in 1781, a horse in George Washington's party fell into this gorge while making the crossing. Washington's own financial accounts record "getting a horse out of Bull's Bridge falls, $215.00." The high price suggests that the horse was probably the general's.

▶ *Continue on* **Route 7** *to Kent.*

SCENIC ROUTES

From New Milford north to Canaan is one of Connecticut's prettiest drives. Running parallel to the Housatonic River the entire way, Route 7 is bordered by the Litchfield Hills to the east and the Taconic Mountains to the west. Housatonic is an Indian word meaning "place beyond the mountains," and it offers tempting photo opportunities.

SPECIAL TO...

White Flower Farm is an emporium of gardening located 3½ miles (5.6km) out of Litchfield via South Street (Route 63 South). Open from April to October, its 5 acres (2ha) are a technicolor extravaganza, with the begonia displays a high point. Its *Garden Book*, a weighty catalog published twice a year, offers a wealth of horticultural information.

---

and West streets was the Litchfield County Jail. Built in 1812, it was in use until the 1990s.

Also on North Street is a red saltbox house. On this site lived two 19th-century personalities: the charismatic preacher Rev. Henry Beecher and his sister, the author Harriet Beecher Stowe. The Litchfield History Museum on The Green has a fine collection of early paintings, decorative arts, and furniture, and The Green is lined with trendy shops, galleries and restaurants. The West Street

6 Kent

Just as Litchfield was once industrial, so Kent was known for its iron foundries. Where pig iron was smelted in the early 1800s, the Sloane-Stanley Museum and Kent Furnace now stands. A dedicated historian and fine artist, Sloane chronicled all aspects of early American life, from the building of barns to his favorite subject, the making and using of tools. The museum, housed in a big barn, includes a dog-powered butter churn, an authentic frontier cabin, and a re-creation of his art studio, right down to his paint-splattered telephone. Ruins of the furnace stand on the grounds, recalling a vanished local industry. Next door is the Connecticut Antique Machinery Association Museum, a mining museum, and an agricultural museum, with exhibitions on local traditions.

▶ *Stay on* **Route 7** *north for 5 miles (8km) to Kent Falls State Park. Continue to Cornwall Bridge.*

RECOMMENDED WALKS

Kent Falls State Park is one of 34 state parks and forests in this corner of Connecticut. All are popular spots for picnics and hiking. Here, the special attraction is a broad view over Connecticut's wild terrain.
For a grand view, climb the steep 200-foot (60m) path beside the falls, which are often used for commercials and feature in the TV soap opera *The Guiding Light*.

---

7 Cornwall Bridge

From here north, the valley narrows and the hills steepen. Hardly more than an intersection and the bridge, the hub of this little community is Baird's General Store, a well-known stopping point for Appalachian Trail hikers. The "world's longest continuous footpath" stretches 2,175 miles (3,500km) from Georgia to northeast Maine. It crosses Route 7 only a few steps from the front porch where weary walkers stack their backpacks.

SPECIAL TO...

You can visit the workshop of the Cornwall Bridge Pottery, south of Cornwall Bridge, to see the craftspeople at work and view the huge wood-fired kiln in which their stylish pots are fired. Seconds are on sale here; the main shop is in West Cornwall.

▶ *Cross the Housatonic again; bear right after the bridge and continue north to West Cornwall on* **Route 7**.

SPECIAL TO...

The only covered bridges for cars in the state are here: at West Cornwall and Bulls Bridge, Kent

Clarke Outdoors, a log cabin on the left. Although U.S. Olympic teams may make this their home base, Clarke's also outfits day trips for recreational paddlers and provides a shuttle service to and from the entry/exit points. The favorite "playground" for the kayakers is beneath the covered bridge at West Cornwall, built in 1837.

▶ *Stay on **Route 7** north for 4¹/₂ miles (7km), bearing left on **Route 112** for ¾ mile (1km) to Lime Rock Park.*

9 Lime Rock Park

Deep in the rural idyll, the self-styled "Road Racing Center of the East" comes as a surprise. The deceptively simple 1¹/₂-mile (2.4km) track has tested the best from every category of motorsport. Drivers from Formula 1 to NASCAR and sports car racing have all taken the wheel here. Among celebrity competitors often seen here are the actors Paul Newman and Tom Cruise.

▶ *Continue west for 3³/₄ miles (6km) on **Route 112**. Climbing out of the Housatonic Valley, grand views open up of magnificent farms. To the north and west, the Berkshire Hills continue and blend into the Catskill Mountains of New York and the Green Mountains of Vermont. Turn north onto **Route 41** and drive for 1¹/₂ miles (2.4km) to Lakeville.*

10 Lakeville

It is hard to believe that this pretty area was once industrial. Back in 1762, settlers discovered that a local hill was almost totally pure hematite, virtually free of impurities. Close to this iron deposit, called Ore Hill, Ethan Allen and Samuel Forbes built Connecticut's first iron blast furnace, producing everything from potash kettles to pig iron.

During the American Revolution, the furnace was operated by the Connecticut Committee on Safety and produced over 800 iron cannons

to fight the British. Today, Lakeville is at the heart of the Upper Housatonic Valley National Heritage Area, a peaceful preservation area embracing 29 communities stretching from northwestern Connecticut up into southwestern Massachusetts.

▶ *Continue north on **Routes 41** and **44** for 2 miles (3km) to Salisbury.*

11 Salisbury

Salisbury is best known for having two prep schools, and the students add a buzz to the atmosphere of this pretty town. Nearby is the venerable Salisbury Ski Jump, where the annual winter festival in February brings competitors from as far as Norway. In summer, the population doubles with weekenders.

▶ *Follow **Route 44** for 7 miles (11km) to Canaan and on for another 7 miles (11km) to Norfolk.*

12 Norfolk

Connecticut's highest town, tucked away in the northwestern corner, has an elevation of 1,770 feet (540m). Here, the Battell Chapel, with its Tiffany glass windows, faces the central Green that sits atop the hill. Each summer, the Norfolk Chamber Music Festival, with the Yale Summer School of Music, attracts music fans as it has for almost a century. Rachmaninov, Caruso and Paderewski are among the legends who have performed during the season. Many of the town's street signs, painted by hand, have been brightened up with engaging pictures of animals.

▶ *From The Green take the tranquil country drive back to Torrington on **Route 272**. This is a peaceful stretch of hilly evergreen and oak forest, dotted with lovely homes and farms. Return to Hartford.*

Water tumbles down a 200-foot (60m) flight of natural steps in Kent Falls State Park

8 Cornwall Bridge to West Cornwall

This is one of the prettiest stretches of the Housatonic, known as a fly-fisherman's paradise. Throughout the summer, anglers come here to practice the elegant art of casting and placing the fly delicately on the water.

Somewhat rougher are the sports of white-water canoeing and kayaking. Paddlers meet at

HARTFORD HARTFORD

DEVILS
HOPPYARD
STATE
PARK

East **7** Haddam
82
8 Gillette Castle
82

COCKAPONSET
STATE
FOREST

Deep River

91

Lake
Gaillard

CHATFIELD
HOLLOW
STATE PARK

Ivoryton

Essex
6

Mill

Quinnipiac

Muddy

NEW
HAVEN

Saltonstall
Lake

95

Eight Mile

154

156

Old
Lyn

NEW
YORK

East
Haven

Branford **1**

2

Guilford
3

146

**Stony
Creek**

Indian
Neck

Thimble
Islands

East
River

Whitfield
House

Madison **4**

HAMMONASSET
BEACH STATE
PARK

Clinton

95

Westbrook

Saybrook
Manor

Knollwood

Old
Saybrook
5

Saybrook
Point
Fenwick

Long Island Sound

The
Connecticut
Shore

2 DAYS • 158 MILES • 254KM

New Haven is a mixture of industry and academia. Some areas still recall the might of the Industrial Revolution that had its roots here; other areas are a delight, thanks to the ivied walls and grassy quadrangles of Yale University (see pages 66–70). East of New Haven, the Connecticut shore is dotted with some surprisingly sleepy villages, sheltered from traffic by I–95, the interstate highway that speeds traffic on its way and diverts it from the coast.

Uncle Tom's Cabin, stayed in Guilford on her grandmother's farm where she got to know the African American servants.

▶ Continue on **Route 146** and turn onto **Route 1** east.

◳ Madison

On the Green at the entrance to the town is the late 17th-century Deacon John Grave House, which has been a school, infirmary, arsenal, tavern and courtroom in its time.

Madison also has one of the few beaches on this shore that is open to all. The 2 miles (3km) of sandy shore is in the enormous Hammonasset Beach State Park. The area also includes a nature reserve.

▶ Continue on **Route 1** east, then turn right to Old Saybrook.

◳ Old Saybrook

Though busy and commercially developed, Saybrook still has many fine Colonial homes, including the General William Hart House (1767), with its corner fireplaces and herb garden. Saybrook's most famous son is David Bushnell (1742–1824), credited with building the first "sub-marine" (see below).

▶ Return north on **Route 154** and drive for 5 miles (8km) to Essex.

FOR HISTORY BUFFS

In the 1770s, Yale student David Bushnell was fascinated by explosives. Tests of his limpet mine, in Otter Cove near Old Saybrook, impressed George Washington and renowned inventor Benjamin Franklin. But Bushnell's pride and joy was his *American Turtle*. Reconstructed at the Connecticut River Museum in Essex, this self-propelled underwater capsule is considered the first "sub-marine." It was lost in battle against the British.

⊡ 1000 Chapel Street

▶ Start in New Haven on **Route 95** east. Take exit 53 and at the rotary take **Route 146** east to Branford (7miles/11km).

◳ Branford

The pleasant town of Branford has an old-fashioned green with an unusually opulent library, church and school nearby. The only historic mansion open to the public is the Nathaniel Harrison House on South Main Street, a restored 1724 home with beautiful period furnishings and flower and herb gardens.

▶ Stay on **Route 146** for 6 miles (10km), following the shoreline through Indian Neck to Stony Creek.

◳ Stony Creek

Millions of Americans and foreigners have seen the pink granite produced from the local quarry: it was used in Grand Central Station and for the pedestal of the Statue of Liberty. Just off shore, the water is speckled by the tiny Thimble Islands. Called the "Hundred Islands" by the Colonists, there are actually over 300 of them scattered throughout Long Island Sound. Some are barely big enough to

accommodate the cottages built on them, often on stilts. With names like Treasure Island and Money Island, it is no surprise that the pirate Captain Kidd supposedly hid out here. Small boats are ready at Stony Creek harbor to give tours.

▶ Continue on **Route 146** for 4 miles (6km) to Guilford.

◳ Guilford

There is a particularly English feeling about this town, founded in 1639 and built around an unusually large green. Luckily, it escaped serious damage during the War of Independence, and around 80 pre-Revolutionary houses still stand.

The oldest, the 1639 Henry Whitfield State Museum, is also the oldest stone building in New England. Sitting on a slight rise in the middle of a large lot, this originally looked more like a fortified manor house, but the steeply pitched roof and small, leaded, lattice windows reflect its remarkable age.

Other homes with history include the 1660 red saltbox Hyland House, and the 1774 Thomas Griswold House, now a museum, occupied by Griswold descendants until 1958. Harriet Beecher Stowe, who later wrote

❻ Essex

In a 1996 book called *The 100 Best Small Towns in America*, Essex came out number one. Founded in 1648, it became quite wealthy due to the skill of its carpenters and shipwrights. The splendid Colonial, Georgian and Federal homes on Main Street were built by their bosses, the shipbuilders and sea captains. The town's social hub is the 200-year-old Griswold Inn. Here, collections of marine art and 19th-century firearms add to the atmosphere of "the 'Gris,'" a busy, though jolly, hotel-restaurant. At the end of the street, in an old warehouse on Steamboat Landing, is the Connecticut River Museum. This tells the story of Essex and of the Connecticut River, from its source in northeastern New Hampshire to the mouth. Star attraction is the reproduction of

Cruising on the Connecticut River near East Haddam

David Bushnell's remarkable underwater craft, *American Turtle*. A stone's-throw away, the keel was laid for the *Oliver Cromwell*, the colony's first custom-built warship, back in 1776. From then on, Essex was an important ship-building center. The tradition continues nearby at the Brewer Dauntless Shipyard, which produces sleek modern yachts. The 1732 Pratt

House Museum portrays an 1800s home with a herb garden.

▶ *Return to* **Route 154** *and drive north to* **Route 82** *east. Turn right and cross the Connecticut River on the turntable bridge to East Haddam.*

SCENIC ROUTES

The Essex Steam Train and Riverboat Ride is organized by the Valley Railroad Company, whose volunteers restore, maintain, and operate old steam engines and cars. They puff through the countryside for the hour-long trip up to Chester and then stop at Deep River to connect with a river boat for an hour-and-a-half-long cruise.

SPECIAL TO...

No prizes for guessing how Ivoryton, 2 miles (3km) west of Essex, got its name. In the old days, ivory from Africa was unloaded in Essex and driven here in horse-drawn carts. It was then cut and polished into piano keys, buttons and combs. On the National Register of Historic Places, the Ivory Town Playhouse once attracted stars such as Katharine Hepburn, and Marlon Brando. The hamlet is tranquil, with beech trees on its main street, a general store, and a summer theater.

BECKY THATCHER

7 East Haddam

Just at the end of the bridge, high above the river, stands the Goodspeed Opera House. This six-story, white "wedding cake" is a grand reminder of the late 19th century, when East Haddam was a resort town, used by Mr. William Goodspeed's very own steam ships. Restored in the 1960s, the house's specialty is musical comedies. It hosted pre-Broadway runs for brand-new shows such as *Man of La Mancha*, in 1966, and *Annie*, in 1977. Now, new musicals are presented in a second theater in Chester, while this house concentrates on revivals. Land for East Haddam's original 17th-century settlement was sold to the English by local Native Americans in exchange for 30 coats. The one-room schoolhouse, where Nathan Hale once taught, is next to the cemetery.

navigation

▷ Continue on **Route 82** south to Gillette Castle.

8 Gillette Castle

At the turn of the century, actor William Gillette (1853–1937) had superstar status, drawing huge audiences to see his 1,300 performances portraying Sherlock Holmes. By 1919, he had poured a million dollars into this extraordinary fake medieval stone castle. An amateur inventor with an odd sense of humor, he made many of the "puzzle locks" on its doors and designed a system of mirrors to be able to see who was visiting. After a major renovation, which included a new visitor center, the castle has plenty to see. The 184-acre (74-ha) grounds make a fine picnic spot, high on the bank overlooking the Connecticut River.

▷ Continue on **Route 82** for 5 miles (8km) to **Route 156** south. Drive to Old Lyme.

9 Old Lyme

Old Lyme, one of America's first art colonies, is the unofficial home of American Impressionism, thanks to Florence Griswold. At the turn of the century, "Miss Florence" decided to take in boarders; first one, then more artists moved into her fine, late Georgian home, drawn by the light and the serenity of the surrounding beaches and marshes. Instead of signing the visitors book, guests such as Willard Metcalf, Childe Hassam, and William Chadwick painted scenes on their landlady's doors and wall panels. This 1817 house, in the heart of the Old Lyme Historic District, is now a museum; the Krieble Gallery has regularly changing

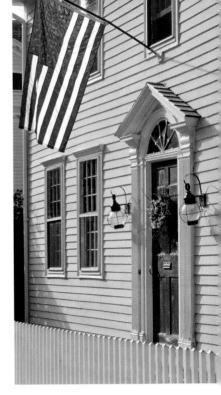

Housefront in Essex

exhibitions from the collection. Next door, the Lyme Academy College of Fine Arts is one of America's leading art schools.

▷ Leave town and follow **Route 156** east, crossing Niantic Bay, with a view of the Millstone Energy Center, a nuclear power plant. After 16 miles (26km), arrive in New London.

SPECIAL TO...

Called the "Fresh River" by Dutch explorer Adriaen Block and the "Great River" by English settlers, the waterway for which Connecticut is named was always the Quinnetukut to the Native Americans. The name means "long river whose waters are driven by wind and tide." It starts in the three Connecticut lakes, up in the northeastern corner of New Hampshire, near the Canadian border.

10 New London

Although New London is slowly renewing its image, it still remains a working town, just as it has been for 300 years. While not as attractive as smaller, more gentrified places in New England, the history here is just as impressive. The deep harbor made this an important port in the early 18th century, and the Hempsted Houses offer an insight into the lives of seafarers' families in Colonial times.

During the American Revolution, New London was the headquarters of the patriots' naval resistance, which made it a target for the British Army. Later, the port became one of the world's biggest and busiest whaling ports, with as many as 80 ships in its fleet. Whale Oil Row has four splendid 1832 mansions, grandiose Greek Revival temples of affluence.

The town's nautical history was boosted further in 1876 when the U.S. Coast Guard Academy opened. Its 60-year-old German barque, the *Eagle*, was confiscated from Germany by the U.S. Navy after World War II. Now, this 295-foot (109m) long sail training ship welcomes visitors (see website) when in port.

FOR CHILDREN

The 300-acre (120-hectare) Denison Pequotsepos Nature Center has been educating and entertaining children for some 50 years, with its wildlife sanctuary, nature trails and fun tree house.
For simply letting off steam, take them to Ocean Beach Park, where swimming pools, waterslides, mini-golf and a playground are among the attractions.

FOR HISTORY BUFFS

Benedict Arnold was a brilliant but vain American general who switched sides in the middle of the war. In 1781, he attacked New London with 1,700 British troops. Having grown up nearby, at Norwich, Arnold knew the area and the communication codes of the local militia. He caught the defenders off guard and burned New London. This was the final engagement of the war in New England. Discover more at Fort Griswold Battlefield State Park, Groton.

Near the Coastguard Academy is the Lyman-Allyn Art Museum, known for its fine collection of 18th- and 19th-century American paintings, from Copley and West to the Hudson River School and Impressionism.

Playwright Eugene O'Neill spent unhappy boyhood summers at Monte Cristo Cottage, to the south on Pequot Avenue. Bleak family events there a century or more ago are recalled in three O'Neill plays, including *Long Day's Journey into Night*. On Route 213, 6 miles (10km) south, is the Eugene O'Neill Theater Center, known for presenting staged readings of new productions.

▶ *Follow signs to I–95 east and cross the Thames river. Exit 86 leads north on **Route 12** to the Nautilus Memorial.*

11 USS *Nautilus*

The USS *Nautilus*, dating from 1954, is the world's first nuclear-powered sub and the first to venture under the ice cap at the North Pole. Now open for visitors, it shows just how crowded conditions are when living underwater in a "sub."

▶ *Return on **Route 12** and take **Route 1** east. Turn right on **Route 215** for Noank.*

12 Noank

Noank is as salty and undiscovered a town as there is on the Connecticut shoreline. A fishing and shipbuilding community in the past, it now looks as if every house might have a retired lobsterman or sea captain sitting out on the front porch. Pearl Street is the main thoroughfare and provides all the high points, from the Deacon Robert Palmer House with its whimsical gingerbread architecture and wild colors to Abbott's Lobster-in-the-Rough. This is a lobster house of the traditional sort found in Maine.

Monte Cristo Cottage, named after O'Neill's actor-father's greatest role

SPECIAL TO...

As soon as European settlers arrived in New England, they began to move the Native Americans off their traditional lands. Some were "bought," others taken by force. Finally, tribes were granted reservations to live on. Best known are those in the West, but Connecticut has its own, the home of descendants of the Mashantucket Pequot Tribal Nation. In 1998, the Mashantucket Pequot Museum and Research Center opened. Heralded as "the most ambitious new museum in America," this center includes a huge re-creation of a 16th-century Pequot village, state-of-the-art interactive computer displays and original film footage. This is the largest tribal museum in America.

▷ Continue on **Route 215**, then **Route 1** to Mystic.

Lobster shop in Noank

13 Mystic

The town itself is attractive, but often overlooked by the visitors who swarm to Mystic Seaport, the re-creation of a 19th-century fishing village. A mixture of real and replica, this is much more than a conventional open-air museum, with the largest and most complete maritime collection in the country. Taking full advantage of its waterside location, it has sailing vessels and models of every description and size on display.

The 1841 *Charles W. Morgan*, the last wooden whaling vessel ever to be built, and the *L. A. Dunton*, a sleek 123-foot (45.5m) Gloucester fishing schooner which looks more like an America's Cup race competitor, can be seen.

Every possible craft and trade associated with seafaring life can be found and studied somewhere on the 40-acre (16.6-ha) site. Active craftsmen re-create the workaday world of an early 19th-century fishing village. Nautical terms such as "sandbag-gers," "smacks," "chandlers," "coopers" and "cordage" are all explained. To understand how sailors used to navigate by the stars, take in one of the shows at the Planetarium. You can even board a steam-boat for a trip out onto the river.

Also in town is the Mystic Aquarium, its centerpiece a coral reef stocked with sharks, stingrays and reef fish. You can learn about alligators and other swamp life, then watch Beluga whales in the Alaskan Coast exhibit. Undersea exploration, such as finding the *Titanic*, is the theme of Challenge of the Deep.

▷ Take **Route 1** toward Stonington. After 3 miles (5km), turn onto **Route 1A** for the village.

14 Stonington

Stonington Borough, a peninsula covered in old houses, remains peaceful and untouristy. The docks of this working fishing port, which has Connecticut's largest commercial fleet, provide an atmospheric place to stroll and watch the dragger fleet and lobster boats come in each afternoon. At the end of the long narrow main street is the Land Battery, with two of the cannons that helped repulse a British naval attack in the War of 1812. A few steps farther is the Old Lighthouse Museum (1823), the first Government-operated lighthouse in Connecticut with gear for whaling and "ice harvesting" displayed in the "pocket-size" lighthouse.

Guided tours are available at the home of Captain Nathaniel B. Palmer, who explored Antarctica. Exhibits in the house cover his career and his family life.

▷ Return to **Route 1**, then join **I–95** west and return to New Haven.

THE MARITIME TRADITION

The Atlantic Ocean has had a profound affect on the development of New England. Five of the six states in the region are adjacent to the coastline, and the Europeans who first arrived all had to cross the stormy North Atlantic. Once they arrived, ships maintained the umbilical cord linking them with the Mother Countries, and permanent communities grew up around safe harbors. The abundance of fish offshore made fishing an easy and reliable means of finding food, and it became so vital to the early settlers that fishermen were exempt from military service.

Once the Colonies were established, shipping became an important part of the economy, though strict laws from London insisted that all manufactured goods had to be imported from England, alone. Enforcement was another matter: and not only were "illegal" cargoes landed, but customs duties were, on occasion, evaded.

Ships were a necessity for England, and the navy increasingly relied on lumber from Maine. Soon, the boats themselves were being constructed in the Colonies, since shipbuilding costs were from 20 to 50 percent less than in the Mother Country. Shipbuilding thrived and by 1760, one-third of the total British merchant tonnage was produced in the American Colonies.

By this time, the patterns of triangular trade routes were established. Merchant ships sailed from New England with grain, timber and fish for the West Indies. These were traded for fruit, sugar, and molasses, which were taken on to England. There, the holds were loaded up with manufactured goods to be transported back home. Similar routes connected New England with Africa and the Mediterranean.

After years of lax enforcement, Britain decided to toughen up its policing of the trade laws in order to raise more revenue from the Colonies. Not only did this

hurt the New England economy, but it fostered anti-London feelings. The major ports of Boston and Portland, along with New York to the south, were targets before and during the Revolution.

Shipping again became a contentious issue during the Napoleonic Wars in Europe. Although the U.S. remained neutral, Britain interfered with American shipping, hoping to deprive the French of supplies. In addition, seamen were taken off captured ships and forced to sail for Britain. Eventually, these grievances led to the War of 1812.

From their early days, Colonists learned from the Native Americans how to catch whales when the mammals swam near shore, and towns such as New London and Mystic in Connecticut, and New Bedford and Provincetown in Massachusetts thrived at the expense of the whale. In 1774, 360 whaling ships sailed from Nantucket. Rhode Island developed a huge candle-making industry based on whale products. The oil was used to light streets and homes in Europe, while bones and baleen were used to make anything from umbrella spokes to corset stays. Only the discovery of oil (made into kerosene) in Pennsylvania, in 1859, ended the bloody trade. The business of whaling was epitomized in Herman Melville's novel, *Moby-Dick*,

Above: humpback whales can reach 40 to 50 feet (13 to 16m)

based on his own experiences aboard ship. Today, museums such as Nantucket's Whaling Museum, housed in a former whale oil refinery, record the exploits of American sailors who roamed the oceans in the early 19th century.

Apart from their heavy involvement in the slave trade, "Yankee traders" sailed round South America to do business with China and the Pacific islands, bringing back huge wealth to towns such as Boston, Salem and Portsmouth. Along the Maine coast, at Kennebunkport and Kittery, Bath, Camden and Belfast, shipbuilders continued traditions begun in 1607, when the *Virginia* was the first ship built in the Colonies, near Bath.

Today, New England's nautical traditions concentrate on the pleasure industry, with yachting keeping the shipbuilders and sail-makers of the region at the forefront of technology. For the first half of the 20th century,

Tall ships at Mystic Seaport

Newport rivalled Cowes (in England) as the sailing capital of the world. The rich and famous built ever-larger yachts and raced them. Battles in the wind-swept seas off Newport for the legendary America's Cup were a feature of the town between 1930 and 1983.

In Bristol, Rhode Island, the Herreshoff Marine Museum recalls the Herreshoff Company's contribution to sailing. Between 1893 and 1934, eight consecutive winners in the America's Cup competition were built on the site, as well as the first torpedo boats for the U.S. Navy. In Newport, the Naval War College Museum emphasizes America's rise to power as a world force on the high seas. Out at Fort Adams State Park, at the Museum of Yachting, the America's Cup Gallery traces 150 years of competition for the "Auld Mug."

"Windjammers," old sailing ships, are now a popular way of spending a vacation, afloat along the coast. In Maine, Rockland and Camden are the best-known centers, while summer festivals such as Windjammer Days in Boothbay Harbor and the finish of the Great Schooner Race, at the Rockland Breakwater, celebrate the nautical tradition.

Nowhere records New England's tradition better than Mystic Seaport on the Mystic River in Connecticut. An American whaler, the *Charles W. Morgan*, built of wood in 1841, is one of several sailing vessels on show to visitors.

83

RHODE ISLAND

Rhode Island, "Little Rhody," is the smallest state, yet it also boasts the longest name: officially, it is The State of Rhode Island and Providence Plantations. Wedged between Connectiut and Massachusetts, this state received its title back in 1644, when two colonies were combined. A mere 48 miles by 37 miles (77km by 59km), it is nicknamed the "Ocean State" because of its 400 miles (640km) of shoreline, which includes some 100 beaches with public access. Not all the coast runs along the Atlantic Ocean; it also borders Narragansett Bay, which bites into the southeast corner of the state and stretches 28 miles (45km) inland, to the city of Providence.

Although the Vikings may have visited North America in the 11th century, Giovanni da Verrazano, the Italian explorer, is on record for sailing past what is now Block Island in 1524. He named it after the Island of Rhodes in Greece. When Roger Williams and a band of followers fled the intolerance of the Puritan colony in Massachusetts in 1636, they settled in what is now Providence. Two years later, Anne Hutchinson was similarly banished, and led another group to Aquidneck Island, now better known for the city of Newport. Both communities believed in religious freedom, for Christians as well as non-Christians. One of the first synagogues in the U.S. was built in Newport, while the first Baptist church was founded in Providence.

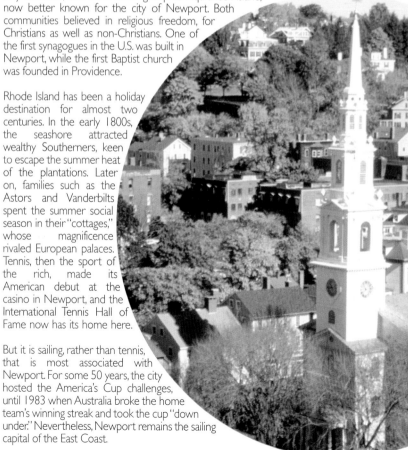

The First Baptist Church, Eastside, Rhode Island

Rhode Island has been a holiday destination for almost two centuries. In the early 1800s, the seashore attracted wealthy Southerners, keen to escape the summer heat of the plantations. Later on, families such as the Astors and Vanderbilts spent the summer social season in their "cottages," whose magnificence rivaled European palaces. Tennis, then the sport of the rich, made its American debut at the casino in Newport, and the International Tennis Hall of Fame now has its home here.

But it is sailing, rather than tennis, that is most associated with Newport. For some 50 years, the city hosted the America's Cup challenges, until 1983 when Australia broke the home team's winning streak and took the cup "down under." Nevertheless, Newport remains the sailing capital of the East Coast.

Tour 12

Providence, the capital of Rhode Island, is a gem of a city, all too often overlooked by visitors to New England. The riverfront and downtown area have been successfully restored and revitalized, while the historic district around Benefit Street is full of 18th- and 19th-century houses, now used for offices and museums, classrooms and private homes. Nearby is Brown University, the seventh oldest in the country, founded in 1764, and the Rhode Island School of Design, one of the country's leading art schools. Not surprisingly, this area is known as College Hill. Across the river is Federal Hill, where Little Italy is full of delicatessens and cafés. With its ethnic mix and large student population, Providence is a lively city, with a thriving music scene, art galleries and numerous restaurants. The good food is a by-product of Johnson and Wales University, which specializes in the culinary arts and hospitality business.

Tour 13

Newport is situated at the southern tip of an island, with a harbor on one side and beaches stretching along the other. This town of contrasts has its share of plain pre-Revolutionary houses as well as opulent summer homes, such as Château-sur-Mer and The Breakers. A century ago, entrance was only for the privileged few; today, visitors are welcome to see the priceless art and grandiose architecture.

Yachting is big on Rhode Island, and in Newport in particular

Sailing has long been popular here, with the most famous race of all, the America's Cup, a long tradition. Even though the cup has been lost to Australians, New Zealanders, and the Swiss, Narragansett Bay still brings in the sailing crowd.

Newport also attracts tennis fans, who visit the Hall of Fame. In summer, you can see one of the few professional tournaments outside the British Isles that is still played on grass. The city also draws music lovers. Since the first Newport Jazz Festival in 1954, the outdoor summer concerts have become important fixtures on the U.S. music calendar.

Providence

Providence, the third largest city in New England, is known as one of New England's most approachable destinations. It has fine examples of pre- and post-Revolutionary architecture, and a lively and artistic student body as well as high-quality restaurants, thanks to the influence of one of America's leading culinary schools. It is compact and walkable, but has steep hills, so wear comfortable shoes.

HALF A DAY

Statue with the State House behind

ℹ *Convention Center, 1 West Exchange Street*

▶ *Start at the Convention Center (park here, or in one of the public parking lots nearby). Walk to Memorial Boulevard.*

❶ Waterplace Park

This ambitious design is the focal point of Providence's extensive riverfront redevelopment. Cobbled walks, amphitheaters and bridges are part of the backdrop for WaterFire Providence, a summer spectacular with some 100 bonfires lighting up the river. This is the perfect place to view the State Capitol, sitting imperially on the hill. Completed in 1904 of Georgia marble, its dome is the fourth largest unsupported dome in the world. On top, the gilded statue *Independent Man* symbolizes the free-thinking founders of Rhode Island. Designed by sculptor George Brewster, the 500-pound (220kg) statue is 278 feet (85m) above the ground. Covered in gold leaf, it stands 11 feet (3.3m) tall and holds a spear that is 14 feet (4.2m) long.

▶ *Continue along Memorial Boulevard, cross the Providence River on Steeple Street Bridge; follow Steeple Street up the hill to No. 75 North Main Street.*

❷ First Baptist Meeting House

Although Roger Williams founded the Baptist congregation in 1638, the first church was not built for nearly 70 years. This house of worship dates from 1775. A plan for St. Martin-in-the-Fields in London provided the inspiration for architect Joseph Brown, but the ability of the 185-foot steeple (56m) to withstand storms was due to the carpenters' extensive shipbuilding experience.

▶ *Turn up Thomas Street to Benefit Street. Turn right to No. 224 Benefit Street..*

❸ Rhode Island School of Design Museum of Art

Rhode Island School of Design, always abbreviated to RISD ("Ris-dee") is one of America's leading art schools. The modern entrance to the school's museum is in the Daphne Farago Wing where the focus is *Mantled Figure*, Howard Ben Tré's sculpture in solid cast glass. Works by Monet and Picasso, an Egyptian mummy and a 9-foot (2.7m) tall Buddha, dating back ten centuries, are among the rich and varied 80,000-piece collection. Must sees include the costume and textile collection, and Pendleton House, whose early American works include paintings and the furniture of Townsend and Goddard.

▶ *Continue along Benefit Street to No. 251, on the corner of College Street.*

❹ Providence Athenaeum

In the old days, a club for learned men was often called an "athenaeum," in honor of Athena, the goddess of wisdom. This Greek Revival building was finished in 1838, and its stern exterior contrasts with the warm intimacy of the main reading room, with its tiers of books. Here, poet Edgar Allen Poe met and wooed local widow Sarah Whitman, who accepted, then rejected him (she is thought to have inspired his poem *Annabel Lee*).

Today, anyone in need of inspiration needs only to look up to busts of the Greek historian Homer, the English authors Milton and Keats, and the American statesman, Daniel Webster.

▶ *Walk up College Street. On the left is the List Art Center and the David Winton Bell Gallery.*

Attractive mansion house in the College Hill district of Providence

5 David Winton Bell Gallery

A distinctive modernistic building on College Street houses the List Art Center and the David Winton Bell Gallery. The gallery has a permanent collecion of more than 4,000 works, from Rembrandt prints to contemporary pieces, and also stages a varied program of exhibitions.

▶ *Continue to the corner of College and Prospect streets.*

6 Libraries

This could be called "library corner." On the right is "the Rock," the bustling J. D. Rockefeller Library, open only to Brown students. Opposite is the "Hay," the hushed John Hay Library, where the public may explore the vast book collection and the small gallery in the lobby.

John Hay graduated from the university in 1858. A poet and

The famous *Brown Bear* statue at Brown University

historian, he was also the U.S. Secretary of State at the turn of the century.

▶ *Cross Prospect Street and enter the campus of Brown University.*

FOR HISTORY BUFFS

Roger Williams founded Providence, but the city's success in the late 18th and early 19th centuries followed the fortunes of the four Brown brothers.

John was a merchant. Joseph, the architect, designed the Market House, First Baptist Church, and a mansion for brother John. Moses founded the Providence Bank and financed the mill at Pawtucket, which started the Industrial Revolution in New England. Nicholas gave land and money to Rhode Island College, which was to be later renamed Brown University in 1804.

---

7 Brown University

The Van Wickle Gates, leading to the quadrangle, open just twice a year: to let new students in and graduates out. Founded in 1764, Brown is the seventh-oldest university in the country, and became co-ed in 1971. The main quadrangle boasts a variety of architecture. At the upper end of the college's grounds is the Carrie Tower, built by Paul Bajnotti of Turin in memory of his wife. It is inscribed: "Love is strong as death."

The oldest building, University Hall (1771), was used as a barracks by French and American troops during the Revolution. Behind is the larger-than-life bronze *Brown Bear* statue. Rearing up, with its rather kindly expression, it supposedly stands on a slate from the rock where Roger Williams first set foot on his arrival from Massachusetts in 1636.

▶ *Return down the hill on College Street and turn left on Benefit Street.*

FOR HISTORY BUFFS

Which Civil War general gave his name to a fashion trend? General Ambrose Burnside, whose statue stands in City Hall Park. So well-known were his side whiskers that the style became known as "sideburns." He went on to be governor and senator for Rhode Island, and lived at No. 314 Benefit Street.

---

8 Benefit Street

Originally known as Back Street, because it ran behind the houses facing the main street, Benefit Street was transformed from a path into a proper road in 1758 "for the common benefit of all." Now it is known as the "Mile of History," with its many 18th- and 19th-century houses: note details such as the old-fashioned street lights and boot scrapers.

At No. 43 Benefit Street, on the corner of Hopkins Street, stands the clapboard Governor

GIVEN BY ALVMNI AND VNDERGRADVATES
TO BROWN VNIVERSITY

Stephen Hopkins House. This delightful example of early 1700s architecture was the home of the ten-time Governor of the state and signatory of the Declaration of Independence.

▷ *Continue along Benefit Street.*

9 First Unitarian Church

John Holden Greene, the architect, rated this 1816 church his finest achievement. High in its steeple hangs the largest ever bell cast by the Paul Revere Foundry. Better known now as the messenger who rode from Boston to Lexington in 1775 to warn the Colonists that the British were approaching, Revere was a silversmith and bell-maker.

▷ *Continue on Benefit to the corner of Power Street.*

10 John Brown House Museum

John Brown was a successful merchant who opened up trade with China after the American Revolution. His brother, Joseph, designed this imposing brick house, whose entrance is at No. 52 Power Street. President John Quincy Adams once called it "the most magnificent and elegant mansion that I have ever seen on this continent." Filled with fine examples of Rhode

Island's furniture-making tradition, it exemplifies the gracious living of the 18th century.

▷ *Continue a few steps along Benefit Street to No. 357.*

11 Nightingale-Brown House

Supposedly the country's largest wood-frame house, this 200-year-old yellow and cream merchant's home has been restored so completely, it could have been built yesterday.

▷ *Return to Power Street and walk down the hill. Turn right on South Main Street; walk to No. 86, the Old Stone Bank, established in 1819.*

12 Old Stone Bank

After the geometric simplicity of most of the buildings on this walk, the art nouveau-style gilt and green dome seems extravagant.

▷ *Continue to Westminster Street, then cross the river to The Arcade.*

13 The Arcade

Shopaholics in the early 19th century had their own indoor shopping malls. This was the U.S.A.'s first, built back in 1828. The stores and goods may have

Brown University's first building, University Hall, is now a National Historic Landmark

changed, but it is still popular with visitors as well as locals. The cantilevered stairways and ironwork are remarkable even today. The Greek Revival porticoes give this building the look of a bank or university library. Imagine teams of oxen dragging the 20-foot (6m) long columns from the granite quarry, 5 miles (8km) away in Johnston.

▷ *Continue on Westminster Street to Dorrance Street. Turn right, heading toward Kennedy Plaza and the Bank of America City Center Skating Rink. Turn left and return to the Convention Center.*

Newport

The original settlement of Newport was founded on the principles of religious tolerance, attracting Jews, Quakers, Baptists and followers of the established Church of England. With its safe, deep-water harbor, it rivaled Boston and Philadelphia by the middle of the 18th century. The city tour route starts with a walk through the Newport of the Colonial days, and finishes with a drive past the grand mansions of the late 19th century, referred to as the "Gilded Age." As well as fine museums, Newport offers wide, flat beaches, making this an appealing destination for families. **HALF A DAY**

ⓘ *Newport Visitor Information Center, 23 America's Cup Avenue (tickets for attractions and special events are sold here)*

▶ *Park in the parking lot behind the Information Center. Walk south along America's Cup Avenue for one block to Long Wharf. Cross the avenue and follow the sign to Washington Square Historic District.*

❶ Museum of Newport History

This handsome three-story building, erected in 1762, was the commercial hub of Colonial Newport. Its arches and columns were radical features in their day, marking a move away from the strictly geometric Georgian style. Now it is the Museum of Newport History, with furniture, tools, interactive computer displays, and the figurehead from the yacht *Aloha*.

❷ Washington Square

In the triangular Washington Square, the statue of Oliver Hazard Perry is a reminder of the naval hero who grew up in Newport. Aged 28, he defeated the British on Lake Erie in what was an important battle during the War of 1812. "We have met the enemy and they are ours," was his victory message.

Around the square are buildings from various periods in Newport's history. What was the city's opera house is now a movie theater; also showing films is the Jane Pickens Theater and Event Center, built as the Zion Episcopal Church back in 1834. Then, there is the Robert and Joseph Rogers House. Recently renovated, it has stood watching the comings and goings of this busy part of downtown Newport, for over 200 years.

▶ *At the top of the square, on the left, you will reach The Colony House.*

❸ The Colony House

In a town constructed primarily of wood, this brick building would have looked even more imposing in the 18th century. The fourth-oldest capitol building in the country, it was the headquarters of government from 1739 until 1900, when the new State House was opened in Providence. Important announcements read from the central second-floor balcony range from the coronation of King George III in 1760, to the results of elections for Rhode Island governors.

FOR HISTORY BUFFS

"...Whereas George the Third ... forgetting his dignity ... instead of protecting is endeavoring to destroy the good people of this colony ..." Those words, read to a crowd waiting outside the Colony House, announced the repudiation of English authority in the colony of Rhode Island. The date was May 4, 1776. Two months later, on July 4, came the Declaration of Independence of all 13 colonies.

▶ *From the Colony House, exit the square and follow*

As well as glamorous mansions, Newport has fun shops and restaurants

▶ *Broadway to No. 17, the Wanton-Lyman-Hazard House. Tours start from the Museum of Newport History.*

❹ Wanton-Lyman-Hazard House

When this house was built around 1697, it was one of more than 260 in a thriving village. Notice that the chimney stack is in the middle of the steep roof, but the front door is off-center; this style was known as the "Rhode Island floor plan." A century later, Tory-enthusiast Martin Howard lived here, but was forced to flee from an angry mob who were protesting against the Stamp Act.

▶ *Return to the square and turn left on Touro Street.*

❺ Touro Synagogue

Dating from 1763, Touro Synagogue enjoys the distinction of being the oldest Jewish place of worship still standing in North America. A community of Sephardic Jews had been in Newport since 1658, led by the Reverend Isaac Touro. Like the Quakers, the Jews were important in building Newport's trading links and wealth. Architect Peter Harrison, who also designed the Brick Market and the Redwood Library, included 12 pillars to represent the 12 tribes of Israel in an interior whose elegant simplicity looks much like a classic New England meeting house.

TOUR 13 Newport

▶ *Continue to the building next door.*

6 Newport Historical Society

The Newport Historical Society, a driving force behind the preservation of Newport's historic buildings, was established in 1854. The Seventh Day Baptist Meeting House, dating from 1730, is the oldest in the country. It was moved here in 1887.

▶ *Return to Washington Square and turn left on Clarke Street. Walk halfway down this street of painted houses to Nos. 23–25, the Armory of the Artillery Company of Newport.*

The moon rises over white-steepled Trinity Church

7 Artillery Company of Newport

Uniforms worn by Field Marshall Montgomery, Prince Philip and President Anwar Sadat of Egypt are among the uniforms, flags, regalia and other artifacts in the museum

contained in this 1836 stone building. The "1741" over the door refers to the date of the artillery's charter, making this the oldest military organization in the country.

▶ *Walk to the corner of Clarke and Mary streets.*

8 Vernon House

In 1781, General Washington met with French Generals Lafayette and Rochambeau to decide tactics for the next stage of the war. Rochambeau, commander of the French troops quartered in Newport, lived in this house. If you look closely you will see that what appears to be weathered stone block is actually wood.

▶ *Continue up Mary Street, turn right on Spring Street and proceed to Trinity Church.*

9 Trinity Church

Since 1726, the tall white spire has been a landmark on the hill above the harbor. In the vestibule is the church's original bell, "probably the first bell that rang over a New England church." The church's organ, made by Richard Bridge, came from London in 1733 and may have been played by composer George Friedrich Handel himself. On the main floor stand box pews, which were privately owned and could be bought and sold. Note the individually chosen cushions and elaborate needlepoint covers for the kneelers. The inscriptions on Pew 81 commemorate the most famous worshippers, from George Washington to Queen Elizabeth II and Archbishop Desmond Tutu of South Africa. Stained-glass windows by Tiffany stand out against a background of white walls and green-gray woodwork. They were paid for by wealthy summer residents such as Cornelius Vanderbilt.

▶ *The next left is Mill Street. Turn left, and walk up the hill past Touro Park and the mysterious Stone Tower. Legend says that*

it was erected by Vikings in the 11th century. More probably, it was a windmill belonging to Governor Benedict Arnold (great-grandfather of the Revolutionary traitor) who owned much of the land. Turn left and cross Bellvue Avenue.

10 Redwood Library

A £500 donation in 1747 bought the first books for what is the oldest continuously used library in the country. The benefactor was Abraham Redwood, a rich trader from the West Indies. The building is typical of the pre-Revolutionary era, with wood painted to look like stone. As well as books, there is a sculpture of Benjamin Franklin

by Jean-Antoine Houdin and paintings by Gilbert Stuart.

▶ *Walk next door.*

11 Newport Art Museum

Clipped gables, airy verandas, scroll-sawed trim and ornamental timbers, or "sticks," epitomize the "stick style" of 19th-century architecture.

Dating from 1864, this is the first of many buildings in Newport designed by Richard Morris Hunt, but it is vastly different from the extravaganzas that made him the defining architect of the later "Gilded Age."

▶ *Cross Bellevue to Touro Park and walk down Pelham Street to the harbor area. Along the way, you pass the tiny Arnold Burying Ground, where the stones date back to 1677. At the bottom, turn right and return to the Visitor Information Center. The rest of the route is followed by car. Drive up Memorial Boulevard and turn right on Bellevue Avenue and head for No. 194.*

cheering tennis fans and the voice of an announcer calling a famous match from the past. The all-encompassing collection of tennis memorabilia is the largest in the world, while the Hall of Fame celebrates champions.

Outside are the world's oldest continuously used grass tennis courts, dating from 1881. (The All-England Club in the U.K. is older, but moved to its present Wimbledon site in 1922.) The annual professional tournament here is played each July, immediately after Wimbledon.

If you feel so inclined, book time on one of the 13 courts and play where the U.S. Open

Stanford White and the McKim, Mead and White architectural firm, its "shingle" style was another popular Victorian trend. There are stores on the ground floor, with the ever-expanding International Tennis Hall of Fame above.

▶ *Drive along Bellevue Avenue. Single. Multiple tickets for Preservation Society houses can be bought at all their properties.*

🄳 Kingscote Mansion
In 1841, the Bellevue Avenue area was only starting to develop as a residential neighborhood, and Kingscote Mansion looks positively simple compared to

Moored boats at sunset in Newport's harbor

🄲 International Tennis Hall of Fame
From an 1876 tennis racquet-bending machine to state-of-the-art computer displays, this museum celebrates the world of tennis. On entering the Hall of Fame, there is the distant roar of

Tennis Championships were born in 1881.

This huge complex was then a social and recreational club, the Newport Casino. As well as tennis, members enjoyed tea parties, archery, dancing and concerts. The name comes from the Italian for "little house" and has nothing to do with gambling. The first major commission for

the grandiose designs of the 1890s. Typical of the Gothic Revival style are the elaborate barge-boards, lancet arch casement window, and sawn cornice trim. Designed by Richard Upjohn and built for George Noble Jones, some say that the expression "Keeping up with the Joneses" originated here.

▶ *Continue on along Bellevue Avenue.*

14 The Elms

When Pennsylvania coal baron Edward Berwind went to France, he was so impressed by the 18th-century Château d'Asnières, near Paris, that he made it the model for this house. The Elms, built in 1901, has furnishings that span the Louis XIV and XV styles, while the formal gardens have spacious terraces and lawns. At the top of the house, a hidden third story contains the servants' quarters.

▶ *Continue on Bellevue Avenue. To the left, on Narragansett Avenue, is Chepstow, an Italianate mansion built for a cousin of the Astors, with a fine collection of 19th-century American paintings.*

15 Château-sur-Mer

In 1857, William Wetmore invited 2,500 guests to a party in his five-year-old home. He paid for those festivities, and for this lavishly decorated mansion, with profits from trading with China. The grounds have some fine old trees, a Chinese moon gate and a Colonial Revival pavilion.

▶ *Continue on Bellevue Avenue.*

16 Vernon Court

This grandiose version of a 17th-century French château is a private home. On the first floor is the National Museum of American Illustration, a pictorial history of American society from 1870 to 1965.

▶ *Turn left at Ruggles Avenue and follow the signs to The Breakers.*

17 The Breakers

This is the ultimate in extravagance and the most famous summer "cottage" of all. Two decades after Richard Morris Hunt renovated Château-sur-Mer, he created this mock 16th-century Italian palace for the railroad tycoon Cornelius Vanderbilt II. Hundreds of

---

SPECIAL TO...

Newport's wealthy loved racing huge yachts. Their money and patronage stimulated interest in the America's Cup, the world's oldest international sporting challenge. The first race was held in England, round the Isle of Wight, in 1851, but from 1920 onward, Newport was the host. The American winning streak finally ended in 1983, when Australia took the cup. In recent decades, the port has acted as the finish line for single-handed transatlantic races. The full story is told in the Museum of Yachting at Fort Adams State Park, home of Newport's jazz and folk festivals.

---

craftsmen were employed, many brought over from Europe, but the grand salon was actually built in France, disassembled, shipped across the Atlantic, and reassembled by the same French craftsmen. In the dining room, a painted ceiling is two stories above the life-sized figures and gigantic marble columns. Although the kitchen is the size of an average house, it looks surprisingly simple and functional, hung with yard after yard of copper cooking pots and pans. The stables house a display of family items, including historic coaches.

▶ *Return to Bellevue Avenue and continue.*

18 Rosecliff

The Grand Trianon of Versailles was the inspiration for the summer home of Mrs. Hermann Oerlich. Soft-white tiles cover the outside; inside, the 80-foot (24m) long ballroom is all cream and gold. Elegant and refined, Rosecliff sits near the ocean and was used for shooting the 1974 movie, *The Great Gatsby* and, in 1994, *True Lies* with Arnold Schwarzenegger.

▶ *Continue along Bellevue Avenue.*

---

19 Astors' Beechwood

At the end of the 19th century, Caroline Astor was the reigning queen of American society. To be invited to her parties meant social acceptance. Her famous list of "The Top 400" people supposedly reflected the capacity of the ballroom in her New York City residence. Today, costumed guides play the parts of the Astors, their guests and their servants, bringing to life the heyday of the country house party.

▶ *Next door is Marble House.*

20 Marble House

Marble House is another Richard Morris Hunt creation, built in 1892 by William Vanderbilt, the brother of Cornelius. The overpowering entrance is covered in Italian marble, while the dining room boasts one-of-a-kind bronze Louis XIV chairs weighing 60 pounds (27kg) each. Most amazing of all is the ballroom, where "all that glisters" really is gold, or gilded. When Alva

Cornelius Vanderbilt's Breakers, Newport's most splendid estate Inset: the Newport coastline

23 Hammersmith Farm

A private home, this shingled 1888 beach house was the location for the wedding reception of Jacqueline Bouvier and John F. Kennedy. From 1961 to 1963 it was also the "Summer White House" for President Kennedy.

Vanderbilt divorced her husband, she took the house, then married Perry Belmont (see below).

▶ *Proceed along Bellevue Avenue to Belcourt Castle.*

21 Belcourt Castle

Alva Vanderbilt did not move far after she divorced William K. Vanderbilt and married his good friend Perry Belmont. Where Vanderbilt was keen on yachts, Belmont followed horse-racing and helped build the Belmont Track in New York.

▶ *Opposite is Rough Point.*

22 Rough Point

This 1889 mansion was built for a Vanderbilt, then owned by the Dukes. It remains a time capsule, left just as it was when the heiress, Doris Duke, lived here. Admire works by Renoir, Reynolds and Van Dyck.

▶ *Ocean Drive starts here and follows a scenic stretch of shoreline, dotted by breath-taking private homes. Bailey's Beach, the first on the left, was the beach favored by the "400." Some 5 miles (8km) farther, also on the left, is Hammersmith Farm.*

SCENIC ROUTES

The 3½-mile (5.6km) Cliff Walk, starting at Cliff Walk Manor on Memorial Boulevard and ending at Bailey's Beach, is an excellent way to see the splendors of the mansions from a different angle.

▶ *To return to the harbor area, follow Harrison, Halidon and Wellington avenues to Thames Street. Turn right, then left on West Narragansett Avenue and left on Spring Street to Memorial Boulevard.*

VERMONT

Vermont has been called "every American's second state" because of the small farms with red barns, and villages with white churches that make up the traditional image of "old-fashioned America." One of the most rural states, it has only one major town, Burlington, with 40,000 inhabitants. The remainder of the half million or so Vermonters are scattered throughout the rolling hills and valleys stretching north–south between Canada and the Massachusetts border.

Although Lake Champlain lies on its western flank and the Connecticut River forms the eastern border, Vermont is the only New England state with no access to the sea. What it does have is mountains. French explorer Samuel de Champlain first remarked on the *verts monts*, the green mountains, back in the 17th century. While still a colony, Vermonters argued over land ownership with neighboring New York; the Vermonters won. When the colonies threw off the yoke of the English crown, Vermont went its own way; from 1777 to 1791 it was a republic, minting its own coins and printing its own stamps.

View of the mountains surrounding Stowe, the area's main skiing and recreation center

The population has always been small. The roller-coaster landscape is difficult to farm, winters are bitter and summers are short. Despite that, Vermont has had its moments of affluence. Early in the 19th century, its wool was in demand world-wide. When that trade was lost, dairy farming took over. Although forests now cover acres of land once cleared for pasture, cattle remain a significant revenue earner. The sharp flavor of Vermont cheddar cheese is rated by gourmets, while a more recent dairy-related success is Ben and Jerry's Ice Cream. Other natural resources such as marble and granite provide a base to the economy, matched by furniture-making, paper production, and computers. Most important of all, however, is tourism.

Each autumn, "leaf peepers" by the millions invade the state, drawn by the natural phenomenon of the maple leaves turning to brilliant shades of red and gold. Since the first ski tow was set up in Woodstock in 1934, the winter season has attracted both downhill and cross-country skiers and snow-boarders.

Tour 14

The southern Vermont town of Bennington rarely rates more than a few lines in the history books, yet it played its part in the Revolution, and a 306-foot (93m) high stone needle commemorates the 1777 battle. Nearby is the grave of one of the country's favorite poets, the 20th-century writer Robert Frost. Bennington's museum displays a fine collection of naive paintings by Grandma Moses. These, along with handsome old houses and business buildings, add up to a town that is worth exploring.

Tour 15

Southern Vermont looks softer than points farther north and is known for its photogenic farms and villages. Weston preserves the atmosphere of a typical 19th-century Vermont village. Ludlow offers skiing at Okemo Mountain Resort, while the center of Grafton, known for its cheese, has been preserved, scrubbed clean, painted white, and seems suspended in time. The only crowded place is Manchester, full of shoppers hunting for bargains at the numerous factory outlet stores.

Tour 16

This part of Vermont is best known for the world-class ski resort of Killington. Apart from that, it is also another peaceful area where artists and craftspeople create minor masterpieces in small villages tucked away in the Green Mountains. Former U.S. president Calvin Coolidge is a local hero, his birthplace and homestead are open to visitors. A few villages, such as Woodstock, have been deliberately "prettied up," but overall, the natural, unhustled pace of life will reward those looking for a relaxed vacation. Take time to bike the back roads.

Tour 17

As well as natural beauty, the northern part of Vermont offers a surprising number of attractions. The Shelburne Museum is an outstanding collection of American folk art, housed in buildings that were moved here lock, stock and barrel from locations all over New England. Celebrities range from Ben and Jerry, whose ice creams have taken the world by storm, to the Von Trapp family of *Sound of Music* fame, who run an inn near Stowe. Teddy bears and Icelandic horses, a house with secret passages, and the Robert Frost Trail are some of the offbeat attractions. The elongated Lake Champlain is fine for a ferry ride, water sports, or for those merely in search of quiet contemplation.

The first pumpkins of the season: they must be picked before the frosts arrive

HALF A DAY

Bennington

Outside the state, Bennington is best known for Ethan Allen and his Green Mountain Boys. This group of feisty Vermonters not only had a grievance against the British, but also against the land-greedy "Yorkers" (New Yorkers) in the state next door. The historic district and its college make this an attractive small town.

i Route 7, north of downtown

▶ Park at the Bennington Museum to start the tour.

❶ Bennington Museum

Grandma Moses (1860–1961) was known as much for her longevity as for her "primitive" portrayals of rural life. This farmer's wife only started to paint when she turned 70, recording countryside activities such as haymaking and maple sugaring. Critical acclaim led to an exhibition at New York's Museum of Modern Art. Although she lived just across the state line, in Eagle Bridge, New York, this Vermont museum has the largest public collection of her work, with 30 paintings shown in a special gallery. A favorite picture, often used on greetings cards, is *Over the River*, which depicts the trip to Grandmother's house for Thanksgiving. Memorabilia are found in the old schoolhouse where she, her grandchildren, and her great-grandchildren all

studied. The museum also houses the 1777 Battle of Bennington flag, thought to be the oldest "Stars and Stripes" in existence. Look for the Bennington pottery and glass collection from the 19th century and the Bennington Wasp (1920s), the only automobile ever to be manufactured in Vermont.

▶ Walk up the hill to the small green in the center of Old Bennington. Look to your left.

The grave of Robert Frost, a simple memorial to the poet, lies in Bennington cemetery

❷ Old First Church

*"And were an epitaph to be my story
I'd have a short one ready for my own.
I would have written of me on my stone:
I had a lover's quarrel with the world."*

The final line of Robert Frost's 1942 poem, *The Lesson for Today*, is engraved on the plain stone marking his grave in the cemetery. One of the best-loved poets of his time (1874–1963), he captured the essential sights, smells, and character of New England.

Also buried here are five Vermont governors and many patriots who fell in the Battle of Bennington. The original 1763

meeting house was replaced in 1805 by this handsome church, with its stylish belfry.

Less than a mile (1.5km) along Route 9 is the Bennington Center for the Arts. Watch a live performance or visit the Vermont Covered Bridge Museum, or browse the rotating art exhibitions.

▶ Turn right on Monument Avenue and head toward the obelisk. Just on the right is a statue.

3 Catamount Tavern

Looking ready to pounce on unwary passersby, this big bronze wild cat commemorates the site of the Catamount Tavern, which was built in 1769. In the 1770s, the meeting place for Ethan Allan and the Green Mountain Boys was named for the stuffed catamount nailed to the pub to taunt "Yorkers", who claimed that Vermont belonged to New York.

▶ *Walk to the top of Monument Avenue.*

4 Bennington Battle Monument

Confusingly, the Battle of Bennington took place in New York. In 1777, the British were running low on food and arms, so General Burgoyne sent troops to capture the American stores that were stashed in a depot in Bennington. Before the Redcoats could reach the town, they were intercepted and overpowered by the patriots led by General Stark and Colonel Seth Warner. This was a significant victory in a regional campaign that ended with the surrender of Burgoyne at Saratoga a few months later.

The statue of local hero, Colonel Seth Warner, stands before the simple monument on the site of the supply depot. Over a century old, the statue,

built of locally quarried limestone, ranks as the tallest manmade structure in Vermont, soaring 306 feet (91.8m). Take the elevator to the observation levels for spectacular views of three states – New York, Massachusetts and Vermont. Each year, the important victory is celebrated in style on Bennington Battle Day Weekend, in mid-August.

▶ *Return down Monument Avenue, noting the fine examples of Federal and Georgian houses on either side. Turn left on West Main Street and head down the hill into the town. On the left is a service station.*

5 Hemmings Sunoco Station

You could be forgiven for thinking this is a museum of classic vehicles. Although it is a functioning Sunoco station, the

The observation platform on top of Bennington's Battle Monument gives excellent views over the city

owners are the publishers of *Hemmings Motor News*. The Car Lover's Store is full of car books, models, toys and artwork, as well as Vermont products. Unusual classic cars, tractors, wreckers, steamrollers and panel trucks from the 1920s to the 1940s are often on display outside.

▶ *Walk on for a block, then turn left on Depot Street. Continue to the junction with River Street.*

6 Historic Bennington Railroad Station

The Bennington and Rutland Railroad was successful a century ago, when this temple of limestone and blue marble was built. However, passenger trains have not stopped here since 1933, although freight trundled through up to the 1950s. The handsome 1897 building survives.

▶ *Turn left on River Street, then right onto Benmont Avenue.*

7 Holden Leonard Mill

Back in the 19th century, Bennington was a manufacturing town, using the river to power grist and paper mills such as the Holden Leonard Mill. This massive building, with a central tower rising four stories high, has been converted to offices, but stands as a legacy to the industrial past.

▶ *Turn right on County Street. At the corner of North Street is the Hawkins House with its contemporary crafts. Cross North Street and continue to No. 324 County Street.*

8 Potters' Yard

In the 19th century, the town was known for its pottery, as the 4,000-piece collection in the museum shows. Today, around 40 potters still work in what was an old grist mill on County Street. This center was founded by David Gil, whose colorful splatterware has been popular since 1948. Although he died in 2002, the Bennington Potters continue to produce the jugs, pitchers and vases, and his dinner services are in great demand, both in restaurants and homes. Take a self-guided tour and watch potters in action (weekdays).

▶ *Return to North Street and turn left. This becomes South Street after the intersection with Main Street.*

9 Pennysaver Building

The houses and churches of 19th-century New England are familiar from postcards and calendars, but the commercial architecture can be just as fascinating. The former Putnam Hotel block curving round from South to Main and the Pennysaver Building at 109 South Street are typical. The

Pennysaver, a free newspaper, still occupies the premises. The huge, globular lights outside were originally gaslit.

▶ *Return to Main Street and turn back west, returning to the car. Drive to the main intersection and go north on **Route 7A**, then left on to Northside Drive (which becomes **Route 67A**). After 3 miles (5km) reach Bennington College.*

10 Bennington College

Founded in 1932 to offer further education to women, Bennington College is now co-ed. It was once the most expensive private college in America, and former students include actress Carol Channing and movie star Alan Arkin, as well as a host of artists. Known for its programs of fine arts, the campus is an attractive blend of mock Colonial and modern buildings in a rural setting.

▶ *Continue on **Route 67A** to North Bennington (2 miles/ 3km). Three covered bridges cross the river on the left: the Silk Road, Papermill Village and the Bert Henry Bridge on Murphy Road. On the right, entering the town, is a fine complex of water-driven mills on Paran Creek. This is a convenient place to park. Cross Main Street and bear left up West Street. At the corner of Park Street is the Park-McCullough House.*

11 Park-McCullough House

With its handsome curving veranda, this early example of an American Second Empire-style mansion (1865) gives some idea of the lifestyle of the wealthy in the second half of the 19th century. The name combines that of lawyer Trenor Park, who built the house, and his son-in-law, John McCullough, one of the two Vermont governors who lived here. The 35-room house contains furniture, clothing and toys, which are all displayed in the original family context. Out in the stables is a collection of old sleighs and carriages. Open to the public, there is a small replica of the mansion on the front lawn.

▶ *Return to Main Street and turn left up the hill, past the imposing Greek columns of the 175-year-old Powers Market. It is no more than a country store inside, but at the top of the hill is the station.*

12 Old Train Station

North Bennington's Victorian railroad station, attractively decorated in shades of green and barn-red trim, dates back to 1880. These days, it functions as an office complex.

▶ *Return to the car at the bottom of the hill.*

Taking a quiet moment in Bennington, once a center of Revolutionary action

THE FALL

While most of the world experiences a dull, even sad end to the year, New England's landscape goes out in a blaze of glory. Due to a combination of soil and trees, sun and rain, the hillsides change from green to a tapestry of scarlet and gold, purple and orange. This is the "foliage season." Rudyard Kipling, who lived for a while in Vermont, felt almost powerless to depict the transformation. "No pen can describe the turning of the leaves – the insurrection of the tree people against the waning year. A little maple began it, flaming blood-red of a sudden where he stood against the dark green of a pine-belt. Next morning there was an answering signal from the swamp where the sumacs grow. Three days later, the hill-sides as far as the eye could range were afire, and the roads paved with crimson and gold." (*Leaves from a Winter Notebook*, 1900.)

in Vermont and New Hampshire. The Columbus Day holiday (second weekend of October) is the most crowded of the year in those states. Hotels and inns tend to have "foliage season rates" that start in mid-September and carry on through mid-October. Of course, there is no promise from Mother Nature that she'll get her paintbrushes out at this time: a dry summer and the leaves could change earlier; a wet summer and the "foliage" could be delayed. To avoid the inevitable crowds,

Photographs cannot prepare you for your first sight of New England in September and October. Millions of visitors, "leaf peepers," visit the region every year, with cameras at the ready. Most go by car or on bus tours, but hot-air balloons and river cruise boats also provide a spectacular experience.

Science
Scientists have a clinical explana-tion for the changes. They say that sunny days, allied with chilly nights, stop the production of chlorophyll, the chemical that turns leaves green. This, in turn, allows other pigments such as anthocyanin (red) or carotenoids (orange, yellow) to show through in the leaves. The Native American explanation is far more entertaining: the Great Bear (in the sky) was killed in a hunt, and its blood dripped down onto the leaves. As for the yellow, that was attributed to the fat of the bear splashing out of the cooking pot.

The time
The leaves change color in a tide that sweeps down from north to south, usually starting in September in Maine, northern Vermont and New Hampshire and reaching Connecticut in the south, around the middle of October. The most intense period is, by tradition, the first two weeks in October, especially

The beautiful colors of fall

a few visitors gamble and go north to Maine, where the weather might not be so gentle, but the roads are almost certainly quiet. Otherwise, the trick is stay off the main roads, and drift along the twisting country lanes which often have poor or even no signs at all. Take warm clothing; leaf watching is warm in the sun, but can turn chilly by the end of the day.

The trees
The dark green is usually provided by fir and spruce.
Scarlet and crimson: dogwood, red (or swamp) maple, sassafras and red oak.
Gold and yellow: poplar, elm, birch and gingko.
Orange: hickory, mountain maple and mountain ash.
Brown: oak.
Purple: sumac.

Hotlines
As well as information on the web, the New England states have special telephone numbers with up-to-date information on the progression of the color, and where to find it. It is also an indicator as to where the most "leaf peepers" are likely to be!

Connecticut (tel: 888/282-4748)
Maine (tel: 888/624-6345)
Massachusetts (tel: 800/227-6277)
New Hampshire (tel: 800/258-3608)
Rhode Island (tel: 800/556-2484)
Vermont (tel: 800/837-6668).

2 DAYS • 151 MILES • 244KM

Southern
Vermont

MAPLE SYRUP ...the Flavor of Vermont

"The Switzerland of North America" was a British ambassador's description of Vermont, yet the southern part is softer than the rest of this rugged state, with hamlets and houses scattered across the landscape. Almost every village has a green, a white steepled church, and an inn and roadside stands selling maple syrup.

RUTLAND
Ludlow
3343ft Okemo Mountain
Proctorsville
GREEN
100
Gassetts
EMERALD LAKE STATE PARK
GREEN Mountains
Weston
Chester Depot
Londonderry
Chester
Peru
Bromley Mountain ski area
Brockways Mills Gorge
3301ft Bear Mountain
3816ft Mount Equinox
Manchester Center
Manchester Village
Manchester Depot
Grafton
MOUNTAIN
SKYLINE DRIVE
Hildene
Cambridgeport
NEW YORK
Batten Kill
Arlington
East Arlington
Stratton Pond
3936ft Stratton Mountain
NATIONAL
Townshend
TOWNSHEND STATE PARK
SHAFTSBURY STATE PARK
Shaftsbury
3748ft Glastenbury Mountain
Somerset Reservoir
3556ft Mount Snow
Newfane
LEBANON
APPALACHIAN TRAIL
FOREST
West Dummerston
3420ft Haystack Mountain
ALBANY
BENNINGTON
Woodford
2767ft Prospect Mountain
Wilmington
Harriman Reservoir
2410ft Hogback Mountain
MOLLY STARK TRAIL
MOLLY STARK STATE PARK
Marlboro
West Brattleboro
Brattleboro

0   5   10 miles
0   5   10   15 km

i *Route 7, 1 mile (1.5km) north of downtown*

▶ *From Bennington drive north on **Route 7A**. Robert Frost lived at the Stone House in Shaftsbury (open to the public).*

❶ Arlington

Illustrator Norman Rockwell, famous for his *Saturday Evening Post* magazine covers, spent the middle part of his life here, from 1939 to 1953, using local people as models for his countless views of everyday life. Although the most complete record of his work is farther south in Stockbridge, Massachusetts, the Norman Rockwell exhibition, in a former church, also has a permanent record, though these are all reproductions. The country doctor who appeared in a Rockwell picture popular in many waiting rooms was one Dr. Russell, whose vast collection of Vermontiana is housed at the library.

Vermont's first grist mill was built here in 1764 by the splendidly named Remember Baker. Only a plaque remains to mark the site.

▶ *Proceed north on **Route 7A** for 4 miles (6km) to the foot of Mount Equinox.*

❷ Mount Equinox

The Carthusian order has a monastery here on the 3,816-foot (1,163m) Big Equinox peak, the highest point in the Taconic Range. The 5-mile (8km) Skyline Drive toll road climbs steeply to the top where memo-

Covered bridges are now recognized as historic landmarks. This example is at West Arlington

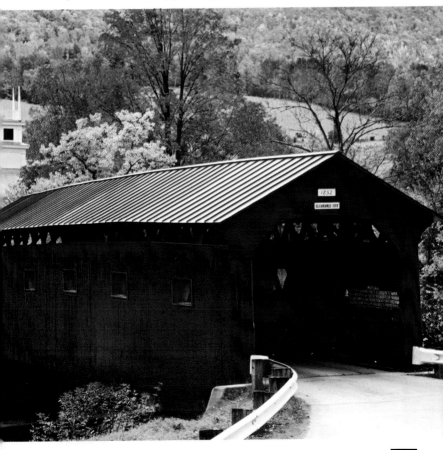

rable views stretch across to Quebec, New York, New Hampshire, and Massachusetts. Cars are warned to have good "brakes, radiators and transmissions" before attempting the drive. Cyclists and sports-car racers frequently test themselves on "hill climbs." The record ascent is 4 mins 28 secs in a Couper Formula 1.

▶ Continue on **Route 7A** to Hildene.

3 Hildene
Robert Todd Lincoln was the son of President Abraham Lincoln. As a child, he visited the Equinox Hotel with his mother, just before his father was assassinated, but only returned to the area many years later. Hildene, Lincoln's summer home, was built in 1905, and it was here that he died in 1926. Lincoln descendants lived here until 1975; the house is filled with authentic memorabilia of the Civil War leader, including Abe's "stovepipe" hat. The stately 24-room Georgian Revival home boasts a huge pipe organ and magnificent grounds. Polo matches are played on summer weekends and, in winter, the former carriage house is a base for visitors who cross-country ski the 9 miles (14km) of trails. Take a picnic and enjoy the garden, farm and walks.

▶ Continue for 2 miles (3km) to Manchester Village.

4 Manchester Village
There are three Manchesters: Center, Depot, and the oldest and highest, the Village. This is where the rich and powerful summered, either in their own luxury mansions, or at the legendary resort hotel, the Equinox. Dating back to 1769, this splendid Victorian hotel has been expanded and renovated over the years and today has 183 rooms and the renowned par-71 Gleneagles golf course.

▶ Drive half a mile (800m) into Manchester Center.

5 Manchester Center
Nowadays Manchester is know for shopping, with bargain-hunters flocking to designer outlet stores such as Polo/Ralph Lauren. More peaceful is the Southern Vermont Arts Center, just outside town. Join an art class or view the galleries and sculpture gardens; or stroll through its 407 acres (165ha).

▶ Drive 2 miles (3km) and turn onto **Route 11** east.

6 Bromley Mountain
The road climbs steadily to Bromley ski area, a pioneer among ski resorts since 1937. Visitors come in summer to try out the alpine slide, the longest of its kind in Vermont.

▶ Continue on **Route 11** east, then turn off to Peru.

7 Peru
Peru, one of the state's little-known hamlets, was featured in the 1987 movie *Baby Boom*, with Diane Keaton. An old-fashioned grocery store shares the street with a church, an antiques shop and several lovely homes.

▶ Return to **Route 11**, east, and drive to Londonderry. Turn left onto **Route 100**, and go north for Weston.

8 Weston
Weston is well known, not only for its prettiness, but also for the two rival stores across the street from one another. The Vermont Country Store and the Weston Village Store both do everything

The Old Tavern Inn, in the pristine village of Grafton

pleasant stores and narrow green. In Chester Depot, the restored 1852 railroad station now welcomes the Green Mountain Flyer. This tourist train has been making the run from its home in Bellows Falls for some 25 years. Popular in summer, seats must be booked well in advance in September/October, when the fall color is spectacular, particularly in Brockway Mills Gorge.

ⓘ *The Green (seasonal)*

▶ *Take* **Route 35** *south for 7 miles (11km) to Grafton.*

⑪ Grafton
In a state of many lovely villages, Grafton is probably the most photogenic of them all. It was once an affluent town on the Boston to Albany post road, with soapstone quarries and a thriving woolen industry, but after the Civil War, its economy collapsed. There was a revival in 1801, when the handsome Old Tavern was built with a California gold miner's money, but by the middle of the century, the village had all but died yet again. Help was at hand, however. In her will, Pauline Fisk instructed her nephews to use her fortune for a good cause of their choice. They came up with the idea of reviving Grafton.

In 1963, the Windham Foundation began the restoration of Grafton's historic charm that draws admiring visitors. For some, the houses are almost too pretty, too perfect for such a rural setting. The village has also revived a former industry: a nutty cheddar-style cheese, made by the Grafton Village Cheese Company. The tiny Grafton Grocery Market also has locally made preserves and hand-knits, and there is a working blacksmith's shop. Two covered bridges complete the scene. On Sunday evenings in summer, the cornet band plays on the green, a tradition dating back to 1867.

but bottle the nostalgia, and both offer an incredible variety of "country" and "Vermont" items that will bring visitors and their wallets to their knees. The circular town green, with its bandstand, inn and brick church on the hill above, is extremely photogenic. The Weston Playhouse is one of New England's oldest and most popular summer theaters.

Just north of the village is the Benedictine monks' religious community of Weston Priory, a tranquil place where visitors are welcome to join in services and walk around the grounds.

▶ *Continue to Ludlow.*

⑨ Ludlow
Where Weston is picture-perfect, Ludlow is full of character, thanks to the restoration and gentrification of century-old buildings and mills. Arts and crafts, antiques and skiing, foliage and fishing draw visitors to this attractive year-round holiday destination on the banks of the Black River, where small

one-of-a-kind shops rub shoulders with B&Bs. The Okemo Mountain Resort is widely acknowledged as having some of the best snow-making and grooming facilities in Vermont.

ⓘ *Clock Tower, opposite Okemo Mountain Access, Route 100/103*

▶ *Take* **Route 103** *south for 13 miles (21km) to Chester.*

⑩ Chester
Hidden away in the woods on the way to Chester was the home of Russian Nobel Prize-winner Alexander Solzhenitsyn. He lived here in isolation during his exile from the Soviet Union. The Stone Village on North Street, has, unusually for Vermont, some 30 cottages built of local stone. Dating from before the Civil War, these had hiding places for slaves escaping from the southern states on the so-called Underground Railroad to Canada.

The heart of Chester is the broad main street, with its inns,

▶ *Leave Grafton on **Route 35** south, which turns briefly into a dirt road after 6 miles (10km). At Townsend, take **Route 30** south for 5 miles (8km) to Newfane.*

12 **Newfane**

In summer, Newfane shows off its classic white Courthouse, church and inns, all of which have gleaming Greek Revival columns. The long-established air of the place is deceptive. Two hundred years ago, the buildings stood 2 miles (3km) away, on Newfane Hill. In 1825, the residents moved the town, using the slippery snow and ice of winter to slide the beams and boards to today's site. Jail accommodations were so comfortable and the food so palatable that paying guests were allowed in to enjoy "good pies and oyster soup" along with the inmates. Excellent fare is still a tradition, with both of the town's inns renowned for their cuisine. During the summer, everyone turns out for the free concerts on the green. Also popular are the flea markets held on summer Sundays; just outside the village on Route 30, this is one of Vermont's biggest and best.

The local museum, the Historical Society Museum of Windham County, is easy to spot, with its mid-19th-century bell standing outside. Inside are simple memorabilia from the area – Victorian dresses, old maps, and a variety of household items.

Beyond town, Route 30 runs parallel to the West River, where rafters and paddlers take up the challenge of high water in spring. In summer, the river is low, but fine for cooling off or "tubing," floating downstream in an inner tube.

▶ *Continue on **Route 30** to Brattleboro.*

13 **Brattleboro**

Fort Dummer, the first site in the state to be settled by Europeans, has now been covered by the waters of the nearby dam. Originally, this was the western frontier of the Bay Colony, used in defense against the French and the Native Americans.

Brattleboro is just down the road. In recent years, there has been a clean-up of the town's industrial infrastructure, centered around the main thoroughfare, Elliott Street. The former Union Railroad Station is now the Museum and Art Center, with five galleries. The focus here is on contemporary art and each year there is a different theme for the regularly changing exhibitions.

Just north of the town at Dummerston, in a house called Naulakha, author Rudyard Kipling lived and worked from 1892 to 1896, after marrying a local girl, Carrie Balestier. Books such as *Captains Courageous*, the *Jungle Books* and the *Just So Stories* were all written here. The house can be rented.

The notorious 19th-century swindler James Fisk, "Jubilee Jim," who once cornered the New York gold market, is buried in the cemetery, with a monument by local sculptor Larken Mead. Mead gained true recognition for his memorial honoring a more reputable man: he carved the statue that graces Abraham Lincoln's tomb in Springfield, Illinois.

▶ *Take **Route 9** west and start climbing into the hills. Pass Whetstone Valley Farm, known for maple sugaring in early spring, to Marlboro.*

14 Marlboro

The countryside looks attractive today, but back in 1763 it must have been daunting for the European settlers. Two families

Newfane's County Courthouse

are credited with founding Marlboro, but neither pioneer family knew the other was nearby for over a year. The focus of town is Marlboro College, with its summer music school. The chamber music festival (mid-July to mid-August, weekend concerts) is a well established highlight, due to the long residency and efforts of cellist Pablo Casals in its early years.

▶ *Continue west on **Route 9**. After 15 miles (24km), there is a panoramic view from one of the highest points on the road. Continue to Wilmington.*

15 Wilmington and Woodford

The alpine-looking village of Wilmington is at the intersection with Route 100, the north–south route that winds its way through the villages and ski resorts of the Green Mountains. Haystack Mountain and Mount Snow are just to the north.

Route 9 climbs on into the Green Mountain National Forest, passing through Woodford, Vermont's highest village. Prospect Mountain offers hiking opportunities.

▶ *Return to Bennington.*

Central
Vermont

The central part of the state gets busy in winter, due to the appeal of internationally known ski resorts such as Killington. In summer, attractions range from the Quechee Gorge, a sudden tear in the landscape, to Plymouth, the home of Calvin Coolidge. Rutland is nicknamed the "Marble City," because local quarries have provided floors and walls for many of America's grand civic buildings.

1 DAY • 109 MILES • 175KM

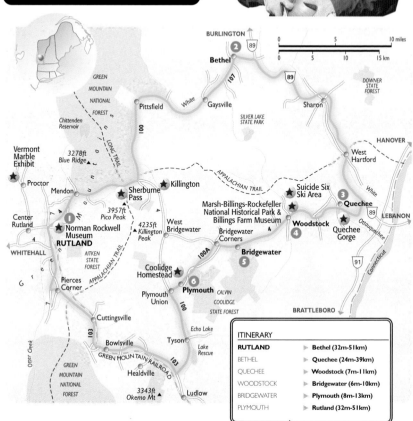

ITINERARY		
RUTLAND	▶	Bethel (32m–51km)
BETHEL	▶	Quechee (24m–39km)
QUECHEE	▶	Woodstock (7m–11km)
WOODSTOCK	▶	Bridgewater (6m–10km)
BRIDGEWATER	▶	Plymouth (8m–13km)
PLYMOUTH	▶	Rutland (32m–51km)

ℹ️ 256 North Main Street, also at junction of Routes 4B and 7 (seasonal)

▶ Leave Rutland on **Route 4** east. After 2 miles (3km) the Norman Rockwell Museum is on the right.

❶ Norman Rockwell Museum of Vermont

Better known collections of the popular illustrator's work can be found in Stockbridge (Massachusetts) and Arlington (Vermont), but you'll find 2,500 reproductions of well-loved covers from magazines such as *Saturday Evening Post, Life,* and *Literary Digest* here. There is enough to keep nostalgia hunters interested for an hour or so. After the museum, the road starts its long climb into the Green Mountains. Just before the Pico/Killington ski area, watch for hikers following the Appalachian Trail and Long Trail which crosses Route 4 but then splits, with the Appalachian Trail heading off to New Hampshire.

▶ Continue on **Route 4** over the Sherburne Pass, turn onto **Route 100** north, then take **Route 107** to Bethel.

❷ Bethel

In 1779, Bethel was the first town recognized by the independent Republic of Vermont. It also lends its name to much-sought after Bethel White granite. A small exhibition at the White River National Fish Hatchery explains an ambitious project to bring back the Atlantic salmon to the Connecticut River. Abundant when the Colonists arrived, the fish had been virtually wiped out by dams, over-fishing and pollution.

▶ Follow **Route 107** and turn onto **I–89** south. After 18 miles (29km) take exit 1. **Route 4** leads to Quechee.

❸ Quechee and Quechee Gorge

Quechee (Kwee-chy) Gorge is 162 feet (49m) deep. Jagged

The Ottauquechee River runs wild as it cuts its way through the Quechee Gorge

chunks of schist rock protrude from the walls. While the best view of Vermont's "Little Grand Canyon" is from the old railroad bridge that spans the ravine, there is also a half-mile (800m) hike to the bottom. The Ottauquechee River that used to drive the woolen mills of Quechee now powers the converted Downer's Mill. It is here that Simon Pearce's well-known glass is made. Visitors can watch his craftsmen at work blowing glass. The Irishman opened his studios in 1981 and has since added a restaurant. All around the town are retirement communities.

RECOMMENDED WALKS

Two of the Northeast's most famous hiking trails part company near Pico Peak. The Long Trail runs the length of the state, some 270 miles (435km) from the Massachusetts line to Québec. This "Footpath in the Wilderness" opened in 1926. The southern part of it overlaps with the even longer Appalachian Trail, which runs from Maine down to Georgia. Be warned! These hikes are only for the hearty. They are administered by the Green Mountain Club, in Waterbury (tel: 802/244–7037) and have simple shelters on the trails.

▶ *Continue on **Route 4** for another 7 miles (11km) to Woodstock.*

FOR HISTORY BUFFS

Although Joseph Smith is always connected with Salt Lake City and Utah, the founder of the Mormons (Church of Jesus Christ of the Latter Day Saints) was actually born in 1805 on a farm near Sharon, 10 miles (16km) southeast of Bethel. His family left the state in 1816, but a huge granite monument at the top of a steep hill is a tribute to the prophet. Each foot of the 38½-foot (11.4m) high obelisk represents a year of his life.

From Thanksgiving to Christmas, 100,000 lights brighten the visitor center. Brigham Young, the other great Mormon leader, was another Vermonter, born in Whitingham, near the Massachusetts border.

❹ Woodstock

This is New England as most people imagine it: a covered bridge, bandstand on the green, shuttered Colonial homes and an elegant inn. Regularly voted one of America's prettiest towns, Woodstock was one of the first in the state to develop as a two-season resort. In 1934 a Model T Ford car engine, set up at the bottom of a hill, was hooked up to a piece of cable on a wheel and Woodstock had the first ski tow in the U.S.A. The colorfully named Suicide Six Ski Area still tests even the most competent of skiers.

Woodstock has been a cultural center from its early days. One of the most intellectual of all its sons was George Marsh (1801–82), the lawyer, diplomat and fervent conservationist. His friend, Frederick Billings, promoted modern farming techniques.

The Marsh-Billings-Rockefeller National Historical Park is named in honor of the

SPECIAL TO...

Fans of birds of prey flock to see the snowy owls, peregrine falcons, red-tailed hawks, bald eagles and more at the VINS Nature Center. This 40-acre (16ha) attraction opened in 2004 between Quechee Gorge and Woodstock. It is as educational as it is fun, particularly if you join one of the naturalist-led walks.

two people who, along with Laurence and Mary Rockefeller, did so much to shape the landscape we see here today. Tours of the mansion show the countryside in art, with a fine collection of American landscapes, while tours of the surrounding forests interpret the way in which the estate has been carefully managed in order to balance the requirements of woodcrafts, recreation, education and ecology.

Everyday exhibits at the Billings Museum, Woodstock
Right: red barns and silos are a common sight in Vermont

The park is in partnership with Billings Farm and Museum, a working 1871 dairy farm where visitors can watch work in progress, including butter churning and ice-cream-making. An excellent introduction to both the park and the farm can be seen in the visitor center, where the Academy Award-nominated movie *A Place in the Land* is shown hourly.

Four bells cast by patriotic hero Paul Revere are at the Congregational Church.

▶ *Continue for 6 miles (10km) to Bridgewater.*

❺ Bridgewater

Bridgewater and its namesakes farther upstream, West Bridgewater and Bridgewater Corners, were all mill towns. As well as visiting artisans, you can

One of the dozens of Victorian stained-glass windows in Wilson Castle, northwest of Rutland

SPECIAL TO...

Little more than a dot on the map, Healdville, just off Route 103 near Ludlow, is the home of one of Vermont's best cheeses. Nothing has changed in the rickety old wooden barn where the cheese makers begin their day at 8am, making Crowley cheese by the same methods the Crowley family used back in 1882. Around midday, the curds are cut and raked by hand to produce the sharp, tangy, cheddar-like cheese that matures well.

watch furniture and pottery makers at Shackleton Thomas in The Mill in Bridgewater.

The Long Trail Brewing Company has a pub-style visitor center at Bridgewater Corners, where you can tour, taste and eat, either inside or on the deck overlooking the river.

▶ *Turn left on* **Route 100A** *south for Plymouth.*

❻ Plymouth

Calvin Coolidge (1872–1933), the 30th president of the United States, was born here on July 4. The five-room Coolidge Birthplace, his father's general store next door, the Coolidge Homestead, and the Wilder House, his mother's childhood home, have been kept much as they would have been when Coolidge was a boy. The summer White House, used in 1924 by Coolidge, has been re-created nearby. He and many other Coolidges are buried in Plymouth cemetery.

The President's father founded the Plymouth Cheese Company more than a century ago; in 1960, a descendant revived the tradition so, happily, the classic New England cheese lives on at Frog City Cheese.

▶ *Continue on* **Route 100A**, *then turn left on* **Route 100** *toward Ludlow, passing the Green Mountain Sugar House. Set on the shore of Lake Pauline, the Sugar House is a good place for maple-related products. Turn right on* **Route 103** *and return to Rutland.*

FOR HISTORY BUFFS

Vermont farms are built to cope with the extremely cold weather. The early settlers soon realized that the less they went outside in winter, the warmer they would stay. The farmhouses were often joined to the barn with a small hallway, an idea developed by the Dutch. In this way, the farmer could tend to his animals without having to go outside.

FOR HISTORY BUFFS

Despite the esteem with which he is held in his native state, Coolidge made his political career in Massachusetts, where he was Governor. Coolidge was visiting his father on the family farm in Plymouth when President Warren Harding died suddenly on August 3, 1923. At 2.47am, Col. John Coolidge took up the old family Bible and, in his role as a justice of the peace, administered the presidential oath to his son. Harding's administration had been tainted by corruption, so Coolidge's frugal New England virtues were welcomed. Famous for his quote that "the business of America is business," Coolidge believed that government should not interfere with industry.

Northern Vermont

In this sparsely populated part of the state, there are a surprising number of attractions.

2 DAYS • 134 MILES • 215KM

ST ALBANS

89

Winooski

BURLINGTON

South Burlington
Williston

89

Richmond

NEW YORK

Shelburne
Museum ★ **Shelburne**

Lake Iroqois

Jonesville

Essex

② **Charlotte**
MT PHILO STATE PARK

Vermont Wildflower Farm

Lewis Creek

③ Rokeby Museum

Ferrisburgh

BUTTON BAY STATE PARK ④

Vergennes

22A

D.A.R STATE PARK

Morgan Horse Farm

Vermont State Craft Center ⑤

Middlebury

GREEN MOUNTAIN

⑥ **Ripton** ⑦

East Middlebury

Robert Frost Trail

Middlebury Gap

Lake Dunmore

RUTLAND

0   5   10 miles

0   5   10   15 km

4393ft
Mount Mansfield

★ Stowe Mountain Resort

108

MOUNT MANSFIELD STATE FOREST

Stowe

⑪

100

Waterbury Reservoir

2

Ben and Jerry's ○ Colbyville

CAMEL'S HUMP STATE PARK

Waterbury

⑩

4083ft
Camel's Hump

Duxbury

89

100

MONTPELIER

Mad

LONG TRAIL

Moretown

G r e e n   M o u n t a i n s

Mad River Glen ★

⑨ **Waitsfield**

Irasville

4135ft
Mount Ellen

N o r t h f i e l d   M o u n t a i n s

⑧

Sugarbush Ski Area ★ ● **Warren**

ROXBURY STATE FOREST

3975ft
Lincoln Peak

100

3661ft
Mount Grant

Moss Glen Falls ★

3823ft
▲ Bread Loaf Mountain White ○ Granville

Bread Loaf

Texas Falls ★

Lower Granville

125

Hancock

100

N A T I O N A L ╱ F O R E S T

Lake Champlain

Otter Creek

i **60 Main Street**

▶ *From Burlington, take **Route 7** south for 5 miles (8 km) and turn right for Shelburne Farms.*

❶ Shelburne

Most Vermont farms are humble affairs, with red barns, a white silo and a low-slung farmhouse. Shelburne Farms is the opposite, a millionaire's toy built in the 1880s and 1890s on a giant scale and using all the latest technical equipment available.

After William Webb married Lila Vanderbilt, daughter of the

landscaped New York's Central Park, to map out their property. Like so many millionaires of the late 19th century, the Webb's "summer cottage" was extraordinary – a 110-room Queen Anne-style manor house. It is now the Inn at Shelburne Farms. The farm continues to be an experimental and working farm, where visitors can watch cheese- and butter-making, or wool-spinning. Old-fashioned pleasures such as hay rides will entertain small children.

When J. Watson Webb, the son of the Webbs of Shelburne

Fascinating exhibits of folk art in the Shelburne Museum

railroad tycoon, they created a European-style estate. The Webbs called upon Frederick Law Olmsted, the man who

FOR CHILDREN

Children (and lots of adults) always love a boat trip, and there are plenty of opportunities to cruise Lake Champlain. One of the most popular trips is from Burlington Boathouse aboard the *Spirit of Ethan Allen III*, a three-deck cruise ship with narration and on-board meals. Or you can go your own way. Waterfront Boat Rentals in Burlington rent canoes, kayaks and motor boats.

SPECIAL TO...

Lake Champlain is shaped like a sausage, 120 miles (192km) long and anything from 400 yards (400m) to 12 miles (19km) wide. Samuel de Champlain, the 17th-century French explorer, recorded seeing a 20-foot-long (6m) serpent with a head like a horse, and visitors have been trying to spot "Champ" ever since. Lake Champlain has four ferry services that cross from Vermont to the New York shores: from Grand Isle to Plattsburgh (12 minutes), from Burlington to Port Kent (an hour), from Charlotte to Essex (20 minutes) and from Shoreham to Ticonderoga (6 minutes).

Farms, married Electra Havemeyer, they began collecting art objects, large and small, and these now form the remarkable Shelburne Museum. The 37 buildings in which the quilts, paintings, toys and farm equipment are displayed are themselves collector's items. These buildings, each a historical landmark, have been rescued from all over New England and reassembled. You'll find a schoolhouse, railroad station, general store, barn, jailhouse and inn, now serving as galleries. Most arresting of all is a boat – the 220-foot (66m) long sidewheel steamer *Ticonderoga*. It was hauled for 2 miles (3km) from Lake Champlain to its final landlocked berth here on the farm. Although the folk art collection is justifiably high-

Church Street market, Burlington

houses in the historic district remain, along with three covered bridges.

Slightly farther along Route 7 is the Vermont Wildflower Farm with 6 acres (2.4 ha) of woodland and flower fields. Self-guiding trails explain the folklore of wildflowers and how Native Americans used them for herbal remedies. Visitors can also buy seeds. This stretch of Route 7 has magnificent views across Lake Champlain to the Adirondack Mountains.

▷ *Continue to Ferrisburgh. On a hill to the left is the Rokeby Museum.*

3 Ferrisburgh

One of the state's underrated museums is the Rokeby, home of the Robinson family for generations. Beautifully furnished, the house is a tribute to their own artistic talents, with portraits and landscapes they have personally painted lining the walls. Rokeby was also one of the last stops on the Underground Railroad, the escape route for slaves from the American South to Canada. It contains a secret passage and hiding room.

▷ *Continue south to Vergennes.*

4 Vergennes

Vergennes was named after France's foreign minister, a great supporter of the Americans in the Revolution. It is one of the smallest cities in the country, just one square mile (259 ha) with 2,700 inhabitants. On Basin Harbor Road, in a 19th-century stone schoolhouse, you'll find Lake Champlain Maritime Museum. During both the Revolution and the War of 1812, American and British warships battled for supremacy on this elongated strip of water. Benedict Arnold (see page 80), later a notorious traitor, delayed the British in 1776 with a series of clever ploys, as explained in the museum. A full-size floating

replica of his gunboat, the *Philadelphia II*, is the highlight.

▷ *Continue on **Route 7** south to Middlebury.*

5 Middlebury

Middlebury is best known for its college, founded in 1800. Visitors who come to visit old buildings such as Painter Hall and the Henry Sheldon Museum of Vermont History use it as a base. For more contemporary culture, the Vermont State Craft Center, in Frog Hollow, on Otter Creek Falls, is a modern showcase for the talents of some 250 artists and craftspeople from all over the state. (There are also branches in Manchester and Burlington.) Across the creek are the old marble works, filled with stores.

Middlebury College claims to be the birthplace of the Frisbee in 1938. Yale students may dispute this (see page 68), but the Vermonters have a handsome statue of a dog leaping to catch a flying disk. It was unveiled in front of Monroe Hall on what they insist was the 50th anniversary of spinning pie dishes at one another.

ℹ *2 Court Street*

▷ *Follow **Route 7** south, then turn onto **Route 125** for East Middlebury.*

6 East Middlebury

Two hundred years ago the hamlet of East Middlebury was

lighted as one of the finest in the world, the Shelburne art collection is equally impressive. Pieces by American painters Andrew Wyeth and Winslow Homer are on display, as are European artists Rembrandt and Goya. You need a full day here to do justice to the museum.

The town of Shelburne has a more recent industry: the Vermont Teddy Bear Company, which exports its furry friends world-wide. Children can decorate and stuff "new born" bears.

▷ *Continue to Charlotte.*

2 Charlotte

Pronounced char-LOT, the town's heyday was in the early 19th century, when it was a stage-coach stop on the journey from Burlington to Troy. The old

> **RECOMMENDED WALKS**
>
> Split by the Mad River and the Moss Glen Falls, Granville Gulf State Reservation borders the eastern boundary of the Green Mountain National Forest. There is a 6-mile (10km) scenic drive, as well as two hiking trails. The easy 1-mile (1.6km) loop on the east side of the road contrasts with the shorter, but tougher half-mile (800m) hike to the west.

little more than a spot for stage coaches to Boston to change horses. In the 1980s television cameras arrived to film the hit TV comedy series *Newhart*, starring comedian Bob Newhart, at the Waybury Inn. Rooms in this quaint 1810 inn have been refurbished in period style.

▶ *Continue for 4 miles (6km) to Ripton on* **Route 125**, *the Robert Frost Memorial Drive.*

❼ Ripton

The poet Robert Frost summered in the woods near Ripton for 23 years, and today the mountain to the north is named after him. Just after the

hamlet of Ripton is a picnic area on the left, and a rough track leading to his cabin. On the other side of the road is the Robert Frost Interpretive Trail, a 1¼-mile (2km) walk studded with plaques of quotes by the great man.

Seven miles (11km) after leaving Middlebury is the Bread Loaf Campus of Middlebury College. Once a hotel in the shadow of Bread Loaf Mountain, the campus is now well known for its summer writing schools and conferences. In winter it is a base for cross-country skiing.

▶ **Route 125** *climbs steadily, passing Bread Loaf and the Snow Bowl, a challenging ski area. Beyond the summit of Middlebury Gap the road*

The densely wooded Green Mountains clothed in fall foliage

*drops down to Hancock, passing Texas Falls recreation area. At Hancock, turn left on **Route 100** north, alongside the White River. After 4 miles (6km) is Granville, and another 10 miles (16km) farther turn right to Warren and Mad River Valley.*

8 Warren

Despite the popularity of the neighboring Sugarbush Resort ski area, Warren has changed little. The simple exterior of the Warren Store belies a sophisticated little emporium of gourmet foods and fine wines for the city folk who visit. Simpler pleasures survive, such as glider rides from the little airport.

Just north of Warren is the left turn for Sugarbush, the heart of one of Vermont's premier ski destinations. Opened in 1958, this affluent resort has expensive condominiums and a busy restaurant scene. Vermont's third highest peak, Mount Ellen (4,135 feet/1,260m), and Lincoln Peak (3,975 feet/1,211m) are the two mountains that provide the ski thrills. In summer, golfers test themselves on the course designed by Robert Trent Jones, Sr. There are also tennis courts.

▶ *Continue to Waitsfield.*

9 Waitsfield

The Mad River Glen Ski Resort is smaller, older and less formal than the nearby Sugarbush Resort, but it offers more challenging runs for the advanced skier. Mad River Valley also attracts cross-country enthusiasts, thanks to a total of four cross-country touring centers. As for Waitsfield, what was once a lumber and dairy town a long time ago is now a vacation destination both in winter and summer. First there are the stores selling the work of local artists and craftspeople; then there is the photogenic old covered bridge. Nearby, the Vermont Icelandic Horse Farm offers trail rides.

▶ *Take **Route 100** north to Waterbury (15miles/24km). Ben and Jerry's is 1 mile (1.6km) north of **I–89**.*

10 Waterbury

Waterbury means just one thing to ice cream aficionados: Ben and Jerry's. Ben Cohen and Jerry Greenfield's rags-to-riches story is the American dream, set deep in the Vermont countryside. In 1977, they started by producing home-made ice cream in Burlington, in a disused and dismantled service station. These days, the factory is in Waterbury, where tours with tastings are a constant draw. In summer, old-fashioned ice cream machines and real cows, ready for milking, keep children entertained.

Waterbury has expanded to include other tasty attractions: Lake Champlain Chocolates, the Cabot Annex Store for Cheese and the Cold Hollow Cider Mill, with its excellent pure pressed apple juices. The Green Mountain Club, half way to Stowe, administers the Long Trail and other outdoor activities.

▶ *Continue to Stowe, then follow **Route 108** to the Mount Mansfield Ski Area.*

11 Stowe

The Stowe Mountain Resort is one of New England's premier ski resorts, built on Mount Mansfield, Vermont's highest peak (4,393 feet/1,338m). In summer, a historic toll road, the Stowe Auto Road, leads to the summit, a 4½-mile (7km)

COLD HOLLOW CIDER MILL

Low mist over Stowe, the main skiing and recreation center for this popular area

journey. This steep route, with numerous tight curves, is a test of both car and driver. For a more relaxed journey use the Gondola Skyride, a 10- to 15-minute scenic swing over the forested slopes. With tennis courts, a swimming pool and children's programs, this is a summer destination for the active.

Another attraction is the Trapp Family Lodge in Stowe, built by the real-life family of *The Sound of Music* fame. Also popular is the Vermont Ski Museum, which traces the century-old history of the sport

in the state. Inside the 1818 Old Town Hall, Vermont's first single chair, double chair, quad chair and gondola hang from the ceiling, like a mobile, above old photos and memorabilia.

[i] *Main Street, Stowe*

▶ *Return on **Route 100** to I–89 and drive to Burlington.*

RECOMMENDED WALKS

The Stowe Recreation Path is a 5-mile (8km) trail alongside a mountain stream. Used for walking, cycling and skating in summer as well as cross-country skiing and snowshoeing in winter, this trail is used for walking, cross-country skiing and snowshoeing and is a tribute to the generosity of local residents, who have donated the right of way past meadows, woods, and cornfields for visitors to cross their land.

SPECIAL TO...

Justin Morgan was a Vermont teacher who created the country's first horse breed. A hardy colt called Figure was born in 1793, a mixture of Arabian and thoroughbred. The Morgan, as it became known, with its deep chest and powerful hindquarters, stands some 14 to 15 hands (1.42–1.52m) high.

Usually long-lived, mild-mannered, and bay in color, this multi-use equine was a boon to the army, who rode it and also used this hardy breed to pull guns and equipment. Now owned by the University of Vermont and open to the public, the Morgan Horse Farm is 2 miles (3km) north of Middlebury. The grounds are immaculate, with a slate-roofed 19th-century barn, lush meadows, and parade grounds, and is home to the 70 stallions, mares and foals.

FOR CHILDREN

Stowe is a wonderful area for children with an adventurous spirit. They can hurtle 2,300 feet (700m) down Spruce Peak on the Alpine Slide, for instance, or head off on two wheels into the countryside to explore the 70 plus miles (112km) of mountain bike trails in the area. As for younger children, they will love the public playground at the Stowe Elementary School. Local children raised the funds for it, including a donation from "Superman" (actor Christopher Reeve).

NEW HAMPSHIRE

New Hampshire's nickname is the "Granite State." Some say it refers to the rocky scenery, others maintain it describes the implacable nature of the residents. Certainly, the terrain is the very opposite of the English county that lent it its name. New Hampshire has only an 18-mile (29km) strip of Atlantic coastline, and a mere 80 miles (128km) away are the White Mountains, the tallest in New England. Hundreds of lakes, often bearing the Native American names given by earlier residents – Sunapee, Winnipesaukee and Squam – are scattered throughout the thick pine forests. Fifty four covered bridges stretch across tumbling streams.

The early settlers were "economic refugees," who had left Europe to make a better life rather than to find religious freedom. The land and climate made the early days a struggle. Later, the Scots-Irish added their resolute character to the New Hampshire persona. Today, car license plates bear the state motto: "Live Free or Die." The rest of this Revolutionary rallying cry is "death is not the worst of evils." The fiery words are attributed to farmer-turned-general, John Stark, one of the New Hampshire men who formed the backbone of the American troops in the early days of the Revolution.

The Kancamagus Highway, in the White Mountains, is famous for its fall foliage

Today, the politics in New Hampshire are notably "grass-roots," with the 234 towns and cities often regarded as "little republics." The state scorns income tax and sales tax, preferring to raise money by taxing liquor and betting. This tax – or lack of tax – structure has attracted businesses to move across the state line from Massachusetts. Shoppers also drive over the border from neighboring states to load up and save money. Since most of the 1.3 million inhabitants cluster near the Massachusetts border, the rest of the state seems sparsely populated. While agriculture has long been a mainstay of the economy, it has been the fast-flowing streams driving machinery that have benefited residents most. Towns like Manchester may not manufacture locomotives and fire engines any longer, but plastics, electronics, and paper products have successfully taken their place.

Tour 18

Portsmouth, New Hampshire's port, is wedged between Massachusetts and Maine. With a bustling waterfront and historic architecture, it is one of the country's oldest cities. Decades ago, enthusiastic residents made a far-reaching decision. Instead of tearing down the old buildings, they started a major restoration project. Now the merchants' houses and warehouses, meeting houses and bankers' offices are the attractive heart of the city and a source of civic pride. Small parks and museums reflect Portsmouth's role as a ship-building center, others are filled with fine antique American furniture. Best known is Strawbery Banke, a collection of houses that show what everyday life was like over a period of four centuries.

Above: Strawbery Banke
Below: The Flume, a giant chasm where a mountain stream tumbles in a series of waterfalls

Tour 19

The White Mountains are a popular destination all year round. The focus is Mount Washington, first climbed by a European 350 years ago. It is now deluged by 250,000 enthusiastic tourists every summer. A cog railroad crawls its way up to the top. Those wanting to avoid the "madding crowds" can explore the numerous well-marked trails throughout the mountains, either for a day hike or a longer trek. In winter, "the Whites" attract both downhill and cross-country skiers and boarders. The spectacular scenery on this route includes "the Kanc," the famous Kancamagus Highway, one of America's prettiest drives.

Tour 20

Since 1981, Squam Lake has become a "must see" for fans of the film *On Golden Pond*. Nearby, larger Lake Winnipesaukee has long been a popular destination for summer visitors wishing to escape the heat and humidity of Boston. The western shore has become over-popular and built-up, but for the most part, this is a peaceful drive, with villages, craft shops, and museums en route. Anyone interested in top-quality crafts should plan to spend time in Center Sandwich, while Meredith is best known for its dolls.

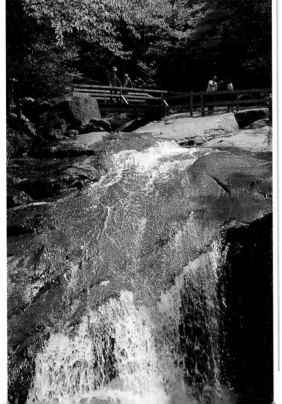

Portsmouth

Portsmouth has one of New England's finest natural harbors and became wealthy on the lumber trade, exporting to Britain and the West Indies. Huge fortunes were made and spent on grandiose mansions, many of which still stand. Recently named a "distinctive destination" by the National Trust for Historic Preservation, this city is perfect for anyone interested in the architecture and craftsmanship of 18th- and 19th-century America.

HALF A DAY

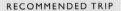

i *500 Market Street*

▷ *Start at Market Square, the heart of the city.*

❶ Market Square

The lottery may seem a new idea but it has long been a means of raising money. Back in 1762, the militia's training ground was paved with funds from a public lottery. The Athenaeum, at No. 9, was originally the headquarters of a fire and marine insurance company, but became a private library in 1823. The classic pointed spire of North Church can be seen from anywhere in the downtown area, especially when it is illuminated at night. On the east side of the square stands the impressive wall of Bankers Row, the guardians of civic wealth for

The John Paul Jones House, where the Scots-born navy officer lived

nearly 200 years. No. 24/26 is thought to be the oldest bank in America, and it was extensively rebuilt in 1904.

▷ *Leave Market Square, heading south on Pleasant Street. Turn right on State Street.*

❷ State Street

Contrasting with the elegant white spire of North Church is the squat tower of South Church, at No. 292. This solid-looking granite building dates from 1826 and is still used for worship by the Unitarian Universalists. Nearby was the starting point of the 1813 fire, which blazed toward the waterfront. Some houses survived, only to be lost to a 1950s urban planning project. Still standing is the Abraham Shaw House (1810) at No. 379. A few doors farther on is the former Rockingham Hotel (No. 401),

RECOMMENDED TRIP

Just off the coast are nine islands, the Isles of Shoals, partly in Maine, partly in New Hampshire. Take a picnic on the delightful one-hour boat ride. Visit Star, an island used as a church retreat which also has the Vaughn Cottage Memorial and Celia Turner Museum, or Appledore, once an artists' colony.

whose lions became the personal emblem of Frank Jones, a flamboyant brewer and entrepreneur whose bust is on the right. You can still appreciate the grandeur in the Library Restaurant, with its marble and mahogany.

▷ *At the corner of State and Middle streets is Haymarket Square, with its enclave of elegant homes. At No. 43 Middle Street is the John Paul Jones House.*

❸ John Paul Jones House

Scottish-born John Paul Jones is known as the "father of the U.S. Navy." He did not own this handsome clapboard house, but rented rooms from Mrs. Sarah Purcell. The naval hero was in Portsmouth in 1777 to supervise the fitting out of the *Ranger*, and once again in 1781, for the building of the *America*. The house is now the headquarters of the local historical society.

▷ *Turn south on Middle Street. Cross the square to No. 18 Court Street.*

❹ John Peirce Mansion

This is "the best" of the city's 19th-century houses, according to some critics. No expense was spared when Peirce built this home in 1799. It was handed down through the family for generations until 1955, when the Baptist Church bought the property.

▷ *Two blocks farther along Middle Street is No. 364.*

5 Rundlet-May House

James Rundlet started out as a farm boy but ended up a wealthy man. With the money he made from importing textiles and wallpaper, he built this mansion in 1807. The garden, pet cemetery, and stables add an extra dimension to the period furniture.

▶ *Retrace your steps to Court Street; bear right and walk two blocks to Pleasant Street. On the corner of Pleasant and Court streets is No. 93 Pleasant Street.*

6 Ann Treadwell Mansion

This house was built to comply with the 1814 law specifying that structures of more than one story had to be made of brick. The previous year, yet another fire had taken its toll, this time along Court Street, with hundreds of houses ruined.

▶ *Retrace your steps. Cross Court Street, then go south on Pleasant Street to No. 143.*

7 Governor Langdon House

John Langdon was one of New Hampshire's founding fathers who made his money in ship-building and buying and selling goods captured from the British.

Langdon became President of the Senate, delegate to the Constitutional Convention of 1787, and finally state governor for three terms. He built this mansion, one of the finest in New England, and the garden to impress, and it still does today. Note the exquisitely carved pale green fireplace in the drawing-room, where Langdon hosted parties. One guest was President George Washington, who commented that, among the town's houses "Col. Langdon's may be esteemed the finest."

▶ *Walk next door to No. 145.*

8 Thomas Thompson House

Portsmouth's importance to the New Hampshire economy is reflected in the state seal and flag, which show shipbuilders at work on a frigate. The first frigate was the *Raleigh*, often called the "first ship in the U.S. Navy." Its owner, Thomas Thompson, erected this house in 1784, and his business part-ner, John Langdon, put up his mansion next door a year later.

▶ *Continue on Pleasant Street, then bear left on Gates Street.*

Inside one of the many houses that make up Strawbery Banke

9 Gates Street

James T. Fields (1817–81), the publisher of *The Atlantic Monthly* magazine, gave American writers a boost onto the world literary stage. He was born and lived in the house at 83/85 Gates Street. A few doors down, No. 130 is another fine old place, built as early as 1731 by the Peirce family. This street was one of the first to be saved back in the 1960s rebirth of Portsmouth.

▶ *Continue to the end of Gates Street, then turn left on Mechanic Street and walk to No. 50.*

FOR CHILDREN

Portsmouth has a long history of building warships. At Albacore Park, there is a rare chance to explore a submarine, the 205-foot (61m) long USS *Albacore*. The cramped space did not allow room for beds for each of the crew, so, men "hot bunked": when one shift finished, they slept in the bunks of those going on duty. The submarine never fired a shot in anger.

10 Wentworth-Gardner House

Tiled fireplaces, fine carving, and paneling make this a "must" for those interested in 18th-century craftsmanship. The owner, Thomas Wentworth, was the younger brother of the last royal governor of New Hampshire.

▶ *Continue on Mechanic Street, which bears left; turn right on Marcy Street.*

11 Liberty Pole

Colonials showed dissent by putting up a liberty pole on their village or town green. The residents of Portsmouth first did this in 1766, to protest against the infamous Stamp Act. The pole became a permanent reminder of that feisty spirit in 1824. Each season, the gardens in Prescott Park are planted with varieties developed by botanists from the University of New Hampshire.

▶ *Across from the liberty pole is Strawbery Banke.*

12 Strawbery Banke

Close to the waterfront, the site of the original 1630 settlement is now one of America's finest outdoor museums. Some 40 buildings, examples of Portsmouth's architecture from 1695 to World War II, stand on this 10-acre (4-ha) site, once a slum. It all comes colorfully to life, with the potter and cooper working at their trades. A favorite spot is the 1766 William Pitt Tavern, which shows the

---

SPECIAL TO...

When English settlers arrived in 1623, the meadows running down to the Piscataqua River were so thick with strawberries they called their new home Strawbery Banke. Thirty years later, with shipbuilding becoming the established industry, they changed the name to the more appropriate Portsmouth.

---

role of the pub in everyday life. By contrast, one of the first televisions in the U.S. is on show at the Drisco House.

▶ *Continue on Marcy Street to the end. Turn left, then right across the parking lot to No. 150 Daniel Street.*

13 Warner House

The oldest brick house in town was once part of a row of splendid brick mansions built around 1716. The museum-quality furniture behind the 18-inch (45cm) walls was used by the same family for two centuries, while the hall staircase is covered with extensive murals. These murals, possibly the oldest in the country, date from 1720, and include biblical scenes and portraits of two members of the Mohawk tribe. A lightning conductor set into the west wall was supposedly installed by the inventor Benjamin Franklin.

▶ *Turn right on Chapel Street.*

14 St. John's Church

Designed by Alexander Parris to replace a church burned in the fire of 1806, St. John's boasts America's oldest working organ, the 1708 Brattle Organ, as well

The Old Country Store at Strawbery Banke

as splendid *trompe-l'oeil* paintings of biblical scenes.

▶ *Continue on Chapel Street to Bow Street. Turn left, then right on Ceres Street. At the end, take the steps to No. 154 Market Street.*

15 Moffatt-Ladd House

Little imagination is needed here to visualize the life of a wealthy Portsmouth family. The Moffatts built their home in 1763 directly across from their warehouses. The counting house next door, with its wall safe, was a more recent addition – in 1830. Now a museum, family mementos range from wedding dresses and portraits, to jewelry and silver. Two inventories of household goods in the late 18th century provided the curators with the details to re-create the Moffatt home, where the family lived until 1913.

The beautiful gardens are a highlight: the plan is 18th-century but the interpretation is 19th-century.

▶ *Return to Market Square via Market Street.*

The White
Mountains

Weekend hikers and serious climbers come to test themselves against the mountains, of which Mount Washington is only one of 86 named peaks.

2 DAYS • 188 MILES • 302KM

SPECIAL TO...

The Old Man of the Mountain was long the craggy symbol of New Hampshire. Sadly, it crumbled away in May, 2003. First spotted by road builders back in 1805, this curious rock formation inspired the clever Nathaniel Hawthorne short story, *The Great Stone Face*. When the New Hampshire senator Daniel Webster saw it, he reportedly said that "Men hang out their signs indicative of their respective trades; shoemakers hang out a gigantic shoe; jewelers a monster watch ... but up in the mountains of New Hampshire, God Almighty has hung out a sign to show that there He makes man." Eventually, near the museum in Franconia State Park, The Old Man of the Mountain Memorial will feature five granite sculptures recreating the profile.

i *Chamber of Commerce, exit 26, off I–93*

▶ *Starting in Plymouth, proceed north on I–93, noting the frequency of the "moose crossing" signs and warnings. After 20 miles (32km), exit 32 heads off for North Woodstock and Lincoln.*

❶ North Woodstock

With storefronts that look like movie sets for Hollywood westerns, North Woodstock is not your typical New England village. The main attraction is Clark's Trading Post, a theme park from the days before theme parks were a "dime-a-dozen." Florence Clark took the unlikely title of "first woman to reach the summit of Mount Washington using a dog sled." The Clark family still runs the show after 80 years. The attraction, which began as a dog ranch, now features performing bears, Merlin's Mystical Mansion, a garage from yesteryear, an old fire station, and other eccentric and eclectic Americana. Clark's

Trading Post also claims to have the world's last remaining Howe Truss railroad bridge (1904) in the world, a covered, 120-foot (36m) long affair.

▶ *At this point I–93 becomes the Franconia Notch State Parkway. Continue north to The Flume and Franconia Notch Pass.*

❷ Franconia Notch

The Notch is the best-known high pass in New England. Ever since the first Europeans saw its towering granite walls 200 years ago, tourists have come to admire the pass, formed by a massive prehistoric glacier. Preserved and protected in their own privately funded State Park, these natural wonders are easily accessible and the park is geared for those who wish to see the sights without much effort. The Flume Gorge and Visitor Center has information on all the attractions in the Notch, as well as a shuttle bus to the Flume itself. Gravel paths and wooden walkways lead through a narrow gorge, 800 feet (240m) long. Its sheer walls stretch 90 feet (27m) straight up on both sides. Through the Notch, the Flume Brook bounces down the side of Mount Liberty and into the glacial pool.

Farther along the road is the viewpoint for the Old Man of

Clark's Trading Post includes a reconstructed New England street

the Mountain, also called the Great Stone Face or Profile. Until 2003, five ledges of granite towering above Profile Lake looked like the silhouette of a man's face. Now it has collapsed (see Special to...)

About a half mile (800m) along is the Cannon Mountain Aerial Tramway. Gondolas whisk 80 passengers at a time up to the top of Cannon Mountain (4,180feet/1,275m), climbing some 2,022 feet (616m) in just 7½ minutes. The view is well worth the fee, and there are plentiful marked walks around the Summit Observatory Platform. Refreshments are available here.

FOR HISTORY BUFFS

New Hampshire claims many firsts in skiing: the first ski club, in Berlin in 1872; the first ski school, in Sugar Hill, in 1929; the first overhead cable ski tow, at Black Mountain, in 1935; and the first trail cut for skiing, right here on Cannon Mountain, in 1930. These historic moments are all described at the New England Ski Museum.

Seats are limited on the Mount Washington Cog Railway, so reservations are recommended

Next to the base of the tramway is the New England Ski Museum. Echo Lake, a little farther on, is a natural mirror, reflecting Cannon Mountain and Mount Lafayette in its still waters. The energetic can cycle through the Notch on the 8-mile (13km) bike path which passes most of the attractions.

▶ Continue on Franconia Notch State Parkway, which becomes I–93 again. Take exit 38 for Franconia.

❸ Franconia

Once a flourishing resort, Franconia has seemingly gone back to sleep. It has been over-taken by the more ambitious towns south of the Notch. Poetry lovers drop by the Frost Place, the 150-year-old, white clapboard hillside farmhouse to which Robert Frost returned in 1915, upon his homecoming from England. Aged 40 and still virtually unknown, he farmed the land, wrote three books of verse and won a Pulitzer prize, all in the next five years. Visitors can see his writing desk, signed first editions and a rare collec-tion of his Christmas card

5 Gorham

Gorham is a useful stop for those who are keen on wildlife. At dawn and dusk, guides take visitors on a 3-hour explanatory Moose Tour in search of these big beasts, which are abundant in the woods.

▶ *Leave town on* **Route 16** *south to Glen House, at the foot of Mount Washington.*

Inset: a young moose

poems. In summer, there are readings by a poet in residence and a Festival of Poetry in late July and early August. A half-mile (800m) nature trail, highlighted with plaques along the way, presents 15 of Frost's favorite poems.

▶ *Return to* **I–93** *and drive 6 miles (10km) to exit 40 for Bethlehem. Turn on to* **Route 302** *east.*

4 Bethlehem

The little town of Bethlehem is more Victorian-looking than Colonial, reflecting its heyday as a vacation destination a century

ago. Back then, thousands flocked here by train. The air was so clean and clear of pollution that the National Hay Fever Relief Association was started here in the 1920s. Now, apart from its antiques shops, Bethlehem is a base for touring and hiking.

▶ *Stay on* **Route 302** *east for 8 miles (13km) to Twin Mountain. Turn left onto* **Route 3**. *At Carroll, take the* **115** *through Meadows, then join* **Route 2** *and head east to Gorham.*

6 Mount Washington

Mount Washington is the tallest mountain in the East, at 6,288 feet (1,916m). A road and railroad allow visitors access to the bare granite summit. On the eastern face of the mountain, at Glen House, about 8 miles (13km) south of Gorham, is the start of the 8-mile (13km) toll road to the top and an audio tour, on CD or cassette, gives you an in-car commentary. Built back in 1861, the road is advertised as America's first man-made attraction. Six horses used to pull a wagon full of tourists up the grade, which still averages 12 percent. Today, large vans provide the same service. Bolder folk drive up, a test of their automobiles and their nerve.

The top is surprisingly busy with radio and TV transmitters, an observatory and the Summit Building, with its glassed-in viewing area. At the peak is the old Tip Top House, a hotel built in 1853. There is also a museum of mountain memorabilia and local wildlife.

the SnowCoach trip up the mountain.

▶ *Continue for 13 miles (21km), then take the left-hand turn on **Route 16A** to detour into the town of Jackson.*

7 Jackson

Always labeled a "classic White Mountain village," Jackson (population 880) lives up to expectations, with its covered

> ### SPECIAL TO...
>
> The Jackson Ski Touring Foundation is dedicated to cross-country skiers. An unusual co-operative effort by the towns of Jackson and Bartlett has produced a network of some 90 miles (145km). The Ellis River Trail (5 miles/8km) is ideally flat for beginners. By contrast, the Wildcat Valley Trail is an 11-mile (18km) run for experts.

and Cranmore mountains offer more than 100 trails, enough to satisfy all levels of ability from mogul masters to modest beginners. Strict controls on building have kept this a picturesque village, with an emphasis on lodging and dining, rather than motels and fast food.

▶ *Continue south to Glen.*

8 Glen

The resort town of Glen has a popular attraction. Story Land, a well thought-out theme park, is aimed at a younger audience with re-creations of fairy-tales, and rides and flumes.

▶ *Continue to North Conway.*

9 North Conway

With no sales tax and an outlet strip mall 3 miles (5km) long, shopping is the number one sport in this popular small town. It's all a far cry from the days when artists would flock to paint Thompson's Falls. The 1874 railroad station, North Conway

Summer skiers willing to endure the tough hike can test themselves on the dangerous chutes and headwall of the Tuckerman's Ravine nearby. Skiing on July 4 is a traditional challenge among the hard-core skiers. At the base of the mountain is the Great Glen Trails Outdoor Center, with a vast trail system for mountain-biking and hiking. In winter, there is cross-country skiing, snowshoeing and

Fun and fantasy at Story Land

bridges, white steepled churches, high mountains and rolling farmland. It could not be prettier. In summer, this is a perfect base for hiking, biking, canoeing, kayaking, or just relaxing by mountain streams. Seasonal festivals add to the fun. In winter, the town offers skiing – downhill and cross-country. The Attitash, Black, Wildcat,

Depot, has survived with much of its Victorian ambience, including the wind-up brass clock, the Telegraph Office, and the separate men's and women's waiting rooms. Now the Conway Scenic Railroad, with its Pullman carriages, runs from here for 11 miles (18km) alongside the Saco River to Conway or through spectacular Crawford Notch. A little way north of the village, the Weather Discovery Center, run by the Mount Washington Observatory, is another attraction. Computer-based interactive displays and audio-visual presentations give a fun insight into the laws of meteorology and how weather affects us.

▶ *Continue south and turn west onto* **Route 112**, *the 37-mile (59km) long Kancamagus Highway to Lincoln.*

🔟 **Kancamagus Highway**
Following alongside the rushing Swift River, "the Kanc" is one of America's National Scenic Byways – there are no private homes, service stations, or other encroachments to spoil the views. The 37-mile (60km) stretch of road, from Conway to Lincoln, climbs to 3,000 feet (900m) on the way, and honors New Hampshire's legendary Native American chief Kancamagus. He was the grandson of Passaconaway, who united and ruled the local tribes from 1627 to 1669. All along the road are Scenic Areas where you can stop. The best known spots include Sabbaday Falls, a short walk from the highway, and the Lower Falls and Rocky Gorge, where you can bathe in the pools and sunbathe on the small beaches.

1️⃣1️⃣ **Lincoln**
The ski resort of Loon Mountain has transformed Lincoln into a busy year-round resort. The skyride, with its four-passenger gondola, is as attractive in summer as in winter, gliding to the summit where there are walking trails and glacial caves. Other popular attractions include the Whale's Tale Waterpark, with its variety of rides on land and in water, and the less frantic Hobo Railroad, which trundles through the Pemi River Valley for some 15 miles (24km).

▶ *Return on* **I-93** *south, 25 miles (40km) to Plymouth.*

The Kancamagus Highway

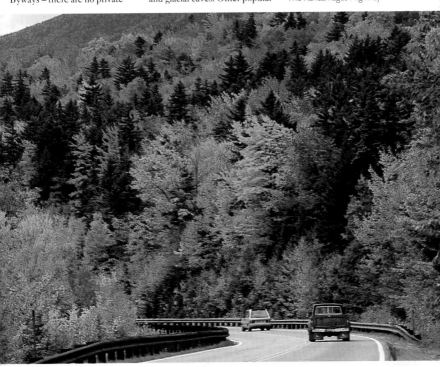

1 DAY • 106 MILES • 169KM

Around Lake
Winnipesaukee

Lake Winnipesaukee is huge, the sixth largest body of water inside the country. The Native American name is "The Smile of the Great Spirit," though some experts prefer the more prosaic translation of "Beautiful Water in a High Place."

ITINERARY

PLYMOUTH	▶	**Ashland (7m-11km)**
ASHLAND	▶	**Holderness (4m-6km)**
HOLDERNESS	▶	**Center Sandwich (12m-19km)**
CENTER SANDWICH	▶	**Moultonborough (5m-8km)**
MOULTONBOROUGH	▶	**Wolfeboro (17m-27km)**
WOLFEBORO	▶	**Alton Bay (13m-21km)**
ALTON BAY	▶	**Weir's Beach (22m-35km)**
WEIR'S BEACH	▶	**Meredith (8m-13km)**
MEREDITH	▶	**Plymouth (18m-29km)**

ℹ *Chamber of Commerce, Exit 26*

▷ *Start in Plymouth and take I–93 south to exit 24 for Ashland.*

❶ Ashland

The small town of Ashland, once an important stop on the old Boston, Concord and Montreal Railroad line, retains the character of an old mill town. The Ashland Historical Society is based in the former home of Dr. George Whipple, the pathologist who won the Nobel prize for medicine in 1934. Next door, the Pauline Glidden Toy Museum has more than 1,000 early toys. A local resident, the late Milton Graton, was one of New England's experts on the restoration and building of covered bridges. His last was built here in his home town, where his son Arnold continues the tradition.

▷ *Continue on **Route 3** to Holderness.*

❷ Holderness

Holderness sits on Little Squam Lake; to the east is the much larger Squam Lake. The Academy Award-winning 1981 movie *On Golden Pond*, starring Katherine Hepburn and Henry Fonda, was filmed here, catapulting Squam Lake to fame, even though the movie was supposedly set in Maine. Small boats cruise the peaceful lake and delight in showing visitors where the scenes were shot. It is a favorite nesting place for loons.

▷ *Follow **Route 113** for Center Sandwich (12 miles/19km). Pass Squam Lake.*

❸ Center Sandwich

Sitting between the Squam Mountains and Squam Lake, this is one of several Sandwich villages in the area. New England poet John Greenleaf Whittier (1807–92) spent time in Center Sandwich. This crusading Quaker championed the anti-slavery cause and used poetry in his emotional campaigns:

"*What! mothers from their children riven!*
What! God's own image bought and sold!
Americans to market driven,
And bartered as the brute for gold!"

Whittier wrote *Sunset* on the Bearcamp, the river that runs through Bearcamp Pond between Center Sandwich and North Sandwich. The Whittier covered bridge crosses the river in West Ossipee.

SPECIAL TO…

Peace and quiet attracts artists to the rural community of Center Sandwich. Sandwich Home Industries, an early collective, opened in 1926 with the aim of helping local craftspeople supplement their incomes. This led to the founding of the League of New Hampshire Craftsmen, known for its seven stores in the state and an annual fair, the oldest in the country, held in August at Mount Sunapee.

BACK TO NATURE

The Squam Lakes Natural Science Center is just to the east of Holderness and enables visitors to observe wild animals such as otters, deer, bears and various birds of prey. All are unable to live in their natural habitats, due to injury. You can follow the trails and boardwalk, try hands-on puzzles, or take a boat trip.

Aerial view of the turreted hilltop Castle in the Clouds

Seaplane on Lake Winnipesaukee

▶ *Drive south on* **Route 109**
for 5 miles (8km) to
Moultonborough.

4 Moultonborough
This typical New England
village has the bonus of the lake
as a backdrop. Apart from its
idyllic setting, the big attraction
is "Castle in the Clouds," a
reminder of the astonishing
wealth garnered a century ago.
Set 750 feet (225m) up in the
Ossipee Mountains, this mock
castle and its extensive estate
offers spectacular views.
Millionaire Thomas Plant, who
made his money from shoes,
designed the $7 million house
himself, which explains the variety of architectural styles, from
Swiss chalet to Norman castle. A
touch of English Tudor is the
coup de grâce. It was built by
hundreds of craftsmen, including Italian stonemasons brought
over from Europe. Water from a
spring on the grounds is bottled
commercially. The nearby Loon
Center and Markus Wildlife

Sanctuary specializes in New
Hampshire's ecology.

▶ *Continue south on* **Route 109**
for 17 miles (27km) to

SPECIAL TO...

West of Alton Bay on Route
140 (12miles/19km) is the
town that shocked America in
1956. Gilmanton was the home
of *Peyton Place* author Grace
Metalious. This high-school
teacher's wife had been unable
to achieve success with her
writing ... until her account of
life and love in small town
America topped the best-seller
lists. Today, the town shows no
signs of the steamy passions
described in the book, movie
and TV series. "You live in a
small town and there are patterns. The minute you deviate
from the pattern you are a
freak," she said, "I wrote a book
and that made me a freak." She
died, aged 39, in 1964.

Wolfeboro. The route passes
through Melvin Village, known
for its antiques shops.
Continue along the shores of
Winnipesaukee, through
Mirror Lake.

5 Wolfeboro
Just before Wolfeboro, on the
edge of Mirror Lake, is the
Libby Museum, with its eclectic
collection. America's oldest
resort began back in 1768, when
Massachusetts Governor John
Wentworth ordered a summer
house here. To reach the house
from Portsmouth, he even had
the "Governor's Road" built.
The retreat burned down in
1820, and people now come to
swim and picnic in Wentworth
State Park, 6 miles (10km) east
of town.

The Wright Museum, in
Wolfeboro, charts the story of
America during World War II.
In addition to its collection of
military vehicles, the museum

reflects life back home, with room settings, costumes and other period items.

▶ Take **Routes 28** and **28A** south for 13 miles (21km) to Alton Bay, right at the foot of Lake Winnipesaukee.

6 Alton Bay

The little town of Alton Bay has much of the appearance it must have enjoyed in its summer heydays. There is a floating bandstand out in the bay, and the railroad station has been spruced up. Scenic lake cruises depart from the docks.

▶ Follow **Route 11** northwest. This side of the lake is much more open, affording great views of the water and to the White Mountains in the north. Weir's Beach is 22 miles (35km) farther on via the Ellacoya State Park, where you get a sense of how large Lake Winnipesaukee really is. Continue to Weir's Beach.

7 Weir's Beach

Weir's Beach is the Coney Island of the region with its amusement park, crowded boardwalks, beaches and a weekly fireworks display. One of New England's last drive-in movie theaters is here too. It is especially busy when the annual motorcycle races take place for one week in June in nearby Loudon. Weir's Beach has a waterslide park, but tamer rides are also available, such as the scenic railroad along the lakeshore.

Another good way to beat the crowds is to take a cruise on the lake, either for its simple scenic value, or to appreciate the wildlife on a special nature cruise.

▶ Take **Route 3** north to Meredith (8 miles/13km).

8 Meredith

Quieter than Weir's Beach, with pretty docks and landings on the lake, Meredith is the home of the popular felt Annalee Dolls. Annalee Davis Thorndike created these cutesy dolls in 1934 and now the factory is a major local employer. The dolls are bought by fans and collectors

---

FOR HISTORY BUFFS

Sport is a high-profile, major ingredient of today's U.S. college life. The first inter-collgiate sporting event, however, was very low key. It took place in 1852, at Center Harbor on Lake Winnipesaukee. Harvard took on Yale in a rowing race over "two miles to windward and straight away," and beat them by two lengths. The ten-minute duel began a rivalry that remains intense more than 150 years later.

---

from all over the world. There is also a museum dedicated to them, which includes the first doll and some valuable pre-war models.

▶ Return to Plymouth via **Route 3** through Holderness and I–93.

Delivering the mail by boat

SCENIC RIDES

Apart from the antique speedboat *Millie-B*, based in Wolfeboro, there are several passenger boats that run in the region. The venerable 1,250 passenger M/S *Mount Washington*, popular for dinner cruises and moonlight cruises, is the largest. Depending on the day, the *Mount Washington* runs across to Wolfeboro, to Meredith, up to Center Harbor or down to Alton Bay. The M/V *Sophie C* doubles as a mailman, delivering mail to the island communities. The Winnipesaukee Railroad is another railroad nostalgia trip, conjuring up the 1920s and 1930s, and runs from Lakeport to Meredith.

MAINE

The Algonquin tribe called this region the "Land of the Frozen Ground" and the summer season is certainly the shortest here in New England, barely covering June through September. No-one knows how or why Maine received its present name. What is known is that it could swallow up the rest of the New England states. One single county, Aroostook, is bigger than the states of Connecticut and Rhode Island combined. Yet the population of Maine is only 1.3 million, mostly in the south and along the coast.

Residents and visitors alike come to Maine to enjoy the unspoiled natural beauty. Geographers estimate that the 230-mile (368km) long coastline would stretch to 3,500 miles (5,600km) if every cove and inlet were measured. Drive down the fingers of land that jut into the sea to find old fishing villages, quiet inlets and rocky cliffs. Offshore lie around 2,000 islands, some linked to the mainland by ferry, the majority barely habitable, and all surrounded by treacherous rocks and ice-cold water.

View over Camden Harbor

The coast is the biggest draw and some parts, such as Oqunquit and Boothbay Harbor, become quite crowded in season. Getting away from it all, however, is easy since 90 percent of the state is wilderness and forest. Maine attracts hikers and canoeists into its hinterland with 32,000 miles (51,200km) of river and 6,000 ponds and lakes dotted around. There are few people, but thousands of moose.

Although many experts assume that the Vikings could have paid a visit a thousand years ago, it was the French and English who first settled here. In 1677, the territory was assigned to Massachusetts, but in the early 19th century, when that state began to struggle economically, it cut the ties and Maine became a state in its own right.

Maine's nickname, the "Pine Tree State," is appropriate. Not only is the coastline wooded, there are vast forests inland. The tall, strong pines once provided masts for the British Navy; now, they are made into paper and pulp. Shipbuilding started in 1607, in Bath, and continues there today.

Tour 21

For many, the "real Maine" begins north of Portland. Here, the coastline breaks up into long skeletal fingers of granite, pointing out to form bays dotted with pine-covered islands. The sea has always been the focus of this region and the earliest Europeans who spent time here were transient fisher folk. Seafaring and boat-building are long traditions that have continued with the U.S. Navy in Brunswick, the huge shipyard in Bath, and numerous smaller boat-builders and museums. Although tourism is a major industry, towns such as Camden, Wiscasset, and Damariscotta have been able to retain their charm.

Tour 22

Portland is often rated as one of the best cities in which to live: small enough to feel friendly, but with a lively cultural scene and innovative restaurants. Years ago, locals made a conscious and successful effort to brighten up the downtown and old harbor by recycling historic buildings and employing novel methods of attracting locals to the stores and galleries. Much of the handsome brick and granite architecture post-dates the devastating fire of 1866, but some earlier buildings remain. Included among these is the home of the writer Henry Wadsworth Longfellow, dating back to 1785. Do take time to explore the myriad islands of Casco Bay, using the regular ferry or mail boat. Take the morning boat, hop off at Chebeague Island, rent a bike and explore.

Tour 23

Getting away from it all is easy when you head for the lakes and mountains of Maine. This long drive explores the state's remote beauty, while also passing through some charming villages. The famous Shaker religious community lives in a village at Sabbathday Lake. Their pious faith still arouses admiration, even though only a handful of the sect survives. By contrast, the nearby Sunday River ski area is one of the liveliest in Maine. Winter temperatures will test a visitor's fortitude. Rangeley is not only the mid-point of this drive, but the town also boasts being precisely halfway between the North Pole and the equator.

The Mid-Coast of Maine

2 DAYS • 260 MILES • 418KM

Rocky bays, cliff-top lighthouses, and peaceful harbors give the mid-coast of Maine its character. This route leads to busy towns and quiet hamlets, past historic houses and old forts. Artists and craftspeople have long been attracted by the area, so there are festivals and fine art galleries as well.

WATERVILLE

95

Searsmont

Augusta

Togus

Appleton

South Windsor

Coopers Mills

17

Stickney Corner

Randolph

Union

Pittson

DAMARISCOTTA LAKE STATE PARK

27

Sheepscot

220

Dresden Mills

Damariscotta Lake

Waldoboro

★ 13
Pownalborough Courthouse

Thomast

Newcastle

4

3

Damariscotta

295

Merrymeeting Bay

Days Ferry

Wiscasset

BRADBURY MOUNTAIN STATE PARK

Topsham

Bristol

Round Pond

Muscongus Bay

1 Brunswick

295

2 Bath

Woolwich

Cooks Corner

5

7 New Harbor

Yarmouth

Freeport

WOLFE'S NECK WOODS STATE PARK

Maine Maritime Museum

Colonial Pemaquid/ Fort William Henry

Pemaquid Point

Cumberland

★ 6
Pemaquid Light and Fishermen's Museum

Falmouth Foreside

REID STATE PARK

Monhegan Island

295

Casco Bay

POPHAM BEACH STATE PARK

0   5   10 miles

0   5   10   15 km

PORTLAND

i *245 Commercial Street*

▶ *Leave Portland on I–295 north. Take exit 20 for Freeport shopping (see left), then follow Route 1. This is the old coastal road; take it into downtown Brunswick.*

❶ Brunswick

Brunswick is an attractive town, centered on Bowdoin College. Originally founded in 1794 as a men's college, Bowdoin has admitted women since the 1960s. Famous graduates range from 19th-century authors Nathaniel Hawthorne and Henry Wadsworth Longfellow to explorers Robert Peary, the first man to reach the North Pole, in 1909, and his colleague Donald MacMillan.

Memorabilia from their expeditions is the focus of the Peary-MacMillan Arctic Museum in Hubbard Hall, decorated with the only gargoyle in the whole of Maine (spot it on the left side of the building). The Museum of Art, located in the imposing Walker Art Building, has a varied collection including Gilbert Stuart's familiar portrait of Thomas Jefferson, author of the Declaration of Independence, and third President of the United States.

i *59 Pleasant Street*

▶ *Leave the campus and turn right on Route 24 north. Continue to Cooks Corner and rejoin Route 1 north. Drive 5 miles (8km) to Bath.*

❷ Bath

The town may be 18 miles (29km) from the Atlantic Ocean, but boats have been launched on the deep Kennebec River since 1607. Bath's glory days were in the 19th century, when sailing ships made fortunes for the merchants, many of whose graceful homes still line Washington Street in the Historic District. Since 1891, the Bath Iron Works and Shipyard, the largest civilian employer in Maine, has built ships for the U.S. Navy. Right on the river, with the tallest crane (400 feet/120m) on the East Coast, it's impossible to miss.

Downriver from the shipyard is the Maine Maritime Museum, a collection of buildings with seafaring memorabilia and hands-on exhibitions. This is the place to learn the history of lobstering, and to understand how the many-masted schooners were constructed. You can watch a demonstration of sailors' skills, or perhaps take a narrated cruise down the Kennebec and Sasanoa rivers, either to look at lighthouses or the wildlife.

i *Route 1 North, just south of Bath (seasonal)*

▶ *Leave Bath on Route 1 northeast and continue for 10 miles (16km) to Wiscasset.*

❸ Wiscasset

The Native American name means "coming out of the harbor but you don't see where." Today, "the Prettiest Village in Maine" is found easily by visitors, who flock to the antiques shops, historic houses, and quirky museums. Wiscasset is the seat of Lincoln County, which once stretched to the Canadian border. Throughout the original colonies, towns pride themselves on the fact that "George Washington slept here." Here, the claim is that General

Lafayette of France ate ice cream at the apothecary store, one of the first places in the U.S. to make the delicacy. That was in 1824, long after Lafayette had helped the Americans during the Revolution.

On High Street is the Musical Wonder House. This is the private collection of Danilo Konvalinka, who calls it "the world's finest museum of restored international antique music boxes and mechanical instruments." The full tour is fascinating, though expensive; but it costs little to wander round the front hall and look at the 19th-century coin-operated music boxes, hurdy gurdies and perforated metal disc players.

At the end of High Street, in a commanding position above the harbor and Sheepscot River, stands Castle Tucker. Built in 1807, it was bought by Captain Tucker in 1858, after he retired from the sea and settled down to married life. From its free-standing switchback staircase to the dramatic southeast façade with

its huge windows, the house is one of a kind, and remains much as Captain Tucker left it. The wallpaper is original, as are the furnishings. A descendant of the captain still lives here.

The Nickels-Sortwell House, on the corner of Route 1 and Federal Street, is another ship-captain's home. Built in the same year as Castle Tucker, it exemplifies the Federal period. Just along Federal Street is Lincoln County Museum and Old Jail. This large and foreboding granite building served as the county jail from 1811 to 1953. Below the tiny barred windows, the cold walls, 41 inches (105cm) thick in places, are covered with graffiti, such as the painstakingly detailed schooner under full sail.

▷ *Continue on **Route 1** northeast to Newcastle and turn right for Damariscotta.*

4 Damariscotta
This attractive yet unpretentious riverside community has

plenty of old wood-frame and brick homes. The restored 1754 Chapman-Hall House on Main and Church streets is the oldest in the region. In summer, guides in period dress conduct you round the 18th-century kitchen and herb garden.

ⓘ *Damariscotta Region Chamber of Commerce, 15 Courtyard Street*

▷ *Leave town on **Route 130** south for 11 miles (18km). Turn right on Huddle Road at signs for Historic Pemaquid and Pemaquid Point. Service stations are few and far between off the main highways, so be sure to fill up before heading down any of the numerous peninsulas.*

5 Colonial Pemaquid/Fort William Henry
The re-creation of Fort William Henry stands guard over the

Typical wood-frame house, near the township of Damariscotta

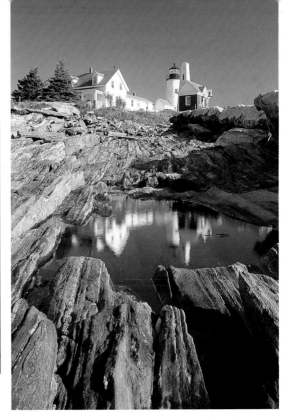

Pemaquid Point Lighthouse juts out on rocky ledges carved by ancient glaciers

FOR HISTORY BUFFS

"Damariscotta" means "the meeting place of alewives." This has nothing to do with women involved in brewing. It refers to a member of the herring family that was popular with Native Americans. They also relished the local oysters and would congregate for "oyster festivals," leaving heaps of shells behind on the banks of the Damariscotta River. These "middens," an Old English word for rubbish dumps, contain shells as large as plates. Ask at the Damariscotta Region Information Bureau for maps of trails leading to the sites.

water, as did four earlier fortresses, and it now houses a museum of artifacts found on the site. Nearby, an on-going archeological dig has uncovered a 17th-century British settlement of houses plus a tavern, jail, burying ground and customs house. It is thought to have been one of the first European settlements in the New World. Although fishing and trapping were productive in the area, raids by the French and their Native American allies, and long, hard winters took their toll.

▶ Follow Snowball Hill Road to **Route 130** and drive south to Pemaquid Point.

⑥ Pemaquid Light and Fishermen's Museum

Maine is famous for its lighthouses. There are 64 lighthouses in the state, but this is one of the most romantic and most photographed. From sundown to sunrise, the Fourth-Order light flashes its warning every six seconds. From as far as 14 nautical miles away, ships take note and adjust their course accordingly. The memorabilia in the small museum gives an insight

into the fishing industry of yesterday and today. The layers of rock show the geological formation of this distinctive coastline. When climbing upon the rocks near the ocean, be careful. The waters are dangerous; the undertow is strong, too.

▶ Take **Route 130** north, then turn onto **Route 32** to New Harbor.

⑦ New Harbor

New Harbor is a truly picturesque and unspoiled Maine fishing village. A memorial here honors Chief Samoset of the local Pemaquid tribe. The chief learned English from British fishermen, and had traveled south to explore the Massachusetts coast in March, 1621, where he discovered the Pilgrim community. Imagine their surprise when he greeted them with the words "Welcome Englishmen."

▶ Continue on **Route 32** north to Waldoboro (20 miles/ 32km). Turn onto **Route 1**

FOR HISTORY BUFFS

Just off Route 32 is Round Pond, another fishing harbor. This once supposedly hid the notorious Captain Kidd, who buried treasure under a huge boulder on a nearby island. Some say it was on Devil's Oven, others on Otter Island. The mystery remains.

RECOMMENDED TRIPS

From New Harbor, take a daytrip out to tiny Monhegan Island, only 1½ miles (2.5km) across at its widest, with the highest cliffs on the East Coast. The energetic can hike through a wildlife sanctuary with hundreds of species of wildflowers and birds, while the less energetic can visit the artists' studios. There are also cruises for watching seals and Atlantic puffins, now a protected species.

northeast and drive for about 12 miles (19km) to Thomaston.

8 Thomaston

This is another ship captain and ship owners' town, although Montpelier, the most imposing house in Thomaston, was built by a general, Henry Knox. He was an important figure in the Revolution and the country's first Secretary of War. He retired here in 1795 and built Montpelier, a mansion high on a hill overlooking the town.

The house was torn down in 1871 but, thanks to the enthusiasm of locals, it was rebuilt in the early 1920s, and is now the General Knox Museum. Original records and descriptions penned by visitors were used to re-create the mansion, which even has many of the original furnishings. Note that the white-painted façade and its two-story bay looks very much like the south front of the White House in Washington D.C., designed in 1792.

▶ *Continue on **Route 1** to Rockland.*

9 Rockland

This is the "Lobster Capital of the World" (though Shediac, north across the Canadian border in New Brunswick, also claims this title). It also boasts a gem of a museum, the result of a 1935 legacy left by an eccentric 96-year-old. The William A. Farnsworth Art Museum specializes in American painters from the 18th, 19th, and 20th centuries, and highlights Maine's role in American art.

The Wyeth Centre, in a historic church near the museum, houses the collection of Andrew and Betsy Wyeth. The new Maine Discovery Center is also home to the Maine Lighthouse Museum, as well as the local information center.

⏲ *1 Park Drive*

▶ *Follow **Route 1** north to Rockport.*

FOR CHILDREN

South of Rockland, in the state park off Route 73, is Owl's Head Light. The 52-step climb is worth it for the view over Penobscot Bay, but vertigo-sufferers should not peer over the 87-foot (26m) sheer cliff. Nearby is the Owl's Head Transportation Museum, a world-class collection of vintage cars, airplanes, motorcycles and carriages in working condition. Demonstrations are held throughout the summer, though the museum is open year round.

SPECIAL TO...

One of the most famous artistic images of Maine is Andrew Wyeth's *Christina's World*, portraying a crippled girl in a meadow looking toward her house. It was just one of his many depictions of members of the Olson family and their house in Cushing, Maine. "I just couldn't stay away from there ... I'd always seem to gravitate back to the house ... It was Maine." The house is administered by the Farnsworth Art Museum and is open, in season, to the public.

10 Rockport

The village of Rockport has a tiny harbor with lots of cultural activities. The musically minded make reservations for chamber music and jazz concerts at the opera house. Photographers head for the internationally known Maine Media Workshops, while the work of local artists and craftsmen is displayed in galleries such as the Center for Maine Contemporary Art, specializing in upcoming contemporary artists.

In the little park down by the

Below: yachts at rest in Camden Harbor
Right: lobsters at Boothbay Harbor

harbor is a statue of André the Seal. A children's book and movie were based on the story of André, who summered here for 20 years.

▶ Leave Rockport on scenic Russell Avenue, going north, with sudden glimpses of the Camden Hills and Penobscot Bay. This becomes East Chestnut Street in Camden.

11 Camden

*"All I could see from where I stood
Was three long mountains and a wood;
I turned and looked another way, and saw three islands in a bay."*
The panorama from the top

of Mount Battie inspired Maine poet Edna St. Vincent Millay to compose this poem in 1917. The views today are still the same of the Camden Hills, Penobscot Bay, and, on a clear day, Monhegan Island.

In the town, below the hill, Millay's statue stands by the harbor in what is, arguably, the state's most popular year-round resort. Conway Homestead, dating from 1770, is one of the oldest houses in the area. It is now a museum that includes the house, barn, smithy, maple sugar house and modern museum building.

i 2 Public Landing

SPECIAL TO...

Lobsters, the specialty of Maine, are caught in the millions of traps set in the cold waters offshore. Traditionally, these box-like contraptions consist of an oak frame with cotton netting. Many visitors take them as souvenirs. However, don't be tempted to pick up any washed on to a beach by the tide: that counts as "molesting a trap" and carries a fine. Buy one from a road-side stand or, better still, stop at a fishing village, look for a pile on the dock or by a house, and make an offer to the owner.

▶ *Follow **Route 1** north 6 miles (10km) to Lincolnville, then on 13 miles (21km) to Belfast.*

12 Belfast

Belfast or Londonderry? A flip of a coin decided the name back in 1765. As usual in New England, a town's name pinpoints the home in the Old World. In this case, the Scots-Irish had come from what is now Northern Ireland. Over the centuries, Belfast has produced ships, axes, pantaloons, sarsaparilla, chickens, rum and shoes. Find out more at 30 stops on The Museum In The Streets® self-guided walking tour.

ℹ️ *Main Street*

▶ *The rest of this route is rural and scenic. Take **Route 3** west to Belmont Corner for 6 miles (10km), then **Route 131** south through scenic farmland, past stone walls and hilly vistas. Pass through Searsmont, Appleton and Union. Take **Route 17** west, then before Togus, turn onto **Route 226** south to Randolph. Follow **Route 126**, then turn onto **Route 27** south. This passes a cluster of privately owned white houses moved here from various parts of the state. Turn right on **Route 128**, an old Native American trail that follows the bay. Continue on **Route 128**.*

13 Pownalborough Courthouse

Now a museum, this is one of only a dozen surviving pre-Revolutionary courthouses in the country. Here, a judge could dispense justice in the court on the middle floor, walk downstairs to drink in the tavern, and retire to his bed on the top floor.

▶ *Continue on **Route 128**. Join **Route 127** south at the pretty village of Days Ferry (the original river crossing) and continue to **Route 1** southwest at Woolwich by the Bath bridge. Return to Portland.*

Portland Head Light, dating from 1791

Portland

Portland aptly deserves its symbol, the phoenix, as well as its motto, *Resurgam*, "I shall rise again." In fact, the city has arisen nearly as often as the sun. Dating back to a settlement called Falmouth, it was virtually destroyed by Native American raids in 1676. After rebuilding, the community flourished until an English fleet bombarded the town in 1775, as punishment for supporting the independence movement. Once again restored, and renamed Portland in 1786, the port buzzed with business and finance, until the Great Fire of July 4, 1866. Again, it was rebuilt, and this tour reflects the development of Portland and the contributions made by prominent citizens to the arts, business and city life.

The Wadsworth-Longfellow House was the first brick house to be built in Portland

i *Convention and Visitors Bureau of Greater Portland, 245 Commercial Street*

▶ *Start at Congress Square.*

❶ Congress Square

This busy five-street intersection is the scene of many summer events, including concerts. On the corner of Congress and Free streets is the Hay Building, described as a flatiron building because of its wedge-shape. Built in 1826, it is one of the recognized icons of Portland.

❷ Portland Museum of Art

The I. M. Pei firm's brick colonnaded building (1983), right on the square, makes an impressive addition to the L. D. M. Sweat Memorial Galleries and rotunda, built in 1911. It houses one of New England's finest art collections and contains pieces by well-known Maine and American painters such as Winslow Homer, Rockwell Kent, Andrew Wyeth and John Singer Sargent. You will also find the Joan Whitney Payson Collection of Impressionist and Postimpressionist works here. One of the best known is Auguste Renoir's *Confidences*. A romantic tête-à-tête, this is a sensitive portrait of one of his favorite models, Margot Legrand.

❸ Children's Museum of Maine

Next door to the art museum, in a former Greek Revival church, is one of the best museums of its kind in New England. The Children's Museum of Maine really is for all ages. Even toddlers have their own play area, and older children can play at pretend in "Our Town," with its market, fire truck, lobster boat, bank, farm and animal hospital. For the technically minded, there are lots of

interactive exhibits and other things to fire the imagination, including the star lab, space shuttle and a climbing wall.

A wonder from the 19th century is a camera obscura, one of only seven in the world. A camera obscura is a dark room where images of objects from outside are projected onto a wall. It may sound simplistic in these days of "virtual reality," but this effective, primitive use of light and lens led to still and motion picture cameras.

▶ *Leave Congress Square and walk north on Congress Street to No. 522.*

❹ Maine College of Art

On the outside, the 1904 Porteous, Mitchell & Braun Building is a beaux arts classic, complete with cherubs. Inside is the Maine College of Art and the ICA, the Institute of Contemporary Art.

▶ *Look across Congress Street.*

❺ Mechanics Hall

This impressive, Italianate, granite-fronted building, with its statues of Archimedes and Vulcan, is the home of the Maine Charitable Mechanic

Association. Dedicated in 1851 to "informing and cultivating the mind and training up a race of mechanics (skilled workmen) of sound moral principle and intellectual power."

▶ *Continue along Congress Street to No. 489.*

❻ Wadsworth-Longfellow House

Three generations of one of the city's most distinguished familes lived here, behind the wrought-iron fence. In 1785, General Peleg Wadsworth, a hero of the Revolution and state senator, built this house, now the oldest surviving residence in Portland, and the first to be constructed of brick. The bricks were shipped in from Philadelphia.

Wadsworth's grandson, the poet Henry Wadsworth Longfellow, grew up here. His childhood flute is on show, and the house is furnished much as he would have remembered it as an adult. "Often I think of the beautiful town that is seated by the sea; often in thought go up and down the pleasant streets of that dear old town, and my youth comes back to me." Next door, the Maine Historical Society Museum has changing exhibitions about the state.

SPECIAL TO...

Henry Wadsworth Longfellow (1807–82) is America's best-loved 19th-century poet. *The Battle of Lovell's Pond*, his first published verses, appeared in the *Portland Gazette* when he was only 12 years old. His best-known works tell all-American tales such as *The Song of Hiawatha* and *Paul Revere's Ride*, but his popularity was not limited to the United States. He had a following in England that included Queen Victoria and, after his death, he was the first American to be commemorated with a bust in Poet's Corner at Westminster Abbey.

Portland's impressive City Hall

▶ *Continue on Congress Street.*

7 Monument Square

This space, originally the town's Market Square, is named for Our Lady of Victories Monument. The monument is a Civil War memorial that was built in 1891, with money raised by local soldiers and sailors. In recent years, the farmers' market has been revived, with stands set out on Wednesdays from May to October. Everyone comes to buy fruit and veg, plants and flowers, cheese and eggs. The summer brings after-work concerts; in December, the city's Christmas tree lights up the square.

▶ *Look across Congress Street.*

8 Maine Bank and Trust

Portland's first skyscraper, built in 1910 in the beaux arts style, was at that time New England's tallest building. Unlike traditional structures of the period, where the exterior walls supported the building, this was constructed with a steel skeleton, allowing the building to achieve a greater height. Inside, the marble lobby soars to a ceiling at least three stories high.

The impression is of solidity and security – perfect for a bank building.

▶ *Continue on Congress Street to No. 425.*

SPECIAL TO...

Congress Street leads to Munjoy Hill, perhaps a derivation of the French *Mont Joie*. Here, the 221-foot (67m) high Portland Observatory was erected in 1807, as a signal tower. Communication by flags announced the identity of approaching merchant ships and enabled the docks to be prepared for their arrival. Views from the top are spectacular.

Nearby is the Eastern Promenade. Turn right for the bandstand. Here, the panorama encompasses Portland Harbor, the best deep-water port north of New Jersey. Watch for an oil tanker or a cruise ferry coming from Nova Scotia. Don't try to count the islands in Casco Bay; supposedly, there are 365 of them, hence the name, the Calendar Islands.

9 First Parish Church

Founded in 1674, this church predates any other house of worship in Portland. The second building on the site took several hits during the British bombardment of the town in 1775. Evidence of the conflict remains inside, where a cannon ball still lodges within the chain supporting the magnificent 600-pound (273kg) cut-glass chandelier. The 1794 clock and 1804 bell were saved and incorporated into the present building, which dates from a reconstruction using granite in 1826.

▶ *Continue on Congress Street.*

10 City Hall

The granite used to build the City Hall was quarried locally in Maine, but the architecture is based on the classic French *hôtel-de-ville*. Within the building is a 1,900-seat auditorium, where the Portland Symphony Orchestra often gives concerts. This is the third municipal headquarters to have been located on this site: the first was destroyed in the Great Fire of 1866, and its successor succumbed to another blaze in 1908.

▶ *Turn right on Exchange Street.*

ⓛ Exchange Street

Exchange Street leads into the six-square-block Old Port Exchange area, the oldest part of the city. Warehouses and offices have now become boutiques, art galleries and ethnic restaurants. Look closely and you'll see another reminder of British shelling in 1775: the cannon ball embedded in the Colesworth building, on the right, just past the entry to the parking garage.

▷ *Continue to the intersection with Middle Street.*

ⓛ Tommy's Park

The *trompe-l'oeil* by two Portland artists on the wall represents architectural elements of the 19th-century marble post office that once stood across the street in what is now the postage-stamp size Post Office Park. In this sunny spot, the granite boulders represent the many islands of Casco Bay, just outside Portland Harbor.

▷ *Turn left on Middle Street and*

walk two blocks to the intersection with Pearl Street.

ⓛ Woodman Block

This was one of the first buildings put up after the Great Fire of 1866. Like its two neighbors with decorative cast iron, it was designed by George Harding. Look for the architect's autograph on the base of the left corner pilaster, on the Middle Street side.

▷ *Continue toward the harbor on Pearl Street. After a block, turn right on cobblestoned Milk Street. Straight ahead is the Regency Hotel.*

ⓛ Milk Street Armory

It is no coincidence that the Regency Hotel, between Silver and Market streets, resembles a fortress. This was originally the armory, and was very active in the late 19th to mid-20th centuries. It also had a tradition of hospitality, as it was the site of musical events and impressive balls. The contemporary dolphin fountain was originally offered

to, and rejected by, the city fathers. Shunted around town, it stood on a variety of sites until it was finally bought by the hotel.

▷ *Turn left on Silver Street.*

ⓛ Boothby Square

At the intersection of Silver and Fore streets is Boothby Square. Directly in front is a row of old buildings, including the 1792 Sam Butts House and Store. It is the second-oldest surviving post-revolutionary house in Portland.

On your left is the 1868 granite U.S. Customs House. In the impressive interior, it is easy to imagine merchants sitting down to negotiate the tariffs on a cargo of molasses being unloaded at the wharf, just down the street.

▷ *Turn right on Fore Street, pass the granite-fronted 1828 Mariner's Church. This impressive building once offered "moral and religious instruction" to seamen; now it houses the Old Port Tavern*

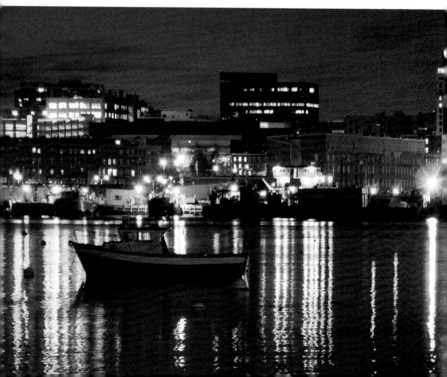

and Billiards Room. Turn left immediately onto cobbled Moulton Street. Turn right on Wharf Street, go right on Union Street, then left at the light on Fore Street. On the corner of Cotton Street is the Tracy-Causer Building.

16 Tracy-Causer Building

Note the old street sign on this building, one of the few survivors of the Great Fire of 1866. The city's Landmarks Association successfully campaigned for its preservation and restoration in 1996. On the harbor side stand some of the few remaining warehouses from the "Golden Age" of the 19th and early 20th centuries.

At the five-street intersection known as Gorham's Corner is a seated statue of John Ford, complete with pipe. He grew up in Portland and the pub owned by this famous Hollywood director's father was here.

▶ *Continue through the five-street intersection onto Pleasant Street. Immediately past the first parking garage, turn right and go up the alley and stairs to Spring Street. On the right is the Civic Center. Cross the street and turn left.*

17 Clapp House and McLellan House

The Great Fire did not reach this area, so these two impressive merchants' homes still stand. Major Hugh McLellan's grand Federal (1801) house was given to the Portland Society of Art in 1908 by Mrs. Lorenzo de Medici Sweat, along with funds to build a "proper" art museum. The Society evolved into the Portland Museum of Art, which also owns the Clapp House, dating from 1832.

▶ *Turn right on High Street. Across the street is another Federal brick residence, built by McLellan's brother, also a successful merchant and auctioneer. Return to Congress Square, at the end of the block.*

RECOMMENDED TRIPS

Portland's waterfront is busy with both working fishermen and pleasure boats. In summer, there are numerous trips going out each day to whale watch or bird watch, to poke around the islands of Casco Bay, or to visit explorer Admiral Peary's former home on Eagle Island. Ferries run a regular service up to Nova Scotia in Canada.

The Portland skyline in the evening

2 DAYS • 268 MILES • 431KM

Mountains &
Lakes of Maine

Nature lovers and sports fans head for the lakes and mountains, just as

vacationers did 150

years ago when

they came by rail-

road to escape the

summer heat of

more southerly

states. Winter also

brings visitors, such

as downhill and

cross-country

skiers.

ⓘ *245 Commercial Street*

▷ *Leave Portland on I–95 (the Maine Turnpike), turning off on Exit 63 at Gray (18m/29km). Follow Route 26 north for 8 miles (13km) to Sabbathday Lake.*

BACK TO NATURE

North of Gray is the Maine Wildlife Park. For those who are not heading out into the wilderness areas of the state, this is a wonderful place to get a close look at moose, bears, deer and porcupines. This is not a zoo; the animals brought here were orphaned or injured.

---

❶ Sabbathday Lake
A cluster of white buildings plus a large red-brick house mark Sabbathday Lake Village, the home of the Shakers, the religious community founded in 1782 by Mother Ann Lee, who voyaged from Manchester, England. Some 30 years later, the Shaker movement had grown to around 7,000, with settlements in New England, Ohio, and Kentucky.

This is the last remaining group. Fewer than a dozen men and women live here, following the credo "Put your hands to work and your heart to God." They aim for self-sufficiency through farming, tending the orchards, knitting and printing. During the summer, outsiders are invited to join the Sunday services at 10am in the Meeting House, with its plain wooden benches. On other days, visitors can tour some of the buildings, including the museum, with examples of ingenious labor-saving inventions.

▷ *Follow Route 26 to Poland Spring.*

❷ Poland Spring
The popularity of bottled mineral waters may seem a recent phenomenon but Poland

Spring water has been prized for more than a century. When its "healing" powers became known, the spring attracted visitors, a hotel was built, and the area developed into a summer resort. Visitors still come to stay at the resort hotel, or to admire the State of Maine Building from the Chicago Expo in 1893, moved and reconstructed here as an attraction for visitors. In Poland Spring Preservation Park, the 1907 bottling plant now houses interactive science displays and memorabilia. The visitor center and café are set on 100 acres (40 hectares) of woods with 4 miles (7km) of nature trails.

▷ *Continue on Route 26 north for 17 miles (27km) through South Paris, where the Celebration Barn Theater puts on vaudeville, mime and juggling in the summer. Turn right to Paris.*

❸ Paris
Few Americans remember Hannibal Hamlin, Vice-President during Abraham Lincoln's first term. His home is the most impressive structure in this cluster of pristine white Federal and Victorian houses on the summit of a hill. Admire the vistas across the valley and to the White Mountains to the west, then tour the tiny library in the former jail. Built in 1822, it is constructed entirely of granite, including the floors. Ask to see

the jail door keys, and to hear how a fat prisoner became stuck while trying to escape.

▷ *Continue and rejoin Route 26 and drive north to the junction of Routes 26 and 219. On the east side of the road is a turn-off for Snow Falls Gorge, where there is a picturesque waterfall, picnic tables and nature trails.*

❹ Trap Corner
"Rockhounds" and gemologists from all over New England know Oxford County because it is rich in minerals and gemstones such as tourmaline, amethyst and quartz.

At the junction of Routes 26 and 219 is Perham's of West Paris, a landmark since 1919. As well as a shop selling local finds, and the museum, this is where modern-day prospectors can get maps of nearby quarries and information about panning for gold in the Rangeley area.

▷ *Continue on Route 26.*

❺ Bryant Pond
The people of Maine are renowned for their stubbornness. This town enjoyed making telephone calls the old-fashioned way, and made national headlines with its campaign to keep its hand-cranked phone system, the last one in the country. They lost their battle in 1983, but the

Reflections at Bryant Pond

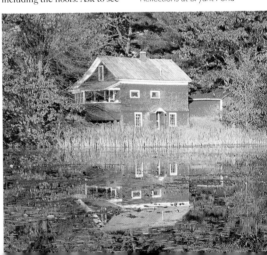

switches and hand-cranked phone are now in the Maine State Museum, Augusta.

▶ Take **Route 26** to Bethel.

❻ Bethel

Founded on the Androscoggin River, the community nearly died after the Revolution. Railroads brought revitalization in the mid-19th century. As well as benefiting agriculture and lumber businesses, the trains carried tourists. Now, vacationers

Main picture: the covered bridge at Newry
Inset: one of Bethel's attractive houses; blueberry leaves in Acadia National Park

come by car to what is a four-season resort. In winter, cross-country and downhill skiers head for Mount Abram and Sunday River, with its 131-trail network over eight different peaks.

The chairlift up the slope provides bird's-eye views of the White Mountains. In summer, the area offers a range of outdoor activities: camping, canoeing, mountain biking, fishing, golf and swimming.

ℹ *Bethel Train Station, 8 Station Place*

▶ *Leave Bethel on* **Routes 26** *and* **2**, *and drive 5 miles (8km) north to Newry.*

SCENIC ROUTES

About 10m (16km) northwest of Newry is Grafton Notch State Park, where the park road has been designated a "Maine Scenic Byway." Moose can be sighted during dawn and dusk hours, while views of Bald Pate Mountain, plus Screw Augur Falls, epitomize the beauties of the region. The Appalachian Trail crosses the road here. This hiking route starts in Georgia and follows the Appalachian Mountains all the way to Mount Katahdin in northeast Maine.

⑦ Newry

Just off the road is the Artist's Covered Bridge, much painted and photographed long before the movie *The Bridges of Madison County* lent cachet to similar bridges in Iowa. This one was built in 1872, over the Sunday River. More than just a scenic spot, it has popular swimming holes as well.

▶ *Continue on scenic* **Route 2** *north to the papermill town of Rumford and cross the river at the mighty Pennacook Falls to Mexico, where much of the country's paper for books is made. Take* **Route 17** *north toward Oquossoc, then turn east on* **Route 4** *to Rangeley.*

⑧ Rangeley

Wilderness and isolation are the hallmarks of the Rangeley region, surrounded by mountains and punctuated by more than 40 bodies of water. The village boasts of being midway between the North Pole and the equator, but there is nothing midway about the winters. A dog-sled mail service used to deliver letters to households cut off by snow; now, snowmobiles provide access to homes and businesses, but they are also raced for fun.

Other winter sports include snowshoeing, dog-sledding and ice-fishing, as well as cross-country and downhill skiing. At Saddleback, the slopes here are less crowded than at most other resorts. When summer comes, there is fishing for landlocked salmon and trout, canoeing, hiking and golfing.

There are also two museums. The Rangeley Historical Society Museum, once a jail, recalls the 19th-century era of lake steamers and lodges that catered to New Yorkers escaping the heat of the city. More unusual is the Wilhelm Reich Museum, the home of the controversial Austrian psychoanalyst who studied with, then broke from, Sigmund Freud. Reich emigrated to the U.S.A. and eventually settled in Rangeley, to pursue "orgonomy, the science of the life energy." His writings and inventions were all to do with sexual energy and personality analysis. In 1956, he was found guilty of violating Food and Drug Administration laws. He died, in prison, a year later. A museum preserves his library, memorabilia and surviving inventions.

i *Rangeley Lakes Region Chamber of Commerce, 6 Park Road*

SPECIAL TO...

When shoppers pick up a pack of wild blueberries, they will be taking home some of the 66 million pounds (30 million kg) grown every year in Maine. That represents 99 percent of the nation's crop. August is the official month of blueberries, and Rangeley's festival is in the middle of the month is a typical celebration, with stands selling pies and muffins, sauces and ice cream. You can even "pick your own" at local farms in the region

---

BACK TO NATURE

At the Hunter Cove Wildlife Sanctuary, just west of Rangeley, on Route 4, there are marked trails through swamps, meadows and thickets where bears, moose and bobcats live. Guides take visitors out for moose-watch canoe trips – as long as they are up by 5am!

▷ *Leave Rangeley via* **Route 4** *south. Note that Smalls Falls, in the Sandy River Gorge, has a good swimming hole, plus a waterfall, picnic site, and hiking trails. At Phillips, take* **Route 142** *northeast to Kingfield.*

❾ Kingfield
What do violins, automobiles and cameras all have in common? They fascinated the ingenious minds of F. O. and F. E. Stanley, twin brothers who

lived here a century ago. Their most profitable discovery was a photographic process which they sold to a company that later became Kodak. Car fans know them for their Stanley Steamers, made by the Stanley Motor Carriage Company. One of their racing cars set a speed record of 127.66mph (204.3km/h) in 1906, and it remained unbroken for many years. The brothers also made fine violins. The Stanley Museum tells their story and displays their inventions, along with photographs taken by their sister, Chansonetta Stanley Emmons.

▷ *Take* **Route 27** *south through New Portland, stopping to see the amazing 1841 Fireproof Wire Bridge, suspended across the Carrabassett River. Rejoin* **Route 4** *and head for Farmington.*

❿ Farmington
It is hard to imagine that this agricultural valley produced an international opera star. A simple farmhouse, just outside Farmington, was the birthplace in 1857 of Lillian Norton. As Madame Nordica, she triumphed in Europe and was the first American woman to take Wagnerian roles at the Bayreuth Festival. Returning to the States, her "liquid purity, exceptional range, and magnificent power" charmed New York critics during numerous seasons at the Metropolitan Opera House. The Nordica Memorial Homestead displays her costumes, annotated scores and other memorabilia.

A branch of the University of Maine is here, continuing a tradition of education dating back to 1864 when the school was founded, the first public college in Maine.

i *Franklin County Chamber of Commerce, 407 Wilton Road*

▷ *Continue on* **Route 4**, *which leads through Dryden, Jay and Livermore Falls, recognized long before arriving by the*

View over Step Falls, Grafton Notch State Park

SPECIAL TO...

Farmington is the home of Greenwood's Champion Ear Protectors, better-known as ear muffs. They were the brainchild of local teenager Chester Greenwood, whose ears had become painfully cold while ice-skating during the winter of 1873. His prototype was made of wire, covered with fur and velvet, but after improvements, he patented the design and opened a factory in town. Each year, the first Saturday in December is Chester Greenwood Day, complete with a parade.

---

sulphurous smell of the papermills.

⓫ Androscoggin River
With its heavy flow and a drop of over 1,000 feet/300m, the 175-mile long (280km) Androscoggin is an important industrial river. Jay, once the home of the biggest paper mill in the world, still has the Androscoggin Mill, producing over 1,000 tons of paper a day.

In the 19th-century, immigrants flocked to the mills from Europe and Québec. Today, Chisholm is the heart of Maine's French-Canadian community. In Livermore Falls, where the river plunges 14 feet (5m), the area's industrial history is explained at the new Maine's Paper & Heritage Museum on Church Street.

Five miles (8km) away, on Route 108, the Washburn-Norlands Living History Center in Livermore reflects Maine's rural heritage, as well as the achievements of the powerful Washburn family. Appointments are required at both museums.

▷ *Follow* **Route 4** *to Auburn and then take* **I–95** *south (Maine Turnpike) for the return to Portland.*

GETTING AROUND
By Car

New England's towns, villages and attractions are close together. From Boston, you are an hour from Providence, Plymouth, Manchester or Portsmouth; two hours from Hartford, Portland, Mystic or Cape Cod; three hours from New Haven, the Berkshires, southern Vermont, the Maine Coast or New Hampshire's White Mountains; and only about four hours to northern Vermont.

By Recreational Vehicle

An alternative way to tour is in an RV (motor home). Hundreds of campgrounds offer electrical, water and sewer hook-ups for $25 to $30 per night. If you travel in high summer, make reservations at the more popular campgrounds.

For more information on RVs, contact the Recreation Vehicle Industry Association (tel: 703/620-6003; www.rvia. org) or the Recreation Vehicle Rental Association (tel: 703/591-7130; www.rvra.org). RV America has a comprehensive website (www.rvamerica.com), as does Go Camping America (www.gocampingamerica.com).

By Plane

As well as major airports in Boston, Providence, Hartford, Portland and Burlington, consider important secondary airports, such as Manchester, NH, and T.F. Green Airport in Warwick, RI, for low-cost airlines. Details on www.flynewengland.com.

By Train

Amtrak (tel: 1–800/872-7245; www.amtrak.com) trains link Boston with the rest of the region. The high-speed Acela Express service runs from Washington D.C. to New York City and Boston.

By Bus

New England is also well-serviced by a network of bus services. As well as covering the region, Greyhound (tel: 800/231-2222; www.greyhound.com) connects New England with the rest of the US. Peter Pan Bus Lines (tel: 617/526-1801 or 800/343-9999; www.peterpanbus.com) cover southern New England; Concord Coach Lines (tel: 603/228-3300 or 1-800/639-3317, www.concordcoachlines.com) service New Hampshire and Maine. With fast, regular services from Boston to Plymouth, Cape Cod and the Islands, check out the Plymouth & Brockton Street Railway Co. (tel: 508/746-0378; www.p-b.com). Megabus has cheap fares between New York City and Boston (877-462-6342; www.megabus.com).

HEALTH SERVICES

Always carry health insurance when you travel. In an emergency, blue road signs bearing a white H mark the way to hospitals.

Hitchhiking

Hitchhiking is not recommended; hitchhiking on expressways is illegal.

Holidays

(LWE = long weekend, including Monday)
1 January – New Year's Day;
Third Monday in January – Martin Luther King Day (LWE);
Third weekend in February – Washington's Birthday (LWE);
First Tuesday in March – Town Meeting Day (Vermont);
Third Monday in April – Patriots' Day (Massachusetts and Maine, LWE);
Easter;
Last weekend in May – Memorial Day (LWE);
4 July – Independence Day;

Second Monday in August – Victory Day (Rhode I, LWE);
16 August – Bennington Battle Day (Vermont);
First Monday in September – Labor Day (LWE);
Second Monday in October – Columbus Day (LWE);
First Tuesday in November – Election Day (some states);
11 November – Veteran's Day;
Fourth Thursday in November – Thanksgiving Day;
25 December – Christmas Day.

Liquor Laws

The minimum age for drinking alcohol is 21. Some New England towns are "dry": no store, restaurant or hotel may sell liquor, but it's not illegal to bring your own (BYO) and to serve yourself. Restaurants might have a full license (liquor, wine and beer), a wine and beer license, or no license. It's illegal to drink alcohol in public areas. Drink/driving laws are very strict.

MOTORING
Driving

Always have your driver's license with you. Outside major cities, cars are often permitted to turn right on a red light at a stop sign. Speed limits, licensing of drivers, and all other rules governing automobile use are set by each state's legislature.

Car Rental

To rent a car, you must have a valid driver's license and be 21, 25 for most major agencies. A credit or charge card is usually required. Non-U.S. residents need an International Drivers Permit. If your own auto insurance covers damage to a rental car, you may not need Collision Damage Waiver (CDW) or Loss Damage Waiver (LDW). Check with your insurer.

All the major car rental chains are represented:
Alamo (tel: 800/462-5266)
Avis (tel: 800/331-1212)

Budget (tel: 800/527-0700)
Dollar (tel: 800/800-3665)
Hertz (tel: 800/654-3131)
National (tel: 800/227-7368)
Thrifty (tel: 800/847-4389).

Breakdowns

Car rental companies tell you what to do in case of a breakdown. The AAA (American Automobile Association) has reciprocal arrangements with many other motoring organizations around the world; check before leaving home. The AAA nationwide, toll-free number is 800-222-4357. In case of a breakdown, lift the hood as a signal, and remain in the car. Only open doors and windows to police in a patrol car.

Accidents

All accidents must be reported to the police. Exchange names, addresses, driver's license number, and insurance details. Non-U.S. residents who have caused, or are held responsible for, an injury, should contact their embassy or consulate.

Safety Belts

The use of safety belts is required by law. Infants and children under 5 must use child safety seats, secured by seat belts (available from car-rental firms at a small extra charge).

Speed Limits

Speed limits are strictly enforced. The speed limit on highways is generally 55 to 65mph (88 to 105km/h). In cities and built-up areas, it is 20 to 40mph (32 to 64km/h), 20mph (32km/h) in school zones. When a school bus stops, all traffic must stop too.

Road Maps

Find maps in bookstores and gas stations. Free state maps are often available from state tourism departments by mail, or from information centers on major highways near state borders. For addresses of the state tourism offices, see Visitor Information below.

PERSONAL SAFETY

New England is safe, but whenever you're traveling in an unfamiliar place, stay alert and watch your possessions.

POST OFFICES

Post offices are usually open Monday through Friday from 8am to 5pm and Saturday from 8am to noon or 2pm. In Boston, the post office at 25 Dorchester Avenue, 02205 (tel: 617/654-5302) is open 24/7.

TAXES

Taxes on hotel rooms, restaurant meals, some transportation, and purchases in general are levied by each state and by some cities. Taxes on rooms, meals, and other purchases (which can be as high as 10 per cent) are not included in the price. Sales tax on clothing and general goods is low to non-existent.

TIPS FOR SPECIAL TRAVELERS

Families

Most attractions offer reduced admission for children or families. Some state parks and beaches charge admission "per car".

Seniors

Senior discounts are available throughout New England at museums, parks, and attractions, so always carry proper identification. However, when making reservations for transport or hotels, always ask for discounts ahead of time, not when you're paying for the services.

For more information about senior discounts, contact the American Association of Retired Persons (AARP), 601 E Street, NW, Washington, D.C. 20049 (tel: 1-888/687-2277; www.aarp.org).

Travelers with Disabilities

By law, all New England's major hotels and attractions must be accessible to visitors with disabilities. However, some historic inns and buildings

cannot always comply. Always check ahead of time whether the level of accessibility is sufficient.

Although Amtrak trains are accessible, not all stations are. Ask when making reservations. Also inquire about help with baggage, special seating, and other assistance. Amtrak grants discounts to disabled travelers of all ages. For full information, go to www.amtrak.com.

VISITOR INFORMATION

Discover New England is the region's official international tourism representative (www.discovernewengland.org). State tourism offices:
Connecticut Commission on Culture and Tourism, 1 Financial Plaza, 755 Main Street, Hartford, CT 06106 (tel: 860/256-2800; www.ctbound.org).
Maine Office of Tourism, State House Station 59, Augusta, ME 04333 (tel: 207/287-5711 or 888/624-6345; www.visitmaine.com).
Massachusetts Office of Travel & Tourism, 10 Park Plaza, Suite 4510, Boston, MA 02116 (tel: 617/973-8500 or 800/227-MASS; www.massvacation.com).
New Hampshire Division of Travel & Tourism, 172 Pembroke Road (P.O. Box 1856), Concord, New Hampshire 03302 (tel: 603/271-2665; www.visitnh.gov)
Rhode Island Tourism Division, 315 Iron Horse Way, Suite 101, Providence, Rhode Island 02908 (tel: 401/222-2601 or 800/556-2484; www.visitrhodeisland.com)
Vermont Department of Tourism and Marketing, National Life Building, 6th Floor, Drawer 20, Montpelier, Vermont 05620 (tel: 802/828-3237; www.vermontvacation.com)

WHEN TO GO

New England is a four-season destination: spring is flowery, summers are hot, fall is spectacular, winter is great for skiing and boarding.

ACCOMMODATIONS AND RESTAURANTS

Following is a selection of hotels and bed-and-breakfasts (✧) which can be found along the routes of each tour, together with suggestions for restaurants (Ⓣ) where you can take a break.

Accommodations prices
Accommodations are divided into four price bands, based on the cost of a double room per night. Where hotels are also identified as a restaurant, prices are in relation to the cost of the bedrooms:

$	under $90
$$	$90–$125
$$$	$125–$200
$$$$	over $200

Restaurant prices
Restaurants are divided into three price categories based on the cost of a three-course meal for one, excluding drink:

$	under $20
$$	$20–$40
$$$	over $40

TOUR I
CONCORD
✧ Ⓣ Colonial Inn $$$–$$$$
48 Monument Square, Concord, MA 01742. Tel: 978/369-9200 or 800/370-9200; www.concord colonialinn.com.
56 rooms.

✧ Hawthorn Inn $$
462 Lexington Road, Concord, MA 01742. Tel: 978/369-5610; www.concordmass.com.
7 rooms.

Ⓣ Walden Grille $–$$
24 Walden Street, Concord, MA. Tel: 978/371-2233. *Modern American cuisine.*

LEXINGTON
Ⓣ La Riviera Gourmet $$
182 Bedford Street, Lexington, MA 02420. Tel: 781/861-2030. *Salads, quiches, daily specials.*

SUDBURY
✧ Longfellow's Wayside Inn $$$–$$$$
72 Wayside Inn Road, Sudbury, MA 01776. Tel: 978/443-1776; www.wayside.org.
10 rooms.

TOUR 2
MARBLEHEAD
✧ Harbor Light Inn $$$–$$$$
58 Washington Street, Marblehead, MA 01945. Tel: 781/631-2186; www.harborlightinn.com.
21 rooms.

Ⓣ The Barnacle $$
141 Front Street, Marblehead, MA. Tel: 781/631-4236. *Fresh seafood in a restaurant overlooking the harbor.*

SALEM
✧ Coach House Inn $–$$$$
284 Lafayette Street, Salem, MA 01970. Tel: 978/744-4092; www.coachhousesalem.com.
11 rooms.

Ⓣ Bella Verona $$
107 Essex Street, Salem, MA. Tel: 978/825-9911. *Classic Italian dishes from the Verona region.*

GLOUCESTER
✧ Cape Ann Motor Inn $–$$$
133 Rockport Road, Gloucester, MA 01930. Tel: 978/281-2900; www.capeannmotorinn.com.
31 rooms.

Ⓣ Franklin Cape Ann $$–$$$
118 Main Street, Gloucester, MA. Tel: 978/283-7888. *Contemporary American food in a bistro setting.*

ROCKPORT
Ⓣ Grand Café $$
Emerson Inn, I Cathedral Avenue, Rockport, MA. Tel: 978/546-6321. *Modern versions of New England dishes.*

IPSWICH
✧ Inn at Castle Hill $$$$
280 Argilla Road, Ipswich, MA 01938. Tel: 978/412-2555; http://innatcastlehill.thetrustees.org.
10 rooms.

Ⓣ Clam Box of Ipswich $
246 High Street, Ipswich, MA 01938. Tel: 978/356-9707. *Serving fried seafood for 70 years.*

NEWBURYPORT
✧ Garrison Inn $$$
11 Brown Square, Newburyport, MA 01950. Tel: 978/499-8500; www.garrisoninn.com.
24 rooms.

TOUR 3
SANDWICH
✧ Dan'l Webster Inn $$–$$$$
149 Main Street, Sandwich, MA 02563. Tel: 508/888-3622; www.danlwebsterinn.com.
48 rooms.

Ⓣ The Belfry Bistro $$–$$$
8 Jarves Street, Sandwich, MA. Tel: 508/888-8550. *New American; great desserts.*

BARNSTABLE
Ⓣ Mattakeese Wharf $$–$$$
271 Mill Way, Barnstable, MA. Tel: 508/362-4511. *Seafood and sunsets. Summer only.*

DENNIS
✧ Isaiah Hall B&B Inn $$–$$$
152 Whig Street, Dennis, MA 02638. Tel: 508/385-9928; www.isaiahhallinn.com.
12 rooms.

EASTHAM
✧ Whalewalk Inn $$$$
220 Bridge Road, Eastham, MA 02642. Tel: 508/255-0617 or 800/440-1281; www.whalewalkinn.com.
16 rooms.

⑪ Arnold's Lobster & Clam Bar $–$$
Route 6, Eastham, MA. Tel: 508/255-2575. *Classic for summer shore dinners.*

PROVINCETOWN
◇ White Wind Inn $–$$$
174 Commercial Street, Provincetown, MA 02657. Tel: 508/487-1526; www.whitewindinn.com. 13 rooms.

◇ The Masthead $$–$$$
31–41 Commercial Street, Provincetown, MA. Tel: 508/487-0523; www.themasthead.com. 19 rooms.

⑪ Level $–$$
386 Commercial Street, Provincetown, MA. Tel: 508/487-7800. *Fun, stylish modern American bistro.*

⑪ Front Street $$–$$$
230 Commercial Street, Provincetown, MA. Tel: 508/487-9715. *Mediterranean fusion.*

⑪ Ross' Grill $$
Whalers' Wharf, Commerical Street, Provincetown, MA. Tel: 508/487-8878. *Bar/bistro on water. Closed Tue, Wed.*

CHATHAM
◇ Chatham Seafarer $$
Route 28 and Ridgevale Road, Chatham, MA 02633. Tel: 508/432-1739; www.chathamseafarer.com. 20 rooms.

⑪ The Wild Goose Tavern $–$$
512 Main Street, Chatham, MA. Tel: 508/945-5590. *From local seafood to Italian favorites.*

TOUR 4
GREAT BARRINGTON
⑪ Castle Street Café $$
10 Castle Street, Great Barrington, MA. Tel: 413/528-5244. *New American; good wine list, jazz.*

STOCKBRIDGE
◇ ⑪ Red Lion $–$$$$
30 Main Street, Stockbridge, MA 01262. Tel: 413/298-5545; www.redlioninn.com. 108 rooms.

LENOX
◇ Apple Tree Inn $–$$$$
10 Richmond Mountain Road, Lenox, MA 01240. Tel: 413/637-1477; www.appletree-inn.com. 34 rooms.

⑪ Bistro Zinc $–$$$
56 Church Street, Lenox, MA. Tel: 413/637-8800. *Stylish modern French bistro, open daily.*

⑪ Church Street Café $$
65 Church Street, Lenox, MA. Tel: 413/637-2745. *Eclectic American cuisine. Book ahead.*

NORTH ADAMS
◇ The Porches Inn at MASSMoCA $$–$$$$
231 River Street, North Adams, MA 01247. Tel: 413/664-0400; www.porches.com. 47 rooms.

⑪ Café Latino $$
11 MASS MoCA Way, Marshall Street, North Adams MA. Tel: 413/662-2004. *Latin American cuisine.*

DEERFIELD
◇ ⑪ Deerfield Inn $$$$
81 Old Main Street, Deerfield, MA 01342. Tel: 413/774-5587 or 800/926-3865; www.deerfieldinn.com. 23 rooms.

TOURS 5 and 6
BOSTON
◇ Beacon Hill Hotel $$$$
25 Charles Street, Boston, MA 02114. Tel: 617/723-7575; www.beaconhillhotel.com. 13 rooms.

◇ Charlesmark Hotel $$–$$$$
655 Boylston Street, Boston, MA 02116. Tel: 617/247-1212; www.thecharlesmark.com. 33 rooms.

◇ Encore B&B $$–$$$
116 West Newton Street, Boston, MA 02118. Tel: 617/247-3425; www.encorebandb.com. 4 rooms.

◇ Fairmont Copley Plaza $$$$
138 St. James Avenue, Boston, MA 02116. Tel: 617/267-5300; www.fairmont.com. 383 rooms.

◇ Liberty $$$$
215 Charles Street, Boston, MA 02114. Tel: 617/224 4000; libertyhotel.com. 298 rooms.

⑪ Legal Seafoods $–$$
100 Huntington Avenue, Copley Place, Boston, MA. Tel: 617/266-7775. *Seafood. Several branches.*

⑪ Metropolis Café $–$$
584 Tremont Street, Boston, MA 02118. Tel: 617/247-2931. *Stylish, modern American. Great brunch.*

⑪ The Paramount Restaurant $–$$
44 Charles Street, Boston MA 02114. Tel: 617/720-1152. *Informal neighborhood restaurant; no reservations.*

⑪ Sel de la Terre $$–$$$
255 State Street, Boston, MA. Tel: 617/720-1300. *Provençal cuisine.*

TOUR 7
CAMBRIDGE
◇ A Cambridge House B&B $$–$$$$
2218 Massachusetts Avenue, Cambridge, MA 02140. Tel: 617/491-6300; www.acambridgehouse.com. 15 rooms.

◇ ⑪ Sheraton Commander Hotel $$$–$$$$
16 Garden Street, Cambridge, MA 02138. Tel: 617/547-4800 or 800/325-3535; www.starwoodhotels.com. 175 rooms.

ⓘ Casablanca $$
40 Brattle Street, Cambridge,
MA 02138. Tel: 617/876-0999.
Mediterranean cooking; well-known bar.

ⓘ UpStairs on the Square £$$–$$$
91 Winthrop Street, Cambridge,
MA 02138. Tel: 617/864-1933.
Outstanding modern New England fare.

TOUR 8
HARTFORD
◇ Goodwin Hotel $$$$
1 Haynes Street, Hartford,
CT 06103. Tel: 860/246-7500
or 800/922-5006;
www.goodwinhotel.com.
124 rooms.

◇ Silas W. Robbins House $$$–$$$$
185 Broad Street, Wethersfield,
CT 06109. Tel: 860/571-8733;
www.silaswrobbins.com.
5 rooms.

ⓘ Bin 228 $–$$
228 Pearl Street, Hartford, CT
06106. Tel: 860/244-9463. *Hip modern wine bar, bistro.*

ⓘ Vito's by the Park $$
26 Trumbull Street, Hartford,
CT 06103. Tel: 860/244-2200.
Italian dishes overlooking Bushnell Park.

TOUR 9
NEW HAVEN
◇ Omni New Haven Hotel at Yale $$$–$$$$
155 Temple Street, New
Haven, CT 06510. Tel: 203/772-6664; www.omnihotels.com.
306 rooms.

◇ Swan Cove B&B $$–$$$
115 Sea Street, New Haven, CT
06519. Tel: 203/776-3240;
www.swancove.com.
6 rooms.

◇ Touch of Ireland Guest House $$–$$$
670 Whitney Avenue, New
Haven, CT 06511. Tel: 203/787-7997; www.touchofirelandguest
house.com.
4 rooms.

ⓘ Foster's $$
56-62 Orange Street, New
Haven, CT 06510. Tel: 203/
859-6666.
Chef Foster's "eccentric American" cuisine.

ⓘ Miso $$
15 Orange Street, New Haven,
CT 06510. Tel: 203/848-6472.
Modern Japanese.

ⓘ Union League Café $$
1032 Chapel Street New
Haven, CT 06510. Tel: 203/562-4299.
Contemporary French.

TOUR 10
LITCHFIELD
◇ ⓘ Tollgate Hill Inn $$–$$$$
Route 202, Litchfield, CT
06759. Tel: 860/567-1233;
www.tollgatehill.com.
20 rooms.

NEW MILFORD
ⓘ Adrienne $$$
218 Kent Road, New Milford,
CT 06776. Tel: 860/354-6001.
*Award-winning American cuisine.
Closed Mon.*

NEW PRESTON
◇ ⓘ Hopkins Inn $$–$$$
22 Hopkins Road, New Preston,
CT 06777. Tel: 860/868-7295;
www.thehopkinsinn.com.
13 rooms.

KENT
ⓘ Bull's Bridge Inn $$
333 Kent Road, Kent, CT.
Tel: 860/927-1000. *Diverse menu including classic grills.*

◇ Inn at Kent Falls $$$–$$$$
107 Kent Cornwall Road, Kent,
CT 06757. Tel: 860/927-3239,
www.theinnatkentfalls.com

SALISBURY
ⓘ White Hart $$
Village Green, Salisbury, CT.
Tel: 860/435-0030. *Modern New England cooking.*

NORFOLK
◇ Manor House $$$
69 Maple Avenue, Norfolk,
CT 06058. Tel: 860/542-5690;
www.manorhouse-norfolk.com.
9 rooms.

TOUR 11
MADISON
◇ Inn at Lafayette $$–$$$
725 Boston Post Road, Madison,
CT 06443. Tel: 203/245-7773;
www.innatlafayette.com.
5 rooms.

OLD SAYBROOK
ⓘ Parthenon Diner $$
809 Boston Post Road, Old
Saybrook, CT. Tel: 860/395-5111. *Classic diner.*

ESSEX
◇ ⓘ Griswold Inn $$$–$$$$
36 Main Street, Essex, CT
06425. Tel: 860/767-1776;
www.griswoldinn.com.
30 rooms.

IVORYTON
◇ ⓘ Copper Beech Inn $$$$
46 Main Street, Ivoryton, CT
06442. Tel: 860/767-0330;
www.copperbeechinn.com.
13 rooms.

OLD LYME
◇ Bee & Thistle Inn $$$–$$$$
100 Lyme Street, Old Lyme,
CT 06371. Tel: 860/434-1667
or 800/622-4946;
www.beeandthistle.com.
11 rooms.

ⓘ Old Lyme Inn $$–$$$
85 Lyme Street, Old Lyme, CT.
Tel: 860/434-2600. *American cooking.*

NOANK
ⓘ Abbott's Lobster in the Rough $–$$
117 Pearl Street, Noank, CT.
Tel: 860/536-7719. *Lobster dishes.
Seasonal specialties.*

MYSTIC
◇ Inn at Mystic $–$$$$
3 Williams Avenue, Mystic,
CT 06355. Tel: 860/536-9604.
67 rooms.

◇ **Taber Inne $$–$$$**
66 Williams Avenue, Route 1,
Mystic, CT 06355. Tel: 860/
536-4904; www.taberinne.com.
32 rooms.

**TOUR 12
PROVIDENCE**
◇ **Christopher Dodge House
B&B $$–$$$**
11 West Park Street,
Providence, RI 02908. Tel:
401/351-6111; www.providence-
hotel.com.
14 rooms.

◇ **Hotel Dolce Villa $$$–$$$$**
63 DePasquale Plaza,
Providence, RI 02903.
Tel: 401/383-7031;
www.dolcevillari.com.
14 rooms.

◇ **Old Court $$$–$$$$**
144 Benefit Street, Providence,
RI 02903. Tel: 401/751-2002;
www.oldcourt.com.
10 rooms.

◇ ⑪ **Providence Biltmore $$$**
11 Dorrance Street, Providence,
RI 02903. Tel: 401/421-0700
or 800/294-7709;
www.providencebiltmore.com.
289 rooms.

⑪ **Local 121 $$**
121 Washington Street,
Providence, RI 02903. Tel:
401/274-2121.
Local produce, fun atmosphere.

⑪ **Providence Oyster Bar $$**
283 Atwells Avenue,
Providence, RI 02903.
Tel: 401/272-8866.
Raw bar, fish.

**TOUR 13
NEWPORT**
◇ **Adele Turner Inn $$$–$$$$**
93 Pelham Street, Newport,
RI 02840. Tel: 401/847-1811
or 800/845-1811;
www.adeleturnerinn.com.
13 rooms.

◇ **Cliffside Inn $$$$**
2 Seaview Avenue, Newport,
RI 02840. Tel: 401/847-1811
or 800/845-1811;
www.cliffsideinn.com.
16 rooms.

◇ **Francis Malbone House
$$$–$$$$**
392 Thames Street, Newport,
RI 02840. Tel: 401/846-0392 or
800/846-0392;
www.malbone.com.
25 rooms

◇ ⑪ **Hotel Viking $$–$$$**
1 Bellevue Avenue, Newport,
RI 02840. Tel: 401/847-3300;
www.hotelviking.com.
209 rooms.

◇ **Mill Street Inn $$–$$$$**
75 Mill Street, Newport, RI
02840. Tel: 401/849-9500;
www.millstreetinn.com.
23 rooms.

⑪ **Black Pearl $$–$$$**
30 Bannister's Wharf, Newport,
RI. Tel: 401/846-5264. *Informal
tavern; posh Commodore's Room.
Seafood.*

⑪ **Clarke Cooke House
$$–$$$**
Bannister's Wharf, Newport, RI.
Tel: 401/849-2900. *On the harbor,
with three floors; three places to eat.*

⑪ **Tucker's Bistro $$**
150 Broadway, Newport, RI.
Tel: 401/846-3449. *Traditional
American.*

⑪ **White Horse Tavern $$$**
26 Marlborough Street,
Newport, RI. Tel: 401/849-
3600. *America's oldest pub.
Seafood a specialty.*

**TOUR 14
BENNINGTON**
◇ **South Shire Inn $$$–$$$$**
124 Elm Street, Bennington,
VT 05201. Tel: 802/447-3839.
9 rooms.

◇ ⑪ **Four Chimneys Inn $$$**
21 West Road, Bennington, VT.
Tel: 802/447-3500.
11 rooms.

⑪ **Blue Benn $–$$**
314 North Street, Bennington,
VT. Tel: 802/442-5140.
American/vegetarian. Diner.

**TOUR 15
ARLINGTON**
◇ ⑪ **Arlington Inn $$–$$$**
Historic Route 7A, Arlington,
VT 05250. Tel: 802/375-6532;
www.arlingtoninn.com.
18 rooms.

MANCHESTER
◇ ⑪ **The Equinox Resort and
Marsh Tavern $$$–$$$$**
3567 Main Street, Manchester
Village, VT 05254. Tel: 802/362-
4700; www.equinoxresort.com.
Regional cuisine.
195 rooms.

◇ **Inn at Manchester $$$**
3967 Main Street, Manchester
Village, VT 05254. Tel: 802/362-
1793;
www.innatmanchester.com.
18 rooms.

◇ **Manchester Highlands
Inn $$$–$$$$**
216 Highland Avenue,
Manchester Center, VT 05255.
Tel: 802/362-4565 or 800/743-
4565; www.highlandsinn.com.
16 rooms.

⑪ **Chantecleer $$$**
Route 7A, East Dorset, VT
(north of Manchester). Tel:
802/362-1616. *Classy Swiss-
inspired cooking.*

⑪ **Sherrie's $**
709 Depot Street, Manchester,
VT 05255. Tel: 802/362-3468.
*Family restaurant, breakfast,
lunch.*

WESTON
⑪ **Inn at Weston $$–$$$**
Route 100, Weston, VT 05161.
Tel: 802/823-6789. *International
cuisine.*

CHESTER
◇ **Fullerton Inn $$–$$$**
40 The Common, Chester, VT
05143. Tel: 802/875-2444;
www.fullertoninn.com.
21 rooms.

◇ **Stone Hearth Inn $$–$$$**
698 Route 11 West, Chester,
VT 05143. Tel: 802/875-2525;
www.stonehearthinnvermont.
com.
8 rooms.

GRAFTON
◇ ⑪ **Old Tavern at Grafton**
$$$$
92 Main Street, Grafton,
VT 05146. Tel: 802/843-2231;
www.old-tavern.com.
30 rooms.

NEWFANE
◇ ⑪ **Four Columns Inn $$$**
21 West Street, Newfane,
VT 05345. Tel: 800/787-6633;
www.fourcolumnsinn.com.
Award-winning gourmet food.
Distinctive blend of New American,
Asian and French cuisine.
15 rooms.

BRATTLEBORO
◇ **Forty Putney Road B&B**
$$$
192 Putney Road, Brattleboro,
VT 05301. Tel: 802/254-6268;
www.fortyputneyroad.com.
6 rooms.

⑪ **Peter Havens Restaurant**
$$$
32 Elliot Street, Brattleboro,
VT. Tel: 802/257-3333.
Seafood, duck and more.

TOUR 16
RUTLAND
◇ **The Inn at Rutland $$–$$$$**
70 North Main Street, Rutland,
VT 05701. Tel: 802/773-0575;
www.innatrutland.com.
8 rooms.

⑪ **Little Harry's $$**
121 West Street, Rutland, VT.
Tel: 802/747-4848. *Global*
cuisines, from steak to Thai. Dinner.

KILLINGTON
◇ **The Inn of the Six**
Mountains $$–$$$
2617 Killington Road,
Killington, VT 05751.
Tel: 802/422-4302;
www.sixmountains.com.
103 rooms.

QUECHEE
◇ **Quechee Inn $$–$$$$**
Mashland Farm, Main Street,
Quechee, VT 05059.
Tel: 1-800/235-3133;
www.quecheeinn.com.
25 rooms.

⑪ **Simon Pearce Restaurant**
$$$
At the Mill, Quechee, VT.
Tel: 802/295-1470. *Contemporary*
New England with international
twist.

WOODSTOCK
◇ **Deer Brook Inn $$**
535 Woodstock Road,
Woodstock, VT 05091.
Tel: 802/672-3713;
www.deerbrookinn.com.
5 rooms.

◇ ⑪ **Jackson House Inn $$$$**
114 Senior Lane, Woodstock,
VT 05091. Tel: 802/457-2065;
www.jacksonhouse.com.
15 rooms.

◇ **Shire Riverview Motel**
$$–$$$
46 Pleasant Street, Woodstock,
VT. Tel: 802/457-2211;
www.shiremotel.com.
42 rooms.

⑪ **Bentleys Restaurant $$**
3 Elm Street, Woodstock, VT.
Tel: 802/457-3232. *Contemporary*
cuisine.

TOUR 17
BURLINGTON
◇ ⑪ **Inn at Essex $$$–$$$$**
70 Essex Way, Essex Junction,
VT 05452. Tel: 802/878-1100 or
800/727-4295;
www.vtculinaryresort.com.
119 rooms.

⑪ **Daily Planet $–$$**
15 Center Street, Burlington,
VT. Tel: 802/862-9647.
Imaginative pub food. Dinner

GOSHEN
◇ **Blueberry Hill Inn $$$**
1307 Goshen-Ripton Road,
Goshen, VT 05733. Tel:
802/247-6735; www.blueberry-
hillinn.com.
12 rooms.

MIDDLEBURY
◇ **Swift House Inn $$$–$$$$**
25 Stewart Lane, Middlebury,
VT 05753. Tel: 802-388-9925;
www.swifthouseinn.com.
21 rooms.

◇ ⑪ **Morgan's Tavern $–$$**
Middlebury Inn, 14 Court
Square, Middlebury, VT. Tel:
802-388-4961. *Steak, fish, game.*
70 rooms.

⑪ **Storm Café $$**
3 Mill Street, Frog Hollow,
Middlebury, VT. Tel: 802/388-
1063. *Chef-owned café with a wide-*
ranging menu.

EAST MIDDLEBURY
◇ ⑪ **Waybury Inn $$$–$$$$**
457 East Main Street, East
Middlebury, VT. Tel: 802/388-
4015; www.wayburyinn.com.
14 rooms.

WARREN
⑪ **The Common Man $$–$$$**
3209 German Flats Road,
Sugarbush, Warren, VT. Tel:
802/583-2800. *Vermont produce is*
given a European touch.

WAITSFIELD
◇ ⑪ **Inn at Mad River Barn**
$$–$$$
Route 17, 2849 Mill Brook
Road, Waitsfield, VT.
Tel: 802/496-3310;
www.madriverbarn.com.
15 rooms.

WATERBURY
◇ ⑪ **Old Stagecoach Inn**
$$–$$$
18 North Main Street,
Waterbury, VT 05676.
Tel: 802/244-5056;
www.oldstagecoach.com.
11 rooms.

STOWE
◇ **Ten Acres Lodge $$–$$$**
14 Barrows Road, Stowe, VT
05672. Tel: 800/327-7357;
www.tenacreslodge.com.
15 rooms.

⑪ **Harvest Market $**
1031 Mountain Road, Stowe,
VT 05672. Tel: 802/253-3800.
Healthy, organic, casual.

TOUR 18
PORTSMOUTH
◊ **Inn at Strawbery Banke $$$**
314 Court Street, Portsmouth, NH 03801. Tel: 603/436-7242 or 800/428-3933; www.innatstrawberybanke.com.
7 rooms.

◊ **The Sise Inn $$$–$$$$**
40 Court Street, Portsmouth, NH 03801. Tel: 603/433-1200; www.siseinn.com.
34 rooms.

⑪ **Portsmouth Brewery $–$$**
56 Market Street, Portsmouth, NH. Tel: 603/431-1115. *Casual; hamburgers and more.*

⑪ **Rosa Restaurant $–$$**
80 State Street, Portsmouth, NH. Tel: 603/436-9715. *Traditional Italian cuisine in an historic setting.*

TOUR 19
FRANCONIA
◊ ⑪ **Franconia Inn $$$–$$$$**
1300 Easton Road, Franconia, NH 03580. Tel: 603/823-5542; www.franconiainn.com.
34 rooms.

BETHLEHEM
⑪ **Restaurant at the Adair Country Inn $$$**
80 Guider Lane, Bethlehem, NH. Tel: 603/444-2600. *Modern American cuisine, tempting desserts.*

BRETTON WOODS
◊ **Bretton Arms Inn $$$–$$$$**
US Route 302, Bretton Woods, NH 03575. Tel: 603/278-1000; www.mountwashingtonresort.com.
34 rooms.

JACKSON
◊ ⑪ **Inn at Thorn Hill $$$–$$$$**
Thorn Hill Road, Jackson, NH 03846. Tel: 603/383-4242 or 800/289-8990; www.innatthornhill.com. *Rates include breakfast, high tea, and gourmet dinner.*
25 rooms.

NORTH CONWAY
◊ **White Mountain Hotel $$–$$$**
Hales Location, 2660 West Side Road, North Conway, NH 03860. Tel: 800/533-6301; www.whitemountainhotel.com.
80 rooms.

◊ **Notchland Inn $$$**
Route 302, Hart's Location, NH 03812. Tel: 800/866-6131; www.notchland.com.
12 rooms.

⑪ **Horsefeathers $**
2679 White Mountain Highway, North Conway, NH. Tel: 603/356-2687. *Pasta and burgers.*

LINCOLN
◊ ⑪ **Mountain Club on Loon $$–$$$**
90 Loon Mountain Road, Route 112, Lincoln, NH 03521. Tel: 800/229-7829; www.mtnclub.com.
351 rooms.

⑪ **Clement Room Grille/ Woodstock Station $$**
Route 3, Main Street, North Woodstock, NH. Tel: 603/745-3951. *Fine dining in the Grille; pub fare in Woodstock Station.*

TOUR 20
HOLDERNESS
◊ ⑪ **The Manor on Golden Pond $$$$**
Shepard Hill Road, Holderness, NH 03245. Tel: 603/968-3348; www.manorongoldenpond.com.
25 rooms.

⑪ **Walters Basin $$**
By the bridge, Holderness, NH. Tel: 603/968-4412. *Cajun cuisine.*

CENTER SANDWICH
⑪ **Corner House Inn $–$$**
22 Main Street, Center Sandwich, NH 03227. Tel: 603/284-6219. *New England country dining.*

WOLFEBORO
⑪ **Wolfboro Inn $–$$**
90 North Main Street, Wolfeboro, NH. Tel: 603/569-3016. *Pub known for seafood and steaks.*
44 rooms

MEREDITH
◊ **Inns and Spa at Mill Falls $$$**
312 Daniel Webster Highway, Meredith, NH 03253. Tel: 603/279-6797; www.millfalls.com.
158 rooms.

TOUR 21
FREEPORT
◊ **Kendall Tavern $$–$$$**
213 Main Street, Freeport, ME 04032. Tel: 207/865-1338; www.kendalltavern.com.
7 rooms.

◊ **Maine Idyll Motor Court $–$$**
1411 US Route 1, Freeport, ME 04032. Tel: 207/865-4201; www.maineidyll.com.
20 cottages.

◊ ⑪ **Harraseeket Inn $$$$**
162 Main Street, Freeport, ME 04032. Tel: 207/865-9377; www.harraseeketinn.com.
84 rooms.

⑪ **Jameson Tavern $$–$$$**
115 Main Street, Freeport, ME. Tel: 207/865-4196. *Mainly seafood classics.*

BRUNSWICK
⑪ **Scarlet Begonias $**
212 Main Street, Brunswick, ME 04011. Tel: 207/721-0403. *Simple seafood bistro.*

BATH
◊ **Galen C Moses House $$–$$$**
1009 Washington Street, Bath, ME 04530. Tel: 207/442-8771; www.galenmoses.com.
5 rooms.

WISCASSET
⑪ **Sarah's Café $**
Main Street, Wiscasset, ME. Tel: 207/882-7504. *Pizzas, lobster, seafood.*

ROCKLAND
◇ **LimeRock Inn $$$**
96 Lime Rock Street, Rockland, ME 04841. Tel: 207/594-2257; www.limerockinn.com. 8 rooms.

⊕ **Café Miranda $$**
15 Oak Street, Rockland, ME. Tel: 207/594-2034. *Fun bistro.*

ROCKPORT
◇ **Samoset Resort $$$–$$$$**
220 Warrenton Street, Rockport, ME 04856. Tel: 207/594-2511 or 800/341-1650; www.samosetresort.com. 178 rooms.

CAMDEN
◇ **Camden Windward House $$–$$$$**
6 High Street, Camden, ME 04843. Tel: 207/236-9656; www.windwardhouse.com. 8 rooms.

◇ **Maine Stay $$$–$$$$**
22 High Street, Camden, ME 04843. Tel: 207/236-9636; www.mainestay.com. 8 rooms.

⊕ **Atlantica $**
I Bayview Landing, Camden, ME. Tel: 207/236-6011. *Seafood bistro. Dinner. Closed Tue, Wed.*

TOUR 22
PORTLAND
◇ **The Danforth $$–$$$**
163 Danforth Street, Portland, ME 04102. Tel: 207/879-8755 or 800/991-6557; www.danforthmaine.com. 7 rooms.

◇ ⊕ **Portland Regency Hotel $$$$**
20 Milk Street, Portland, ME 04101. Tel: 207/774-4200 or 800/727-3436; www.theregency.com. 95 rooms.

⊕ **Back Bay Grill $$**
65 Portland Street, Portland, ME. Tel: 207/772-8833. *Modern New England cuisine; innovative appetizers; extensive wine list.*

⊕ **Fore Street Restaurant $$**
288 Fore Street, Portland, ME. Tel: 207/775-2717. *Modern American cuisine.*

TOUR 23
BETHEL
◇ ⊕ **Bethel Inn Resort $$$–$$$$**
On the Common, Bethel, ME 04217. Tel: 207/824-2175 or 800/654-0125; www.bethelinn.com. 40 rooms.

◇ **L'Auberge Country Inn $$–$$$$**
15 L'Auberge Lane, Bethel, ME 04217. Tel: 207/824-2774; www.laubergecountryinn.com. *Also has excellent bistro.* 6 rooms.

⊕ **Sunday River Brew Pub $–$$**
Route 2 at Sunday River Road, Bethel, ME. Tel: 207/824-4253. *Informal brew-pub fare.*

RANGELEY
◇ **Rangeley Inn $$–$$$**
2443 Main Street, Rangeley, ME 04970. Tel: 207/864-3341 or 800/666-3687; www.rangeleyinn.com. 50 rooms.

⊕ **The Red Onion $**
Main Street, Rangeley, ME. Tel: 207/864-5022. *Pizzas, steaks; informal.*

KINGFIELD
⊕ **The Orange Cat Café $**
329 Main Street, Kingfield, ME 04947. Tel: 207/265-2860. *Cheerful, soup and sandwiches.*

FARMINGTON
⊕ **Homestead Bakery $**
186 Broadway Street, Farmington, ME. Tel: 207/778-6162. *Down-home dishes.*

Practical Information

The addresses, telephone numbers, websites and opening times of the attractions and Tourist Information Offices mentioned in the tours, are listed below tour by tour.

TOUR 1

ⓘ Cambridge Visitor's Information Center, Harvard Square, Cambridge, MA 02138. Tel: 617/441-2884; www.cambridge-usa.org

ⓘ Lexington Visitor Center, 1875 Massachusetts Avenue, Lexington, MA 02421. Tel: 781/862-2480; www. lexingtonchamber.org

ⓘ Minute Man Visitor Center, Route 2A, Lexington, MA 02420. Tel: 978/369-6993; www.nps.gov/mima

ⓘ Concord Visitor Center, 58 Main Street, Concord, MA 01742. Tel: 978/369-3120; www. concordchamberof commerce.org

ⓘ North Bridge Visitor Center, 174 Liberty Street, Concord, MA 01742. Tel: 978/369-6993; www.nps.gov/mima

❶ National Heritage Museum
33 Marrett Road (Route 2A), Lexington. Tel: 781/ 861-6559; www.monh.org. Open Mon–Sat 10–5, Sun noon–5.

❷ Munroe Tavern
1332 Massachusetts Avenue. Lexington. Tel: 781/862-1703; www.lexingtonhistory.org. Open Apr to mid-Jun weekends; mid-Jun to Nov 2 11–3.

❸ Lexington
Buckman Tavern 1 Bedford Street. Tel: 781/ 862-1703; www.lexington-history.org. Open Apr–Nov 2 daily 10–4.

Hancock-Clarke House 36 Hancock Street. Tel: 781/861-0928; www.lexingtonhistory.org. Open Apr–Jun weekends; Jul–Oct daily 11–2.

❹ Minute Man National Historical Park
Route 2A, Lexington. Tel: 978/369-6993; www.nps.gov.mima

❺ Concord
The Wayside 455 Lexington Road. Tel: 978/318-7862; www.nps.gov/mima/ wayside. Open May–Oct.

Orchard House 399 Lexington Road. Tel: 978/369-4118; www.louisamayalcott.org. Open Mon–Sat 10–4.30, Sun 1–4.30; shorter hours on winter weekdays. Closed first 2 weeks Jan.

Concord Museum 200 Lexington Road. Tel: 978/369-9763; www. concordmuseum.org. Open Mon–Sat 9–5, Sun 1–4. Shorter hours in winter.

Ralph Waldo Emerson House 28 Cambridge Turnpike. Tel: 978/369-2236. Open mid-Apr to mid-Oct,Thu–Sat 10–4.30, Sun 1–4.30.

Sleepy Hollow Cemetery Bedford Street, Concord. Tel: 978/318-3233.

Old Manse 269 Monument Street. Tel: 978/369-3909; www.old manse.org. Open mid-Apr to Oct, 10–5. Sun noon–5.

❻ Walden Pond
Walden Pond State Reservation, Route 126 Walden Street. Tel: 978/ 369-3254.

❼ Gropius House
68 Baker Bridge Road, Lincoln. Tel: 781/259-8098; www.historicnewengland. org. Open Jun to mid-Oct, Wed–Sun. Weekends in winter. Phone for hours.

❽ DeCordova Museum
51 Sandy Pond Road, Lincoln. Tel: 781/259-8355; www.decordova.org. Open Tue–Sun 10–5. Park daily, daylight hours.

Recommended trips
South Bridge Boathouse 496 Main Street, Concord. Tel: 978/369-9438; www.canoeconcord.com. Open Apr–Oct daily.

TOUR 2

ⓘ Boston Common Visitor Information Center, 147 Tremont Street. Tel: 617/536-4100; www.bostonusa.com

ⓘ Marblehead Information Booth, Pleasant and Spring streets, Marblehead, MA 01945. Tel: 781/631-2868; www. marbleheadchamber.org

ⓘ National Park Service Regional Visitor Center, New Liberty and Essex streets, Salem, MA 01970. Tel: 978/740-1650; www.nps.gov/sama

ⓘ Stage Fort Park Information Center, Hough Avenue, Gloucester, MA 01930. Tel: 978/281-8865 (seasonal); 33 Commercial Street. Tel: 978/283-1601; www.gloucesterma.com

ⓘ Rockport Chamber of Commerce, 3 Whistlestop Mall, Rockport, MA 01966. Tel: 978/546-6575; www.rockportusa.com

❷ Marblehead
Jeremiah Lee Mansion 161 Washington Street. Tel: 781/631-1768; www. marbleheadmuseum.org. Open Jun–Oct, Tue–Sat 10–4.

Marblehead Museum and Historical Society 170 Washington Street. Tel: 781/631-1768. www. marbleheadmuseum.org. Open Tue–Sat 10–4. Closed Fri Nov–May.

❸ Salem
Salem Witch Museum Washington Square

North. Tel: 978/744-1692; www.salemwitchmuseum. com. Open daily 10–5 (till 7pm Jul, Aug).

Salem Witch Village 282 Derby Street. Tel: 978/740-9229; www.salemwitchvillage.net. Open Apr–Oct, daily 10–6 (extended hours Jul, Aug, Oct). Nov–Mar 11–4.

Witch House 310 Essex Street. Tel: 978/744-8815; www. salemweb.com/witch-house. Open mid-May to Nov 10–5 (extended hours in Oct).

Peabody Essex Museum East India Square. Tel: 978/745-9500; www. pem.org. Open daily 10–5.

Salem Maritime National Historic Site 193 Derby Street. Tel: 978/ 740-1660; www.nps.gov/ sama. Open daily 9–5.

❻ Hammond Castle Museum
80 Hesperus Avenue, Gloucester. Tel: 978/283-2080; www.hammond castle.org. Open. Mon–Fri 10–4. Seasonal.

❼ Gloucester
Cape Ann Museum 27 Pleasant Street. Tel: 978/ 283-0455; www.cape annmuseum.org. Open Tue–Sat 10–5, Sun 1–4. Closed Feb.

Gloucester Maritime Heritage Center 23 Harbor Loop. Tel: 978/ 281-0470; www.gloucester maritimecenter.org. Open end May to mid-Oct daily 10–5. Off-season weekends 10–5.30.

❽ Rocky Neck and Beauport
Beauport Sleeper-McCann House 75 Eastern Point Boulevard, Beauport, Gloucester. Tel: 978/283-0800; www. historicnewengland.org. Open Jun to mid-Oct Tue–Sat 10–4, till 7pm Thu Jul–Aug.

Practical Information

[9] Rockport
Rockport Art Association Gallery
12 Main Street. Tel: 978/546-6604; www.rockport artassn.org

[10] Pigeon Cove
Paper House
52 Pigeon Hill Street. Tel: 978/546-2629; www. paperhouserockport.com. *Open daily Apr–Oct, 10–5.*

[11] Essex
Shipbuilding Museum
66 Main Street. Tel: 978/768-7541; www.essexship buildingmuseum.org. *Open Jun to mid-Oct Wed–Sun 10–5; rest of year weekends.*

[12] Ipswich
Whipple House Museum
Route 1A, 1 South Village Green. Tel: 978/356-2811; www.ipswichmuseum.org. *Open May–Oct, Wed–Sat 10–4, Sun 1–4 (last tour 3).*

Heard House Museum
Route 1A, 54 South Main Street. Tel: 978/356-2811; www.ipswichmuseum.org. *Open May–Oct, Wed–Sat 10–4, Sun 1–4 (last tour 3).*

Castle Hill/Crane's Beach
290 Argilla Road. Tel: 978/356-4351 (beach 4354); www.thetrustees.org

[13] Plum Island and the Parker River National Wildlife Refuge
Plum Island Turnpike, Newburyport. Tel: 978/465-5753; www.fws.gov/ northeast/parkerriver

[14] Newburyport
Custom House Maritime Museum
25 Water Street. Tel: 978/462-8681; www.custom housemaritimemuseum.org. *Open mid-May to mid-Dec Thu–Sat 11–4, Sun 12–4.*

Cushing House Museum
98 High Street. Tel: 978/462-2681; www.newbury hist.com. *Open May–Oct, Tue–Fri 10–4, Sat noon–4.*

For history buffs
Abbot Hall
188 Washington Street. Tel: 781/631-0000; www. marblehead.org. *Open daily 8–5; end May to mid-Oct weekends 10–5.*

Special to…
The House of the Seven Gables
115 Derby Street. Tel: 978/744-0991; www.7gables. org. *Open daily 10–5 (to 7, Jul–Oct). Closed early Jan.*

Woodman's of Essex
121 Main Street, Essex. Tel: 978/768-6057 or 800/649-1773; www.woodmans. com. *Open summer 11–10 (closes 8/9pm in winter).*

Recommended walks
Halibut Point State Park
Off Route 127, Rockport. Tel: 978/546-2997.

Back to nature
Wolf Hollow
144 Essex Road, Ipswich. Tel: 978/356-0216; www. wolfhollowipswich.org

---

TOUR 3

[i] Cape Cod Chamber of Commerce, Hyannis, MA 02601. Tel: 508/362-3225; www.capecodcham ber.org

[i] Cape Cod Canal Chamber of Commerce, 70 Main Street, Buzzards Bay, MA 02532.
Tel: 508/759-6000; www. capecodcanalchamber.org

[i] Yarmouth Area Chamber of Commerce, 424 Route 28, West Yarmouth, MA 02673. Tel: 508/778-1008; www. yarmouthcapecod.com

[i] Dennis Chamber of Commerce, Routes 134/28, West Dennis, MA 02760.
Tel: 508/398-3568; www.dennischamber.com

[i] Brewster Chamber of Commerce, Brewster Town Hall, 2198 Main Street, Brewster, MA 02631. Tel: 508/896-3500; www.brewstercapecod.org

[i] Eastham Tourist Information Booth, Route 6 at Governor Prence Road, Eastham, MA 02642. Tel: 508/255-3444; www.

easthamchamber.com (seasonal).

[i] Wellfleet Chamber of Commerce Information Booth, off Route 6, South Wellfleet, MA 02667. Tel: 508/349-2510; www. wellfleetchamber.com

[i] Provincetown Chamber of Commerce, 307 Commercial Street, Provincetown, MA 02657. Tel: 508/487-3424; www ptownchamber.com

[i] Chatham Chamber of Commerce, 533 Main Street, Chatham, MA 02633. Tel: 508/945-5199; www.chathaminfo.com. Also at 2377 Main Street, South Chatham (same telephone number as above).

[2] Sandwich
Thomas Dexter Grist Mill
Water Street. Tel: 508/888-4910 (town hall). *Open mid-Jun to mid-Sep, daily 10–4.*

Hoxie House
18 Water Street. Tel: 508/888-4910. *Open Jun to mid-Sep, daily 10–4.45.*

Thornton W. Burgess Museum
4 Water Street (Route 130). Tel: 508/888-4668; www.thorntonburgess.org. *Open May–Oct, Mon–Sat 10–4, Sun 1–4.*

[3] Barnstable
Sturgis Library
Route 6A. Tel: 508/362-6636; www.sturgislibrary. org. *Call for hours.*

[4] Yarmouth
Captain Bangs Hallet House
11 Strawberry Lane. Tel: 508/362-3021; www.hsoy. org. *Open Jun to mid-Oct, Thu–Sun.*

Winslow-Crocker House
250 Route 6A. Tel: 617/227-3957, ext. 256; www. historicnewengland.org. *Open Jun to mid-Oct.*

[5] Dennis
Josiah Dennis Manse Museum

77 Nobscusset Road, Dennis. Tel: 508/385-2232; www.dennishistsoc.org. *Open end Jun–Aug. Phone for times.*

Cape Playhouse
820 Main Street, Dennis. Tel: 508/385-3838; www. capeplayhouse.com. *Open mid-Jun to mid-Sep.*

Cape Cod Museum of Art
Route 6A, Dennis. Tel: 508/385-4477; www.ccmoa. org. *Open end May to mid-Oct Tue–Sat 10–5 (Thu till 8), Sun noon–5.*

[6] Brewster
Brewster Historical Society Museum
Route 6A, 3171 Main Street, East Brewster. Tel: 508/896-9521; www. brewsterhistoricalsociety. org. *Open Thu–Sat 1–4.*

[8] Eastham
Cape Cod National Seashore
Salt Pond Visitor Center, Route 6. Tel: 508/255-3421; www.nps.gov/caco. *Open daily 9–4.30 (later in summer).*

Eastham Windmill
Opposite Town Hall. www.easthamhistorical.org. *Open Jul–Aug Mon–Sat 10–5, Sun 1–5.*

[12] Provincetown
Pilgrim Monument and Provincetown Museum
High Pole Hill Road. Tel: 508/487-1310; www.pilgrim-monument. org. *Open Apr–Nov daily 9–5 (later mid-Jun to mid-Sep).*

[13] Chatham
Chatham Lighthouse
Chatham Harbor. Tel: 508/430-0628; www.lighthouse.cc/ chatham. *Call for details.*

Special to…
Sandwich Glass Museum
129 Main Street. Tel: 508/888-0251; www.sandwich glassmuseum.org. *Open Feb–Mar, Wed–Sun 9.30–4; Apr–Dec, daily 9.30–5.*

For children
Heritage Museums and Gardens
67 Grove Street. Tel: 508/888-3300; www.heritage museumsandgardens.org. *Open Apr–Oct daily 10–5.*

Green Briar Nature Center & Jam Kitchen
6 Discovery Hill Road, East Sandwich. Tel: 508/888-6870; www.thornton burgess.org. *Open Jan–Mar, Tue–Sat 10–4; Apr–Dec, Mon–Sat 10–4, Sun 1–4.*

Cape Cod Museum of Natural History
Route 6A, Brewster. Tel: 508/896-3867; www.ccmnh.org. *Open Jun–Sep daily 9.30–4; Feb–Mar 12–4; rest of year Wed–Sun 10–4. Closed Jan.*

Scenic route
Cape Cod Central Railroad
252 Main Street, Hyannis. Tel: 508/771-3800; www.capetrain.com. *Scenic excursions daily end May–Oct; also lunch and dinner trains.*

TOUR 4

ℹ️ Greater Springfield CVB, 1441 Main Street, Springfield, MA 01103. Tel: 413/787-1548; www.valleyvisitor.com

ℹ️ Riverfront Park Information Center, 1200 West Columbus Avenue, Springfield, MA 01115. Tel: 413/750-2980.

ℹ️ Stockbridge Information Booth, Main Street, Stockbridge, MA 01262. Tel: 413/298-5200; www. stockbridgechamber.org

ℹ️ Lenox Chamber of Commerce, 5 Walker Street, Lenox, MA 01240. Tel: 413/637-3646; www.lenox.org

ℹ️ Pittsfield Visitor Information Center, 109 South Street, Pittsfield, MA 01201. Tel: 413/743-4500; www.berkshires.com

ℹ️ Williamstown Information Booth, Routes 2 and 7.

ℹ️ Williamstown Chamber of Commerce, 70 Denison Park Drive, Williamstown, MA 01267. Tel: 413/458-9077; www.williamstownchamber.com

ℹ️ Shelburne Falls Village Information Center, 75 Bridge Street, Shelburne Falls, MA 01370. Tel: 413/625-2544; www.shelburnefalls.com

ℹ️ Upper Pioneer Valley Visitors Center, 18 Miner Street (exit 26, I–91), Greenfield, MA 01301. Tel: 413/773-9393; www.mohawktrail.com

ℹ️ Northampton Area Visitors Center, 99 Pleasant Street, Northampton, MA 01060. Tel: 413/584-1900; www.explore northampton.com

5 Stockbridge
Red Lion Inn
30 Main Street. Tel: 413/298-5545; www.redlioninn.com

Norman Rockwell Museum
Route 183. Tel: 413/298-4100; www.nrm.org. *Open daily 10–5 (4 on weekdays Nov–Apr).*

Chesterwood
Off Route 183. Tel: 413/298-3579; www.chester wood.org. *Open mid-May to mid-Oct, daily 10–5.*

Naumkeag
Prospect Hill Road. Tel: 413/298-8146; www. thetrustees.org. *Open end May to mid-Oct, daily 10–5.*

Berkshire Botanical Garden
Junction Routes 183 and 102. Tel: 413/298-3926; www.berkshirebotanical. org. *Open May to mid-Oct, daily 10–5.*

7 Lenox
Tanglewood
Tel: 617/266-1492; www. bso.org. *Season early Jul–end Aug.*

8 Arrowhead
780 Holmes Road, Pittsfield. Tel: 413/442-1793; www.mobydick.org. *Open end May to mid-Oct. daily 9.30–5 or by appointment.*

9 Hancock Shaker Village
Junction Routes 20 and 41, Pittsfield. Tel: 413/443-0188; www.hancockshaker village.org. *Open end May to mid-Oct, daily 10–5; rest of year guided tour only; phone for times.*

10 Williamstown
Sterling and Francine Clark Art Institute
225 South Street. Tel: 413/458-2303; www.clarkart. edu. *Open Tue–Sun 10–5; also Mon Jul–Aug.*

Williams College Museum of Art
Main Street. Tel: 413/597-2429; www.wcma.org. *Open Tue–Sat 10–5, Sun 1–5.*

Williamstown Theatre Festival
Tel: 413/597-3400; www.wtfestival.org. *Open Jul–Aug.*

L North Adams
MASS MoCA
87 Marshall Street. Tel: 413/662-2111; www.mass moca.org. *Open Wed–Mon 11–5 (daily 10–6 Jul–Aug).*

13 Deerfield
The Street. Tel: 413/775-7214; www.historic-deefield.org. *Open Apr–Dec daily 9.30–4.30.*

For history buffs
Emily Dickinson Museum
280 Main Street, Amherst. Tel: 413/542-8161; www. emilydickinsonmuseum.org

Special to...
Basketball Hall of Fame/ Naismith Memorial
1000 West Columbus Avenue, Springfield. Tel: 413/781-6500; www.hoop hall.com. *Open Mon–Fri 10–4, Sat–Sun 10–5.*

For children
Six Flags New England
Route 159, Agawam. Tel: 413/786-9300; www. sixflags.com. *Open summer daily; spring, fall weekends. hours vary.*

Magic Wings Butterfly Conservatory and Garden
Routes 5 and 10, South Deerfield. Tel: 413/665-2805; www.magicwings. com. *Open daily 9–5 (to 6 end May–early Sep).*

For history buffs
Col John Ashley House
Cooper Hill Road, Ashley Falls. Tel: 413/298-3239; www.thetrustee.org. *Open Jun to mid-Oct, Sat–Sun 10–5.*

Back to nature
Barthlomew's Cobble
Weatogue Road off Route 7A, Ashley Falls. Tel: 413/229-8600; www.thetrust ees.org. *Open daily dawn–dusk, museum 9–4.30. Closed Sun, Mon Dec–Mar*

Pleasant Valley Wildlife Sanctuary
472 West Mountain Road, Lenox. Tel: 413/637-0320; www.massaudubon.org. *Open Tue–Fri 9–5, Sat–Sun 10–4 (also Mon in summer).*

TOUR 5

ℹ️ Boston Common Visitor Information Center, 147 Tremont Street. Tel: 617/536-4100; www.bostonusa.com, www.thefreedomtrail.org

ℹ️ Boston National Historical Park Visitor Center, 15 State Street. Tel: 617/242-5642; www.nps.gov/bost

ℹ️ Charlestown Navy Yard Visitor Center. Constitution Road, Charlestown. Tel: 617/242-5601; www.nps.gov/bost

2 State House
Beacon Street. Tel: 617/727-3676; www.sec.state. ma.us/trs. *Tours weekdays.*

Practical Information

ⓘ Tourist Information Office
⑫ Number on tour

⑨ Old South Meeting House
310 Washington Street.
Tel: 617/482-6439;
www.oldsouthmeeting
house.org. *Open daily.*

⑩ Old State House
Corner of State and
Washington streets. Tel:
617/720-1713; www.
bostonhistory.org. *Museum
open daily 9–5 (6 Jul–Aug).*

⑪ Faneuil Hall
Merchants Row. Tel: 617/
242-5642; www.thefree
domtrail.org. *Open daily
9–5.*

⑮ Paul Revere House
19 North Square. Tel:
617/523-2338; www.paul
reverehouse.org. *Open
daily 9.30–4.15 (5.15 mid-
Apr to Oct). Closed Mon,
Jan–Mar.*

⑱ USS Constitution
Pier 1, Charlestown Navy
Yard. Tel: 617/242-5670/
5671; www.ussconstitu-
tion.navy.mil/. *Tours Tue–Sun
10–4.30*

⑲ Bunker Hill Monument
Monument Square,
Charlestown. Tel: 617/242-
5641; www.nps.gov/bost.
Open daily 9–5.

Special to…
Omni Parker House
60 School Street. Tel: 617/
227-8600; www.omni
hotels.com

TOUR 6

ⓘ Boston Common
Visitor Information Center,
147 Tremont Street.
Tel: 617/536-4100;
www.bostonusa.com

ⓘ Boston National
Historical Park Visitor
Center, 15 State Street.
Tel: 617/242-5642;
www.nps.gov/bost

❶ New England Aquarium
Central Wharf. Tel: 617/
973-5200; www.neaq.org.
*Open daily 9–5 (6 Sat–Sun);
later in summer.*

❸ Faneuil Hall
See Tour 5.

❻ Otis House Museum
141 Cambridge Street.
Tel: 617/227-3956; www.
historicnewengland.org.
Open Wed–Sun 11–4.30

❼ Black Heritage Trail
Museum of African
American History/Abiel
Smith School
46 Joy Street. Tel: 617/720-
2991. *Open Mon–Sat 10–4.*

❽ Nichols House Museum
55 Mount Vernon Street.
Tel: 617/227-6993; www.
nicholshousemuseum.org.
*Open Tue–Sat noon–4
(Thu–Sat only Nov–Mar).*

Special to…
Durgin-Park
340 Faneuil Hall Market-
place. Tel: 617/227-2038;
www.durgin-park.com

Scenic routes
Boston Duck Tours
Prudential Center or
Museum of Science. Tel:
617/267-3825; www.
bostonducktours.com. *Late
Mar–Nov.*

TOUR 7

ⓘ Cambridge Visitor's
Information Center,
Harvard Square,
Cambridge, MA 02139.
Tel: 617/497-1630;
www.cambridge-usa.org

ⓘ Harvard Information
Center, Holyoke Center
Arcade, 1350
Massachusetts Avenue,
Cambridge, MA 02138.
Tel: 617/495-1573;
www.harvard.edu

❼ Fogg and Busch-Reisinger Art Museums
32 Quincy Street.
Tel: 617/495-9400.
Currently closed.

❽ Arthur M. Sackler Museum
485 Broadway.
Tel: 617/495-9400. *Open
Mon–Sat 10–5, Sun 1–5.*

❾ Memorial Hall
45 Quincy Street for
Sanders Theater perfor-
mances. Tel: 617/496-2222.

❿ Museum of Natural History
26 Oxford Street. Tel: 617/
495-3045. *Open daily 9–5.*

⓭ Brattle Street
Hooper-Lee-Nichols
House
159 Brattle Street.
Tel: 617/547-4252; *Open
Tue, Thu 2–5.*

⓮ Longfellow House
105 Brattle Street.
Tel: 617/876-4491;
www.nps.gov/long. *Phone
for tour details.*

TOUR 8

ⓘ 45 Pratt Street,
Hartford, CT 06103.
Tel: 860/244-0253;
www.enjoyhartford.com

❷ Old State House
800 Main Street. Tel: 860/
522-6766; www.ctosh.org.
Open Tue–Sat 11–4.

❸ Travelers Tower
1 Tower Square Tel: 860/
277-4208. *Tours mid-May
to Oct, Mon–Fri 10–2.30.*

❹ Wadsworth Atheneum
600 Main Street. Tel: 860/
278-2670; www.wads
worthatheneum.org.
Open Tue–Sun 11–5.

❼ Bushnell Park Carousel
Jewell Street. Tel: 860/585-
5411; www.thecarousel
museum.org. *Open late
Apr–late Oct, Tue–Sun 11–5.*

❽ State Capitol
210 Capitol Avenue. Tel:
860/240-0222; www.
cga.ct.gov/capitoltours.
*Tours Mon–Fri 9.15–1.15
(2.15 Jul–Aug); also Sat
10.15–2.15 Apr–Oct.*

❾ Museum of Connecticut History
231 Capitol Avenue.
Tel: 860/617-6535; www.
museumofhistory.org.
*Open Mon–Fri 9–4, Sat
9–3.*

❿ Mark Twain House and Museum
351 Farmington Avenue.
Tel: 860/247-0998;
www.marktwainhouse.org.
*Open Mon–Sat 9.30–5.30,
Sun noon–5.30. Closed Tue
Jan–Mar.*

⓫ Harriet Beecher Stowe Center
77 Forest Street. Tel: 860/
522-9258; www.harriet
beecherstowecenter.org.
*Open Mon–Sat, 9.30–4.30,
Sun noon–4.30. Closed Mon
mid-Oct to May.*

⓬ Connecticut Historical Society Museum
1 Elizabeth Street. Tel: 860/
236-5621; www.chs.org.
*Open Tue–Fri 12–5, Sat
9–5.*

⓭ Noah Webster House
227 South Main Street,
West Hartford. Tel: 860/
521-5362; www.noah
websterhouse.org. *Open
Thu–Mon 1–4.*

Back to nature
Elizabeth Park Rose
Garden
Prospect Avenue. Tel: 860/
231-9443; www.elizabeth
park.org. *Open daily.*

For history buffs
Historic Wethersfield
www.historicwethers
field.org

TOUR 9

ⓘ Greater New Haven
Convention and Visitors
Bureau, 169 Orange Street,
New Haven, CT 06510.
Tel: 203/777-8550;
www.visitnewhaven.com

ⓘ INFO New Haven,
Downtown New Haven's
Visitor Info Center, 1000
Chapel Street, New
Haven, CT 06510. Tel:
203/773-9494; www.visit-
newhaven.com.

ⓘ Yale University Visitor
Information Center, 149
Elm Street, New Haven,
CT 06520. Tel: 203/432-
2300; www.yale.edu

5 Yale University Art Gallery
1111 Chapel Street at York Street. Tel: 203/432-0600; www.artgallery.yale.edu. Open Tue–Sat 10–5, Sun 1–6.

6 Yale Center for British Art
1080 Chapel Street. Tel: 203/432-2800; www.yale.edu/ycba. Open Tue–Sat 10–5, Sun noon–5.

7 Yale Repertory Theatre
Corner of Chapel and York streets. Tel: 203/432-1234; www.yale.edu/yalerep. Open Sep–May.

11 Beinecke Rare Book and Manuscript Library
121 Wall Street Tel: 203/432-2977; www.library.yale.edu/beinecke. Open Mon–Thu 8.30–8, Fri 8.30–5.

TOUR 10

$\boxed{i}$ 45 Pratt Street, Hartford, CT 06103. Tel: 860/244-0253; www.enjoyhartford.com

$\boxed{i}$ Litchfield Hills Information Booth, Route 202, On-the-Green, Litchfield, CT 06759. Tel: 860/567-4506; www.litchfieldhills.com

1 Litchfield
Tapping Reeve House and Law School
Route 63 South, 82 South Street. Tel: 860/567-4501; www.litchfieldhistoricalsociety.org. Open Apr–Nov, Tue–Sat 11–5, Sun 1–5.

Litchfield History Museum
7 South Street. Tel: 860/567-4501 www.litchfieldhistoricalsociety.org. Open mid-Apr to mid-Nov, Tue–Sat 11–5, Sun 1–5.

3 Lake Waramaug
Hopkins Vineyard
25 Hopkins Road, New Preston. Tel: 860/868-7954; www.hopkinsvineyard.com. Open May–Dec daily;
Jan–Feb Fri–Sun; Mar–Apr Wed–Sun. Phone for times.

6 Kent
Sloane-Stanley Museum and Kent Furnace
Route 7. Tel: 860/927-3849; www.cultureandtourism.org. Open mid-May to Oct, Wed–Sun 10–4.

Connecticut Antique Machinery Association Museum
Route 7. Tel: 860/927-0050; www.ctamachinery.com. Open May–Oct, Wed–Sun 10–4.

8 Cornwall Bridge to West Cornwall
Clarke Outdoors
163 Route 7, West Cornwall. Tel: 860/672-6365; www.clarkeoutdoors.com. Open mid-Mar to Dec.

9 Lime Rock Park
Routes 7 and 112, Lakeville. Tel: 860/435-5000; www.limerock.com. Regular meets Apr–Nov.

Special to…
White Flower Farm
Route 63. Tel: 800/503-9624; www.whiteflowerfarm.com. Open daily Apr–Oct, daily 9–5.30.

Henderson Cultural Center at Hunt Hill Farm
44 Upland Road, New Milford. Tel: 860/355-0300; www.hunthillfarmtrust.org. Open daily 10–5.

Cornwall Bridge Pottery
Route 7, between Routes 45 and 4. Tel: 800/501-6545; www.cbpots.com. Open Mon–Fri noon–5, Sat–Sun 10.30–5.30.

Recommended walks
Kent Falls State Park
Route 7. Tel: 860/927-3238; www.dep.state.ct.us. Open daily 8am–dusk.

TOUR 11

$\boxed{i}$ Greater New Haven Convention and Visitors Bureau, 169 Orange Street, New Haven, CT 06511; www.visitnewhaven.com. Tel: 203/777-8550.
$\boxed{i}$ Info New Haven, 1000 Chapel Street. Tel: 203/773-9494.

1 Branford
Nathaniel Harrison House
124 Main Street. Tel: 203/488-4828; www.branfordhistory.org. Phone for hours.

3 Guilford
Henry Whitfield State Museum
248 Old Whitfield Street. Tel: 203/453-2457; www.whitfieldmuseum.com. Open Apr to mid-Dec, Wed–Sun 10–4.30.

Hyland House
84 Boston Street. Tel: 203/453-9477; www.hylandhouse.com. Open Jun–Oct, Tue–Sat 10–4.30, Sun noon–4.30.

Thomas Griswold House Museum
171 Boston Street. Tel: 203/453-3176; www.thomasgriswoldhouse.com. Open Jun–Sep, Tue–Sun 11–4; Oct weekends.

4 Madison
Hammonasset Beach State Park
Route 1. Tel: 203/245-2785; www.dep.state.ct.us. Open daily 8–sunset.

5 Old Saybrook
General William Hart House
350 Main Street. Tel: 860/388-2622; www.oldsaybrook.com. Open limited hours.

6 Essex
Connecticut River Museum
67 Main Street, Steamboat Dock. Tel: 860/767-8269; www.ctrivermuseum.org. Open Tue–Sun 10–5.

Pratt House Museum
19 West Avenue. Tel: 860/767-1191; www.essexhistory.org. Open Jun–Sep, Sat–Sun 1–4.

7 East Haddam
Goodspeed Opera House
Route 82. Tel: 860/873-8668; www.goodspeed.org. Open Apr–Dec, Wed–Sun.

Nathan Hale Schoolhouse
Main Street. Open end May–early Sep, Sat–Sun noon–4.

8 Gillette Castle
Gillette Castle State Park
67 River Road. Tel: 860/526-2336. Open, castle: Jun to mid-Oct, daily 10–5; park: daily 8am–sunset.

9 Old Lyme
Florence Griswold Museum
96 Lyme Street. Tel: 860/434-5542; www.flogris.org. Open Tue–Sat 10–5, Sun, 1–5.

Lyme Academy College of Fine Arts
84 Lyme Street. Tel: 860/434-5232; www.lymeacademy.edu. Open Mon–Sat 10–4.

10 New London
Hempsted Houses
11 Hempsted Street. Tel: 860/443-7949; www.ctlandmarks.org. Open mid-May to mid-Oct, Thu–Sun noon–4.

US Eagle (when in port)
US Coast Guard Academy, Mohegan Avenue. Tel: 860/444-8270; www.cga.edu. Open 1–5. Museum daily 9–5.

Lyman-Allyn Art Museum
625 Williams Street. Tel: 860/443-2545; www.lymanallyn.org. Open Tue–Sat 10–5, Sun 1–5.

Monte Cristo Cottage
325 Pequot Avenue. Tel: 860/443-5378; www.theoneill.org. Open end May–early Sep, Thu–Sun 10–5.

Eugene O'Neill Theater Center
305 Great Neck Road, Waterford. Tel: 860/443-5378; www.theoneill.org

11 USS *Nautilus*
Naval Submarine Base, 1 Crystal Lake Road, Groton. Tel: 860/694-3174; www.ussnautilus.org. Open daily 9–5, Tue 1–5; Nov to mid-May 9–4, closed Tue.

Practical Information

12 Noank
Abbott's Lobster-in-the-Rough
117 Pearl Street.
Tel: 860/536-7719; www.abbotts-lobster.com. *Open Jun–Aug, daily; weekends in May and Sep to mid-Oct.*

13 Mystic
Mystic Seaport
75 Greenmanville Avenue.
Tel: 860/572-5315; www.mysticseaport.org. *Open daily 9–5, winter 10–4.*

Mystic Aquarium
55 Coogan Boulevard. Tel: 860/572-5955; www.mysticaquarium.org. *Open daily 9–6 (10–5 Mon–Fri winter).*

14 Stonington
Old Lighthouse Museum
7 Water Street. Tel: 860/535-1440; www.stoningtonhistory.org. *Open May–Oct, daily 10–5.*

Scenic routes
The Essex Steam Train and Riverboat Ride
Valley Railroad, 1 Railroad Avenue (off Route 9). Tel: 860/767-0103; www.essexsteamtrain.com. *Open May–Dec.*

Special to…
Mashantucket Pequot Museum and Research Center
110 Pequot Trail, Mashantucket. Tel: 800/411-9671; www.pequotmuseum.org. *Open daily 10–4.*

For history buffs
Fort Griswold Battlefield State Park
57 Fort Street, Groton. Tel: 860/449-6877 (seasonal); www.dep.state.ct.us. *Open daily, 8am–sunset.*

For children
Denison Pequotsepos Nature Center
109 Pequotsepos Road.
Tel: 860/536-1216; www.dpnc.org. *Open Mon–Sat 9–5, Sun 10–4.*

Ocean Beach Park
1225 Ocean Avenue, New London. Tel: 860/447-3031; www.ocean-beach-park.com. *Open late May–early Sep, daily 9am–11pm.*

TOUR 12

i Providence and Warwick Convention and Visitors Bureau, 1 West Exchange Street, Providence, RI 02903. Tel: 401/456-0200 or 800/233-1636; www.pwcvb.com

3 Rhode Island School of Design
Museum of Art
224 Benefit Street. Tel: 401/454-6500; www.risd.edu. *Open Tue–Sun 10–5.*

4 Providence Athenaeum
251 Benefit Street.
Tel: 401/421-6970; www.providenceathenaeum.org. *Open Mon–Thu 9–7, Fri–Sat 9–5, Sun 1–5 (Jun–Aug, Sclosed 1pm Sat, all day Sun). Also closed 2 weeks Aug.*

5 David Winton Bell Gallery
64 College Street. Tel: 401/863-2932; www.brown.edu. *Open Mon–Fri 11–4, Sat and Sun 1–4.*

6 Libraries
John Hay Library
Prospect and College streets. Tel: 401/863-3723. *Open Mon–Fri 9–6, Sun 1–5. Phone in summer, academic holidays.*

7 Brown University
45 Prospect Street, College Hill. Tel: 401/863-1000; www.brown.edu. *Phone for tour dates. and times.*

8 Benefit Street
Governor Stephen Hopkins House
Benefit/Hopkins streets. Tel: 401/421-0694. *Open for tours May–Oct Sat–Sun 1–4.*

10 John Brown House Museum
52 Power Street. Tel: 401/273-7507; www.rihs.org. *Open Apr–Dec, Tue–Sat; Jan–Mar, Fri–Sat (phone for times).*

TOUR 13

i Newport Visitor Information Center, 23 America's Cup Avenue, Newport, RI 02840. Tel: 401/845-9123; www.gonewport.com

1 Museum of Newport History
Thames Street/Washington Square. Tel: 401/841-8770; www.newporthistorical.org. *Open Mon–Thu 10–6, Fri–Sat 10–8, Sun 11–5.*

4 Wanton-Lyman-Hazard House
17 Broadway. Tel: 401/846-0813; www.newporthistorical.org. *Open by tour only; phone for information.*

5 Touro Synagogue
85 Touro Street. Tel: 401/847-4794; www.tourosynagogue.org. *Open for tours May–Jun, Sep–Oct Mon–Fri 1–3, Sun 11–3; Jul–Aug Sun–Fri 10–5. Nov–Apr phone for hours.*

6 The Newport Historical Society
82 Touro Street. Tel: 401/846-0813; www.newporthistorical.org. *Open Tue–Fri 9.30–4.30, Sat am only.*

10 The Redwood Library
50 Bellevue Avenue.
Tel: 401/847-0292; www.redwoodlibrary.org. *Open Tue–Thu 9.30–8; Mon, Fri, Sat 9.30–5.30, Sun 1–5.*

11 Newport Art Museum
76 Bellevue Avenue. Tel: 401/848-8200; www.newportartmuseum.com. *Open Mon–Sat 10–5, Sun noon–5 (4 early Sep–end May).*

12 International Tennis Hall of Fame
194 Bellevue Avenue.
Tel: 401/849-3990; www.tennisfame.com. *Open daily 9.30–5.*

13 Kingscote Mansion
Bellevue Avenue. Tel: 401/847-1000; www.newportmansions.org. *Open end May to mid-Oct, daily 10–5.*

14 The Elms
Bellevue Avenue. Tel: 401/847-1000; www.newportmansions.org. *Open early Apr–early Jan daily 10–5 (closes at 4 in Oct).*

Chepstow
Narragansett Avenue.
Tel: 401/847-1000. *Open in season, by reservation only.*

15 Château-sur-Mer
Bellevue Avenue. Tel: 401/847-1000; www.newportmansions.org. *Open early Apr to mid-Nov daily 10–5.*

16 Vernon Court
National Museum of American Illustration
Bellevue Avenue. Tel: 401/851-8949; www.americanillustration.org. *Limited opening; phone for hours.*

17 The Breakers
Ochre Point Avenue. Tel: 401/847-1000; www.newportmansions.org. *Open daily 9–5 (10–4 Nov–Apr).*

18 Rosecliff
Bellevue Avenue.
Tel: 401/847-1000; www.newportmansions.org. *Open early Apr to mid-Oct, daily 10–5; late Oct to mid-Nov closes 4; Jan–Mar open weekends.*

19 Astors' Beechwood
580 Bellevue Avenue.
Tel: 401/846-3772; www.astorsbeechwood.com. *Open daily 10–4. Feb–end May Fri–Sun.*

20 Marble House
Bellevue Avenue. Tel: 401/847-1000; www.newportmansions.org. *Open mid-Apr to mid-Oct, daily 10–5; late Oct–early Jan closes 4. House: open weekends Jan–Mar.*

21 Belcourt Castle
657 Bellevue Avenue. Tel: 401/846-0669; www.belcourtcastle.com. *Open most of year, call for info.*

22 Rough Point
Bellevue Avenue. Tel: 401/849-7300; www.newportrestoration.org. *Open mid-Apr–early Nov. Call for times.*

Special to...
Fort Adams State Park
Fort Adams Drive. Tel: 401/847-2400; www.riparks.com. *Open daily dawn–dusk.*

Museum of Yachting
Tel: 401/847-1018; www. moy.org. *Open mid-May to Oct, daily 10–6; closed Tue.*

Scenic Routes
Cliff Walk
Memorial Bouelvard. www.newportcliffwalk.com. *All year.*

TOUR 14

[i] Route 7, Bennington, VT 05201.
Tel: 802/447-3311; www.bennington.com

1 The Bennington Museum
West Main Street. Tel: 802/447-1571; www. benningtonmuseum.org. *Open Thu–Tue 10–5.*

12 Bennington Center for the Arts
44 Gypsy Lane. Tel: 802/442-7158; www.benning toncenterforthearts.org. *Open Tue–Sun 10–5.*

4 Bennington Battle Monument
Monument Circle, Old Bennington, off Route 9. Tel: 802/447-0550; www. historicvermont.org. *Open mid-Apr to Oct, daily 9–5.*

5 Hemmings Sunoco Station
216 Main Street.
Tel: 802/447-9652; www.hemmings.com. *Open daily 7am–9pm.*

8 Potters' Yard
324 County Street.
Tel: 802/447-7531; www. benningtonpotters.com

11 Park-McCullough House
Park and West streets, North Bennington. Tel: 802/442-5441; www.park mcculloghh.org. *Open for tours mid-May to mid-Oct, daily 10–4. Grounds open most of year.*

TOUR 15

[i] Route 7, Bennington, VT 05201. Tel: 802/447-3311; www.bennington.com

[i] The Green, Chester, VT 05143. Tel: 866/216-8722; www.okemovalleyvt.org

1 Arlington
Norman Rockwell Exhibition
Route 7A. Tel: 802/375-6423; www.vmga.org. *Open May–Oct, daily 9–5; Nov–Apr, daily 10–4.*

2 Mt Equinox
Skyline Drive
Toll Road, Route 7A. Tel: 802/362-1114; www.equi noxmountain.com. *Open May–Oct 9am–dusk.*

American Museum of Fly Fishing
Route 7A, 4104 Main Street, Manchester.
Tel: 802/362-3300; www. amff.com. *Open daily 10–4.*

3 Hildene
Robert Todd Lincoln's Hildene
Route 7A, Manchester. Tel: 802/362-1788; www.hil dene.*Open daily 930–4.30.*

6 Bromley Mountain Ski Area
Bromley Mountain, Route 11. Tel: 802/824-5522; www.bromley.com

8 Weston
Vermont Country Store
Route 100. Tel: 802/824-3184; www.vermont countrystore.com. *Open daily 9–5.30.*

Weston Playhouse
On the Green. Tel: 802/824-5288; www.weston playhouse.org. *Open late Jun to mid-Oct.*

9 Ludlow
Okemo Mountain Resort
77 Okemo Ridge Road. Tel: 802/228-4041; www.okemo.com

10 Chester
Green Mountain Railroad
54 Depot Street, Bellows Falls. Tel: 800/707-3530; www.rails-vt.com. *Open late Jun to mid-Oct, daily.*

11 Grafton
Grafton Village Cheese Company
533 Townshend Road.
Tel: 800/472-3866. *Open Mon–Fri 8–4, Sat–Sun 10–4.*

12 Newfane
Historical Society Museum of Windham County
Tel: 802/365-4148; www. newfane.com/historical. *Open late May to mid-Oct, Wed–Sun noon–5.*

13 Brattleboro
Museum and Art Center
10 Vernon Street. Tel: 802/257-0124; www.brattle boromuseum.org. *Open Wed–Mon 11–5.*

TOUR 16

[i] Rutland Chamber of Commerce, Routes 4B and 7 and 256 North Main Street, Rutland, VT 05701. Tel: 802/773-2747; www.rutlandvermont.com

1 Norman Rockwell Museum of Vermont
Route 4E. Tel: 877/773-6095; www.norman rockwellvt.com. *Open daily 9–5 (4 in winter).*

2 Bethel
White River National Fish Hatchery
Route 107, 2086 River Street. Tel: 802/234-5400; www.fws.gov. *Open daily 8–3.*

3 Quechee and Quechee Gorge
Simon Pearce Glass
Main Street. Tel: 802/295-2711; www.simonpearce. com. *Open Mon–Fri 9–9, Sat–Sun 10.30–7.*

4 Woodstock
Marsh-Billings-Rockefeller National Historic Park
Route 12. Tel: 802/457-3368; www.nps.gov/mabi. *Open May–Oct, daily 10–5.*

Billings Farm and Museum
Route 12. Tel: 802/457-2355; www.billingsfarm. org. *Open Apr–Oct, daily 10–5; Nov, Dec weekends.*

5 Bridgewater
Long Trail Brewing Company
Junction Route 4 and 100A, Bridgewater Corners. Tel: 802/672-5011; www.longtrail.com

6 Plymouth
President Calvin Coolidge State Historic Site
Tel: 802/672-3773; www.historicvermont.org. *Open end May to mid-Oct daily 9.30–5.*

Frog City Cheese
106 Messer Hill Road.
Tel: 802/672-3650; www.frogcitycheese.com. *Tours daily 9.30–5.*

Green Mountain Sugar House
820 Route 100 North, Ludlow. Tel: 800/643-9338; www.gmsh.com. *Open daily 9–6.*

Special to...
Crowley Cheese
Healdville. Tel: 802/259-2340; www.crowley cheese.com. *Shop open daily; factory open Mon–Fri.*

Recommended walks
Green Mountain Club
Route 100 between Stowe and Waterbury. Tel: 802/244-7037; www.green mountainclub.org. *Open Mon–Fri (daily in summer).*

For history buffs
Joseph Smith Birthplace Memorial
357 LDS Lane, South Royalton. Tel: 802/763-7742. *Open daily May–Oct 9–7; Nov–Apr 9–5.*

TOUR 17

[i] Lake Champlain Regional Chamber of Commerce, 60 Main Street, Burlington, VT 05401. Tel: 802/863-3489; www.vermont.org

[i] Addison County Chamber of Commerce, 2 Court Street, Middlebury, VT 05753. Tel: 802/388-7951 or 800/733-8376; www.midvermont.com

Practical information

i Tourist Information Office

12 Tour Number

i Stowe Area Association, Main Street, Stowe, VT 05672. Tel: 802/253-7321; www.gotostowe.com

1 Shelburne
Shelburne Farms
1611 Harbor Road. Tel: 802/985-8686; www.shel burnefarms.org. *Open mid-May to mid-Oct, daily 10–5.*

Shelburne Museum
Route 7. Tel: 802/985-3346; www.shelburnemuseum. org. *Open May–Oct 10–5.*

Vermont Teddy Bear Company
Route 7. Tel: 802/985-3001; www.vermontteddybear. com. *Tours daily 9.30–5 (9–5 Nov–Apr).*

2 Charlotte
Vermont Wildflower Farm
3488 Ethan Allen Highway. Tel: 802/425-3641; www. vermontwildflowerfarm. com. *Open Apr–Oct, daily 10–5.*

3 Ferrisburgh
Rokeby Museum
4334 Route 7. Tel: 802/ 877-3406; www.rokeby.org. *Open mid-May to mid-Oct, Thu–Sun.*

4 Vergennes
Lake Champlain Maritime Museum
4472 Basin Harbor Road. Tel: 802/475-2022; www. lcmm.org. *Open May to mid-Oct, daily 10–5.*

5 Middlebury
Henry Sheldon Museum of Vermont History
1 Park Street. Tel: 802/388-2117; www.henrysheldon museum.org. *Open daily 10–5. Closed Sun, Mon Sep–Jun.*

Vermont State Craft Center at Frog Hollow
1 Mill Street, Middlebury. Tel: 802/388-3177; www. froghollow.org. *Open Mon–Sat 10–5.30, Sun noon–5.*

9 Waitsfield
Vermont Icelandic Horse Farm
3061 North Fayston Road, Fayston. Tel: 802/496-7141;

www.icelandichorses.com. *Open daily. Call ahead for trail ride reservations.*

10 Waterbury
Ben and Jerry's Ice Cream Factory
Route 100, Waterbury. Tel: 802/882-1240; www.benjerry.com. *Open daily, June 9–6, Jul–Aug 9–9, Sep–late Oct 9–7, late Oct–May 10–6.*

Lake Champlain Chocolates
Route 100, Waterbury Center. Tel: 802/241-4150; www.lakechamplainchoco lates.com. *Open daily 9–6.*

Cold Hollow Cider Mill
Route 100. Tel: 802/244-8771 or 800/327-7537; www.coldhollow.com. *Open daily 8–6 (7 Jul–Oct).*

11 Stowe
Stowe Mountain Resort
5781 Mountain Road. Tel: 802/253-3000; www.stowe.com

For children
Spirit of Ethan Allen III
Departs from Burlington Boathouse, College Street, Burlington. Tel: 802/862-8300; www.soea.com. *Boat trips mid-May to mid-Oct.*

Waterfront Boat Rentals
Burlington. Tel: 802/864-4858; www.waterfront boatrentals.com

Special to…
University of Vermont Morgan Horse Farm
74 Battell Drive, Weybridge, off Route 23. Tel: 802/388-2011. *Open May–Oct, daily 9–4.*

TOUR 18

i 500 Market Street, Portsmouth, NH 03802. Tel: 603/436-3988; www. portsmouthchamber.org

3 John Paul Jones House
43 Middle Street (corner of State Street). Tel: 603/436-8420; www.ports mouthhistory.org. *Open end May to mid-Oct, daily 11–5.*

5 Rundlet-May House
364 Middle Street. Tel: 603/436-3205; www.spnea.org. *Open Jun–Oct, 1st and 3rd Sat of month, 11–4.*

7 Governor Langdon House
143 Pleasant Street. Tel: 603/436-3205; www. historicnewengland.org. *Open Jun to mid-Oct, Fri–Sun 11–4.*

10 Wentworth Gardner House
50 Mechanic Street. Tel: 603/436-4406; www. wentworthgardner andlear.org. *Open mid-Jun to mid-Oct, Tue–Sun 12–4.*

12 Strawbery Banke
Marcy Street, On the Waterfront. Tel: 603/433-1100; www.strawbery banke.org. *Open daily 10–5. Nov–Dec phone for hours.*

13 Warner House
150 Daniel Street. Tel: 603/436-5909; www.warner house.org. *Open Jun–Oct, Mon–Sat 11–4, Sun noon–4.*

15 Moffatt-Ladd House
154 Market Street. Tel: 603/436-8221; www.moffatt ladd.org. *Open mid-Jun to mid-Oct, Mon–Sat 11–5, Sun 1–5.*

Recommended trip
Vaughn Cottage Memorial/ Celia Thaxter Museum
Star Island. Tel: 603/430-6272. *Open Jun–Sep, museum daily 1–3.*

For children
USS Albacore
Albacore Park, 600 Market Street. Tel: 603/436-3680; www.ussalbacore.org. *Open end May to mid-Oct, daily 9.30–5; mid-Oct to end May Thu–Mon 9.30–4.*

TOUR 19

i Plymouth Chamber of Commerce, kiosk at McDonald's, exit 26 off I-93. Tel: 800/386-3678; www.plymouth.org

i Visitor Center, North Woodstock, NH 03262, exit 32 off I-93. Tel: 603/745-8720 or 800/346-3687; www.visitwhite-mountains.com

1 North Woodstock
Clark's Trading Post
Route 3, Lincoln. Tel: 603/745-8913; www.clarks tradingpost.com. *Open late Jun to mid-Oct daily; week-ends spring and fall.*

2 Franconia Notch
Franconia Notch State Park
Tel: 603/745-8391; www. franconianotchstatepark. com

The Flume Gorge & Visitor Center
Route 3. Tel: 603/745-8391; www.flumegorge.com. *Open mid-May to Oct (weather permitting) daily 9–5 (5.30 Jul–Aug).*

Cannon Mountain Aerial Tramway
I-93. Tel: 603/823-8800; www.cannonmt.com. *Open mid-May to Oct daily.*

3 Franconia
Frost Place
Ridge Road, Franconia. Tel: 603/823-5510; www.frostplace.org. *Open Jun weekends, Jul–mid-Oct, Wed–Mon 1–5. Closed Tue.*

6 Mount Washington
Mount Washington Auto Road at Great Glen
Route 16, Gorham. Tel: 603/466-3988; www.mountwashington autoroad.com. Open mid-May–late Oct (weather permitting).

Great Glen Trails
Tel: 603/466-2333; www.greatglentrails.com

Mount Washington State Park
Tel: 603/466-3347; www.nhstateparks.org. *Open daily May–Oct, 8–8 (weather permitting).*

Mount Washington Observatory
Tel: 603/356-2137; www. mountwashington.org. *Open daily 8–6.*

❽ Glen
Story Land
Route 16. Tel: 603/383-4186; www.storylandnh.com. *Open early Jun, early Sep to mid-Oct weekends 9–5; mid-Jun to early Sep daily 9–6.*

❾ North Conway
Conway Scenic Railroad
Route 16. Tel: 603/356-5251; www.conwayscenic.com. *Open May–Nov.*

Weather Discovery Center
2779 Main Street, Route 16. Tel: 603/356-2137. *Open end May–Dec daily 10–5. Weekends rest of year.*

⓫ Lincoln
Whale's Tale
Route 3. Tel: 603/745-8810; www.whalestalewaterpark.net. *Open early Jun–Sep, daily 10–6.*

Hobo Railroad
Main Street. Tel: 603/745-2135; www.hoborr.com. *Open late Jun to mid-Oct, daily; weekends mid-May to mid-Jun.*

For history buffs
New England Ski Museum
Franconia Notch Parkway, exit 34B. Tel: 603/823-7177, or 800/639-4181; www.skimuseum.org. *Open Jun–Mar, daily 10–5.*

Scenic routes
Mount Washington Cog Railway
Off Route 302, Bretton Woods. Tel: 603/278-5404; www.thecog.com. *Open year-round.*

For children
Six Gun City
Route 2, Jefferson. Tel: 603/586-4592; www.sixguncity.com. *Open end May–early Sep daily 10–5 (9.30–6 Jul–Aug).*

TOUR 20

ⓘ Plymouth Chamber of Commerce, kiosk at McDonald's, exit 26 off I-93. Tel: 800/386-3678; www.plymouth.org

❶ Ashland
Pauline Glidden Toy Museum
49 Main Street. Tel: 603/968-7289 or 7023. *Open Jul–Aug Wed–Sat 1–4.*

❹ Moultenborough
Castle in the Clouds
Route 171. Tel: 603/476-2352; www.castleinthe clouds.org. *Open Sat, Sun in spring; daily Jun to mid-Oct.*

Loon Center and Markus Wildlife Sanctuary
Lees Mill Road. Tel: 603/476-5666; www.loon.org. *Open daily Jul to mid-Oct; rest of year, Mon–Sat 9–5.*

❺ Wolfeboro
Libby Museum
Route 109. Tel: 603/569-1035. *Open Jun–Sep Tue–Sun 10–4.*

Wentworth State Park
Route 109. Tel: 603/569-3699; www.nhstateparks.org

Wright Museum
77 Center Street. Tel: 603/569-1212; www.wright museum.org. *Open May–Oct, Mon–Sat 10–4, Sun noon–4.*

❻ Alton Bay
Ellacoya State Park
Route 11, Gilford. Tel: 603/293-7821; www.nhstateparks.org. *Open Jun–Aug, 9–dusk.*

❽ Meredith
Annalee Doll Museum
44 Reservoir Road, off Route 104. Tel: 603/279-6542; www.annalee.com. *Open end May to mid-Oct. Phone for hours.*

Back to nature
Squam Lakes Natural Science Center
23 Science Center Road, Route 113, Holderness. Tel: 603/968-7194; www.nhnature.org. *Open May–Oct daily.*

Scenic Rides
Mount Washington Cruises
Weirs Beach. Tel: 603/366-5531; www.cruisenh.com. *Cruises late May–late Oct. Phone for times.*

Winnipesaukee Railroad
Tel: 603/279-5253; www.hoborr.com. *Open late May to mid-Jun weekends; mid-Jun to mid-Oct. daily. Phone to check timetables.*

TOUR 21

ⓘ Convention and Visitors Bureau of Greater Portland, 245 Commercial Street, Portland, ME 04101. Tel: 207/772-5800; www.visitportland.com

ⓘ Southern Midcoast Maine Chamber of Commerce, 59 Pleasant Street, Brunswick, ME 04011. Tel: 207/725-8797; www.midcoastmaine.com

ⓘ Damariscotta Region Chamber of Commerce, 15 Courtyard Street, Damariscotta, ME 04543. Tel: 207/563-8340; www.damariscottaregion.com

ⓘ 1 Park Drive, Rockland, ME 04841. Tel: 207/596-0376; www.therealmaine.com

ⓘ 2 Public Landing, Camden, ME 04843. Tel: 207/236-4404; www.camdenme.org

ⓘ Main Street, Belfast, ME 04915. Tel: 207/338-5900; www.belfastmaine.org

❶ Brunswick
Peary-MacMillan Arctic Museum
Hubbard Hall, Bowdoin Campus. Tel: 207/725-3416; www.bowdoin.edu. *Open Tue–Sat 10–5, Sun 2–5.*

Bowdoin College Museum of Art
Upper Park Row, Walker Art Building. Tel: 207/725-3275; www.bowdoin.edu. *Open Tue–Sat 10–5, Sun 2–5.*

❷ Bath
Maine Maritime Museum
243 Washington Street. Tel: 207/443-1316; www.mainemaritime museum.org. *Open daily 9.30–5.*

❸ Wiscasset
Musical Wonder House
18 High Street. Tel: 207/882-7163; www.musicalwonderhouse.com. *Open Jun–Oct daily 10–6.*

Castle Tucker
Lee Street at High Street. Tel: 207/882-7169; www.historicnewengland.org. *Open Jun to mid-Oct. Tours hourly Wed–Sun 11–4.*

Nickels-Sortwell House
121 Main Street. Tel 207/882-6218; www.historicnewengland.org. *Open Jun to mid-Oct, Fri–Sun, tours hourly 11–4.*

Lincoln County Museum and Old Jail
Federal Street. Tel: 207/882-6817; www.lincoln countyhistory.org. *Open Jul–Aug, Tue–Sat 10–4; Jun, Sep Sat–Sun 10–4.*

❹ Damariscotta
Chapman-Hall House
Main Street. *Open mid-Jun to mid–Sep, 1–5. Closed Mon.*

❺ Colonial Pemaquid/ Fort William Henry
Off Route 130. Tel: 207/677-2423; www.friendsof-colonialpemaquid.org. *Open late May–early Sep, daily 9–5.*

❻ Pemaquid Light and Fisherman's Museum
End of Route 130. Tel: 207/677-2494; www.pema quidlighthouse.com. *Open Jun to mid-Oct, daily 9–5.*

❽ Thomaston
General Henry Knox Museum
Montpelier, junction Routes 1/131. Tel: 207/354-8062; www.knox museum.org. *Open late May–early Oct, Tue–Sat 10–4, last tour leaves at 3.*

❾ Rockland
Farnsworth Art Museum and Wyeth Center
16 Museum Street. Tel: 207/596-6457; www.farnsworthmuseum.org. *Open daily 10–5 (closed Mon mid-Oct to May).*

Practical information

Maine Discovery Center
1 Park Drive. Tel: 207/594-3301; www.mainelight
housemuseum.com. *Open Mon–Fri 9–4.30, Sat–Sun 10–4. Closed Sun in winter.*

$\boxed{10}$ **Rockport**
Opera House
6 Central Street. Tel: 207/236-2514; http://town.
rockport.me.us/opera-house.

Maine Media Workshops
70 Camden Street.
Tel: 877/577-7700;
www.theworkshops.com

**Center for Maine
Contemporary Art**
162 Russell Avenue.
Tel: 207/236-2875;
www.cmanow.org. *Open Tue–Sat 10–5, Sun 1–5.*

$\boxed{11}$ **Camden**
Conway Homestead
Tel: 207/236-2257;
www.crmuseum.org. Open Jul–Aug, Mon–Thu 10–4.

$\boxed{13}$ **Pownalborough
Courthouse**
Lincoln County Historical Association, Route 128, off Route 27. Tel: 207/882-6817; www.lincolncounty
history.org. *Open Jul–Aug, Tue–Sat 10–4; Jun, Sep, Sat–Sun 10–4.*

Special to…
L. L. Bean
95 Main Street, Freeport.
Tel: 800/559-0747;
www.llbean.com

Fat Boy Drive-In
111 Bath Road, Brunswick.
Tel: 207/729-9431.

Moody's Diner
Route 1, Waldoboro.
Tel: 207/832-7785;
www.moodysdiner.com

Olson House
Hathorn Point Road,
Cushing. Tel: 207/596-6457;
www.farnsworth
museum.org. *Open Jun–mid-Oct, daily 10–5.*

Recommended trips
Monhegan Island
Monhegan Boat Line, Port Clyde. Tel: 207/372-8848;
www.monheganboat.com

For children
**Owl's Head
Transportation Museum**
Next to Knox County Airport, off Route 73.
Tel: 207/594-4418;
www.ohtm.org. Open daily 10–5 (4 Nov–Mar).

**Fort Knox State Historic
Site**
Route 174, off US Route 1, Stockton Springs, near Belfast. Tel: 207/469-7719 (seasonal);
www.maine.gov/doc/parks.
Open May–Oct.

TOUR 22

$\boxed{i}$ Convention and Visitors Bureau, 245 Commercial Street, Portland, ME 04101.
Tel: 207/772-5800;
www.visitportland.com

$\boxed{2}$ **Portland Museum
Of Art**
7 Congress Square.
Tel: 207/775-6148;
www.portlandmuseum.
org. *Open daily 10–5 (Fri till 9). Closed Mon mid-Oct to late May.*

$\boxed{3}$ **Children's Museum
of Maine**
142 Free Street. Tel: 207/828-1234; www.childrens
museumofme.org. *Open Mon–Sat 10–5, Sun noon–5. Closed Mon early Sep–May.*

$\boxed{4}$ **Maine College Of
Art**
522 Congress Street.
Tel: 207/775-3052;
www.meca.edu

$\boxed{6}$ **Wadsworth-
Longfellow House**
487 Congress Street.
Tel: 207/774-1822;
www.mainehistory.org.
Open May–Oct Mon–Sat 10.30–5, Sun noon–4. Phone Nov–Dec.

**Maine Historical Society
Museum**
489 Congress Street.
Tel: 207/774-1822. *Open Mon–Sat 10–5, Sun noon–5. Closed Sun in winter.*

$\boxed{9}$ **First Parish Church**
425 Congress Street.
Tel: 207/773-5747;
www.firstparishportland.
org

$\boxed{10}$ **City Hall**
389 Congress Street.
Tel: 207/879-0300;
www.portlandmaine.gov.
Open weekdays 8–4.30.

Portland Symphony
Tel: 207/842-0800 (box office); www.portland
symphony.com

$\boxed{14}$ **Milk Street Armory**
Portland Regency Hotel, 20 Milk Street.
Tel: 207/774-4200;
www.theregency.com

S**pecial to…**
**Gritty's Portland Brew
Pub**
396 Fore Street.
Tel: 207/772-2739;
www.grittys.com

Portland Observatory
138 Congress Street. Tel: 207/774-5561; www.port-landlandmarks.org. *Open late May to mid-Oct, 10–5.*

TOUR 23

$\boxed{i}$ Convention and Visitors Bureau, 245 Commercial Street, Portland, ME 04101. Tel: 207/772-5800; www.visit-portland.com

$\boxed{i}$ Bethel Area Chamber of Commerce, 8 Station Place, Bethel Train Station, Bethel, ME 04217.
Tel: 207/824-2282 or 800/442-5826;
www.bethelmaine.com

$\boxed{i}$ Rangeley Lakes Region Chamber of Commerce, 6 Park Road, Rangeley, ME 04970. Tel: 207/864-5364; www.rangeleymaine.com

$\boxed{i}$ Franklin County Chamber of Commerce, 407 Wilton Road, Farmington, ME 04938.
Tel: 207/778-4215;
www.franklincountycham-berofcommerce.org

$\boxed{1}$ **Sabbathday Lake**
Sabbathday Lake Village Route 26, New Gloucester.
Tel: 207/926-4597;
www.shaker.lib.me.us. *Open late May to mid-Oct, Mon–Sat 10–4.30.*

$\boxed{2}$ **Poland Spring**
State of Maine Building
Tel: 207/998-4142;
www.polandspringps.org.
Open May–Oct Tue–Sat 9–4, Sun 9–noon.

$\boxed{4}$ **Trap Corner**
Perham's of West Paris
194 Bethel Road, Routes 26 and 219. Tel: 207/674-2341. *Open daily 9–5; closed Mon, Tue, Jan–May.*

$\boxed{8}$ **Rangeley**
**Rangeley Historical
Society Museum**
Main Street. Tel: 207/864-5647. Limited opening hours; phone ahead for information.

Wilhelm Reich Museum
Dodge Pond Road, off Route 4/16. Tel: 207/864-3443; www.wilhelmreich
museum.org. *Open Jul–Aug, Wed–Sun 1–5; Sep, Sun 1–5.*

$\boxed{9}$ **Kingfield**
Stanley Museum
School Street. Tel: 207/265-2729; www.stanley-museum.org. *Open Tue–Sun 1–4 (Tue–Fri 10–4, Nov–May).*

$\boxed{10}$ **Farmington**
**Nordica Memorial
Homestead**
Holley Road. Tel: 207/778-2042. *Open Jun–early Sep, Tue–Sat 10–noon, 1–5, Sun 1–5.*

$\boxed{11}$ **Washburn-Norlands
Living History Center**
290 Norlands Road, Livermore Falls. Tel: 207/897-4366;
www.norlands.org. *Phone ahead to confirm opening times.*

Back to nature
Maine Wildlife Park
Route 26. Tel: 207/657-4977; www.maine.gov/ifw.
Open mid-Apr to mid-Nov, 9.30–4.30.

Index

Index & Acknowledgments

The Automobile Association
wishes to thank the following libraries and photographers for their assistance in the preparation of this book.

ALAMY 79 (Jon Arnold Images); 105 (Mike Briner); 146 (Cosmo Condina); 74/5 (Florida Images); 108/9 (Dennis Hallinan); 138 (Robert Harding Picture Library Ltd); 34, 37, 62b, 63, 72, 91, 150/1 (Andre Jenny); 72/3 (Photofusion Picture Library); 139a (Miro Vrlik Photography); MARY EVANS PICTURE LIBRARY 8a, 8b, 56a, 56/7; TOM MACKIE 59, 83, 92, 94/5, 95, 118/9, 120/1, 142, 143, 144/5, 153, 154/5, 154b, 157, 165; MAINE OFFICE OF TOURISM 148, 149; PICTURES COLOUR LIBRARY 9; RHODE ISLAND ECONOMIC DEVELOPMENT CORPORATION 84, 85; SPECTRUM COLOUR LIBRARY 6, 11, 44, 82/3, 97; TANGLEWOOD (BOSTON SYMPHONY ORCHESTRA)/STEVE LISS 33; STOCK MARKET 26/7 (Jean Miele MCMXCII); YALE UNIVERSITY 68, 70

All remaining pictures are held in the Association's own library (AA World Travel Library) with contributions from the following photographers:

C COE 31, 32/3, 38, 81, 86, 86/7, 103, 111, 126, 136/7, 137; R HOLMES 2, 14/5, 18, 29b, 30, 34/5, 36, 39b, 40, 41, 43, 45, 47, 50a, 53, 54, 55, 60, 61, 62a, 66, 76, 78/9, 122, 123b, 124, 125, 130/1, 132/3, 140; J LYNCH 12, 13, 19a, 19b, 20; M LYNCH 4, 5, 7, 23, 25, 27, 28, 29a, 39a, 50b, 52, 58, 64, 65, 67, 70, 80, 88, 89, 92/3, 96, 98, 99, 100, 101, 102/3, 104, 106, 106/7 110, 112/3, 113, 114, 115, 117, 120. 123a. 127, 129, 131, 132, 135, 139b, 145, 147, 154a; T LYNCH 116; C SAWYER 10, 17, 42, 51; J WILLIAMS 57.

Contributors
Copy editors: Larry Dunmire, Karen Bird   **Indexer:** Marie Lorimer
Thanks also to **Kathy Arnold** and **Paul Wade** for their updating work on this book.

Atlas

St Frances
182-183

Clayton Lake
Ashland
184-185
186-187

Jackman
M A I N E
Lincoln
Princeton

Newport
194-195

188-189
190-191
192-193

Burlington
Montpelier
Berlin
Augusta
Belfast
Jonesport

Middlebury
Rockland

VERMONT
Plymouth

NEW
HAMPSHIRE
Portland

NEW
YORK

196-197
198-199

Bennington
Portsmouth

Concord
Boston

MASSACHUSETTS

Springfield
Provincetown

Hartford
Providence
Orleans

200-201
202-203
204

CONNECTICUT

New Haven
RHODE
ISLAND
Newport
Martha's Vineyard
Nantucket

Long Island

══ Toll-free motorway	🛢 101 134 Road numbers
══ Toll motorway	══ International boundary
— Highway	═══ State boundary
— Main road	- - - Admin boundary
— Secondary road	✈ International airport

Built-up area

National park

● Town / Attraction

182-183
0   10   20   30 km
0   10   20 miles

184-204
0   10   20   30 km
0   10   20 miles

Brownville

Milo

MAINE

D

E

F

6,16

186

Howland

2

1

16

Dover-
Foxcroft

Lagrange

6,155

Passadumkeag

South
Lagrange

Olamon

15

95

xter

Exeter
Corners

Hudson

16

7

Corinna

Milford

Orono

Old
Town

178

95

Newport

Etna

Bangor International (BGR)

Bangor

Brewer

9

2

A

100

Carmel

395

Hampden

East Holden

Green
Lake

Hampden
Highlands

202

Dixmont

Winterport

194

Alt
1

Frankfort

Bucksport

1

3

ty

Alt
1

Brooks

*Waldo
County*

Waldo

Searsport

172

3

Belfast

Blue
Hill

ashington

Sedgwick

3

erty

Lincolnville

Deer
Isle

Ba

Union

Camden

*Knox
County*

1

North Haven

Stonington

4

Rockland

194

aldoboro

Thomaston

Owls
Head

Isle Au Haut

Port Clyde

Vinalhaven

Acadia National Park

Penobscot Bay

5

D

E

F

193

McAdam

Brockway

Vanceboro

ookton

Lincoln

⑥

Topsfield

Watt Junction

I

Waite

Moores Mills

①

Princeton

St. Stephen

Woodland

⑨ Calais

2

Washington County

⑨ Alexander

Wesley

⑲¹

①

Perry

Pembroke

Eastport

⑧⁶ Marion

Lubec

3

⑲²

⑱⁹

Whiting

Machias

①

Grand Manan Island

Columbia Falls

①

Cutler

Seal Cove

⑱⁷

4

Jonesport

Bay of Fundy

5

D

E

F

Cumberland County

Kezar Falls
25
Frye Island
114
191
North Windham
Cumberland Center
LL Bea
295
Yarmouth
35
South Windham
Little Falls
4
Falmouth Foreside
Limerick
25
202
302
25
PORTLAND
295
Gorham
Westbrook
Portland International (PWM)
South Portland
Bar Mills
4
11
1
Scarborough
Cape Elizabeth

York County

Springvale
Alfred
111
195
Saco
Old Orchard Beach
Sanford
Biddeford
202
South Sanford
109
9
Kennebunk
11
95
Kennebunkport
4
9
North Berwick
9
Berwick
Rollinsford
Ogunquit
16
4
Dover
Durham
Eliot
Cape Neddick
South Eliot
York Harbor
4
Newmarket
Kittery
1
Portsmouth
101
1A
Rye Beach
Hampton
Hampton Beach
Amesbury
110
Salisbury
113
Newburyport
1A
5
1
Rowley
Pigeon Cove
Ipswich
Rockport
Hamilton
Essex
Wenham
128
Gloucester
Manchester
Beverly
Salem
A
Marblehead
Swampscott

Massachusetts Bay

Edward Lawrence International (BOS)

203

204

North Cohasset

199

D   E   F

1

2

3

4

5

Massachusetts Bay

1

Scituate
Scituate

Ocean Bluff
Green Harbor
Duxbury

2

Plymouth

White Horse Beach

Provincetown

Cape Cod National Seashore

North Truro

Wellfleet

Cape Cod Bay

Eastham

Cape Cod

White Island Shores

3

25

28

Sagamore
Sandwich

East Sandwich

Orleans

Nickerson State Park

Cohasset

28

Forestdale

West Barnstable

Yarmouth Port

Cape Cod Museum of Natural History

Dennis

Brewster

East Harwich

203

Marstons Mills

6

Barnstable

Antiques Center of Cape Cod

28

Chatham

130

132

West Chatham

mouth
28

Centerville

Yarmouth

Dennis Port

Harwich Port

Falmouth

Osterville

Teaticket

East Falmouth

Nantucket Sound

Haven

4

Oak Bluffs

Edgartown

Dukes County

Martha's Vineyard

Nantucket Island

Nantucket

Siasconset

Nantucket County

5

ATLAS INDEX

Atlas Index